The Foster's Market Cookbook

foster's market

The Foster's Market Cookbook

Sara Foster WITH SARAH BELK KING

PHOTOGRAPHS BY JAMES BAIGRIE

RANDOM HOUSE NEW YORK

LIBRARY OF CONGRESS CATALOGING-IN-PUBLICATION DATA

Foster, Sara.
    The Foster's Market cookbook/Sara Foster with Sarah Belk King.
        p.   cm.
    Includes index.
    ISBN 0-375-50546-6
    1. Cookery.   2. Foster's Market.   I. King, Sarah Belk.
II. Title.
TX714 .F685 2002
641.5—dc21   2001041909

Random House website address: www.atrandom.com

Printed in the United States of America on acid-free paper

9 8 7 6 5

Book design by Barbara M. Bachman

In memory of my grandparents, for teaching me to appreciate good food
and to take the time to enjoy and share it with family and friends

Foreword by Martha Stewart

Walk into Foster's Market and you walk right into Sara's World. Sara Foster started Foster's Market twelve years ago, after an illustrious and industrious cooking career in New York and Connecticut. A native of Tennessee, Sara is an intuitive chef, steeped in tradition, expert in the foods of the American South. Those qualities alone could have guaranteed her a place in culinary history, but Sara early on realized the value of education and illumination and moved to New York to cook at the SoHo Charcuterie, a pioneering restaurant specializing in inventive, fine, fresh food. She worked hard and long in my catering business and helped significantly with several of my books. She left to cook with Jonathan Waxman when he moved east from California to open a restaurant that brought New Yorkers a taste of the new American cuisine. When Sara told us that she wanted to open a gourmet food market, I watched with interest as she did her research, zeroing in on those few fast-growing urban centers that had great potential and little competition. When she and her husband, Peter, settled on the Raleigh-Durham area, I thought, "How smart." Good food, entertaining, and interest in fresh ingredients were inherent to that area, university life and corporate expansion were prevalent, and there was nothing like the market Sara planned to open. Just a few years later, there are two busy, thriving, successful, and charming Foster's Markets, and they are popular not just as places to buy beautifully prepared, delicious foodstuffs, but also as relaxed, carefree gathering places where a cup of latte and a huge piece of crumb cake or a giant sticky bun or a bowl of steaming soup can be savored quietly with a book or a newspaper or with a group of friends.

Sara has remained true to her beliefs and conviction that good, honest food can be deliciously simple. Her recipes, though often complex in flavor, are by and large easy to prepare. I've cooked many of the recipes collected for this book and eaten many, many more of Sara's creations, and I've never been disappointed, only elated by the taste and appearance and freshness.

Foster's Markets reflect Sara's casual approach to living and eating. Organized carefully, the Markets sell packaged goods—Sara's own selections—but also seasonally appropriate prepared foods for takeout, special order, or "sit down and eat" right there. The salads, the desserts, and everything else are mouth-wateringly good.

Sara has prepared this cookbook with the same care and attention that she has lavished on the rest of her work. Well written and well tested, each recipe is sure to please. And the best news is that these represent just a small number of Sara's repertoire, so we can look forward to more of her collected recipes.

Acknowledgments

This book would not have happened without all of our customers, who have been there every day and have made Foster's Market possible. We thank all of them for their ongoing support.

A special thanks to my husband, Peter Sellers, for his continuous encouragement, love, and enthusiasm, mixed with a healthy appetite for tasting and critiquing all the recipes, making this a better book.

My gratitude to the team that helped put this book together; it is as much theirs as mine: Pamela Cannon at Random House, for believing in this project and supporting and guiding us through it. Sarah Belk King, my coauthor, for her dedication, wit, endless intellect, and countless hours. James Baigrie, for his wonderful eye and tireless enthusiasm. Judy Edwards, my sister and a wonderfully creative cook, for sharing, testing, and tasting recipes and endless hours of caring. Caitlin Salemi, Alison Attenborough, Karen Steadman, and Edouard Phoulière, for bringing their own style and creativity to the project. Janis Donnaud, for her persistence in getting things done the right way. Robert Malone, for being the link to making it happen and always being there.

A warm and special thanks to Martha Stewart, my friend and mentor, for sharing her knowledge, insight, and great style and encouraging me to develop my own. Also, for her continuous support and generosity.

Thanks to Bruce Claiborne, for teaching me that less is more, and to all the other great cooks I have worked with and learned from over the years.

I cannot thank enough all the cooks and managers, my friends and coworkers, at Foster's Market, past and present. They have all inspired and taught me over the years. Special thanks to Elizabeth Laine, Laura Cyr, and Wendell Wilson, for having the vision to improve and expand the Foster's style and sharing and developing recipes. To Patrick Edwards, not only for running the business, but also for enthusiastically tasting and critiquing. To Shay Charles, Meg deLuca, Jennings Brody, and Jan Vandervort, for sharing their passion and love for great food and quality and seeing it through, from start to finish, day after day, devoting endless hours of time and energy to making Foster's successful. To Eddie Zuniga, Amy Buckner, Donnie Willey, Eric Muhl, Whitney Aichner, Tim Youngblood, Kathy Edwards, and many more, each contributing to the success of Foster's Market in their own way.

To my family and friends, for sharing recipes, props, homes, and more.

—Sara Foster

Thank you, Sara, for giving me the opportunity to work with you and your team on this book. Thanks, too, to my editor, Pamela Cannon, and to my agent, Janis Donnaud, for believing that I could effectively express the philosophy, the heart, and the soul of Foster's Market. This has been a dream assignment.

—Sarah Belk King

contents

Foreword by Martha Stewart   vii

Introduction

I remember the first time I saw the space that would eventually become Foster's Market. It was one of several nondescript buildings on a busy highway lined with gas stations and fast-food restaurants. The space reeked of gasoline and motor oil, which was not surprising, since it had been a lawn mower repair shop for thirty-five years. It didn't exactly fit my vision for the charming takeout food store I'd been dreaming of, one that was inviting and friendly, with doily-lined platters of brownies and eye-catching displays of sumptuous layer cakes.

In time, the old lawn mower shop grew on me—it had a certain charm and plenty of natural light. I began to feel that my dream takeout shop was possible. After the premises received a dozen or so power washings, new pine floors, and a professional kitchen, the doors to Foster's Market opened in May 1990. It was only a matter of days before our modest eight-cup espresso maker was replaced by a state-of-the-art commercial machine that could make hundreds of lattes per hour. The mouthwatering aromas of baked goods and freshly ground coffee beans made the lawn mower shop a distant memory.

In the weeks that followed, I watched with amazement as my business evolved. Although I had opened a takeout store, I noticed that most customers were sipping their coffee and eating their salads and sandwiches right on the premises. Professionals, students, and moms with kids in tow were leaning on counters, perching on the porch steps, or sitting cross-legged outside on the grass. To remedy the situation, I brought in a couple of café tables and some mismatched flea-market chairs. It wasn't long before we expanded by building an area just for dining-in. Today, that area is full all day, every day. The same can be said for the dining area in my second store, which I opened in nearby Chapel Hill in 1998. I really hadn't planned to open another store, but the building—an old grocery store—just felt right. I trusted my instincts.

At both Foster's locations, we serve homemade fare that's simple, fresh, and delicious, the kind of food that everyone seems to crave these days. My cooking style reflects my southern heritage as well as techniques I've learned—and continue to learn—as a professional chef. As a child, I was weaned on newly laid eggs and just-picked produce from my grandparents' farm in Tennessee. Granny

Foster's buttermilk biscuits were so light, so flaky, and so addictive that I used her old-time recipe as a springboard for my own version, which has variations such as adding Cheddar cheese and herbs. And then there were all those made-from-scratch cakes and pies that my mother taught me to make; her bourbon-soaked bread pudding has become somewhat legendary at Foster's Market. Without a doubt, the foods that I grew up with left an indelible mark: nothing less than the best will do.

My recipes are characterized by high-quality ingredients, which means that I insist on cooking seasonally—asparagus in spring, tomatoes in summer, local sweet potatoes in autumn—since food at its peak doesn't need much done to it to taste great. Simplicity is the key: I believe in enhancing flavors, not masking them. I believe that food should taste like what it is, not hide in heavy sauces, dressings, or garnishes.

Layering flavors is also an important element in my cooking. For instance, using *roasted* garlic and tomatoes (which become sweeter and more concentrated in flavor as they cook) makes an entirely different kind of dish from one that calls for raw garlic and uncooked tomatoes. Spreading a sandwich with Basil Mayonnaise—instead of plain mayonnaise—adds dimension, taking a simple B.L.T. to a different level altogether. And as for Grilled Vegetable Ratatouille, grilling adds a delicious charcoal flavor to the peppers, eggplant, and tomatoes that classic ratatouille—cooked in a skillet—simply doesn't have.

I've wanted to share the recipes that have made Foster's Market so popular ever since we opened. This book is not only for our customers (who have been pleading for our recipes for over a decade), but also for those who don't live in the area but have heard about us or visited our website (www.fostersmarket.com). We've made the recipes in this book hundreds—sometimes thousands—of times. They work, and they don't require esoteric equipment, complicated techniques, or hard-to-find ingredients. They taste great, too.

Even though I created these recipes thoughtfully and carefully to result in certain flavors and textures, they're not sacred. I encourage you to use my recipes as inspiration for your own interpretation. Don't like pecans? Substitute walnuts. Peaches out of season? Try apples or pears in that cobbler or muffin recipe. For the most part, there are no hard-and-fast rules; let your personal taste and what's available at the farm stand—or in the cupboard—inspire you.

Along with the recipes, I've included numerous sidebars that cover topics such as cooking techniques, ingredients, and cookware that I find indispensable. I've also included lots of easy cooking tips, such as the many ways to dress up an omelet, and tasty ideas for sandwich fillings. In addition, most of my recipes include variations, because I believe whole-heartedly in cooking with the seasons and using what's best at the supermarket or what's on hand in your own pantry.

Foster's comfortable, home-away-from-home atmosphere and warm, friendly service keep customers coming back day after day. And, of course, there's the food; they love our fresh, seasonal, unpretentious food. I hope you enjoy our recipes as much as our customers do and that this book makes your meals easier, more delicious, and more enjoyable every day.

—Sara Foster, Fall 2001

The Foster's Market Cookbook

breakfast and brunch

Sweet Peach Muffins with Brown Sugar–Walnut Streusel Topping
Country Muffins with Carrots, Coconut, and Pecans   Jalapeño
Corn Muffins   Apple-Walnut Muffins with Maple Syrup
Oatmeal-Banana Muffins with Chocolate Chips   Blueberriest
Muffins   Foster's Scones   Old-Fashioned Buttermilk Biscuits
Molasses Brown Bread   Apple Rum-Raisin Bread   Granny
Foster's Banana-Walnut Bread   Spiced Pumpkin Bread   Sweet
and Spicy Gingerbread   Granny Foster's Refrigerator Rolls
Hot Cross Buns with Raisins, Apricots, and Cranberries   Killer
Pecan Sticky Buns   Sticky Orange-Coconut Pinwheels
New York–Style Crumb Cake   Classic Sour Cream Coffee Cake
Foster's Omelets   Grits Soufflé   Mushroom-Risotto Hash with
Fried Eggs and Grilled Ham   Corn Pancakes with Crispy Fried
Oysters and Cajun Rémoulade   Huevos Rancheros with Granny
Foster's Chili Sauce   Panama Buttermilk Pancakes
Garden Vegetable Frittata   Turkey–Sweet Potato Hash

Sweet Peach Muffins with Brown Sugar–Walnut Streusel Topping

These are best when peaches are at their summer peak, although they're good made with frozen peaches, too. The streusel topping can be made in advance. These muffins are best eaten warm.

MAKES 1 DOZEN MUFFINS

Brown Sugar–Walnut Streusel Topping

1 1/2 cups coarsely chopped walnuts

1/3 cup all-purpose flour

1/3 cup firmly packed light brown sugar

1/2 teaspoon ground cinnamon

3 tablespoons unsalted butter, softened

Combine the walnuts, flour, brown sugar, and cinnamon in a bowl and stir to mix. Add the butter and mix until well blended. Set aside or refrigerate in an airtight container until ready to use.

Muffin Batter

2 cups all-purpose flour

1 cup sugar

1 teaspoon baking powder

1/2 teaspoon baking soda

2 teaspoons ground cinnamon

1/2 teaspoon ground allspice

1/2 teaspoon salt

3 large eggs

3 tablespoons unsalted butter, melted

1 1/2 cups sour cream

1 tablespoon dark rum or pure vanilla extract

1 1/2 cups peeled, pitted, chopped peaches

1 • Preheat the oven to 375 degrees.

2 • Line 12 large muffin cups with paper liners and spray the top part of the pan lightly with vegetable oil spray.

3 • Sift together the flour, sugar, baking powder, baking soda, cinnamon, allspice, and salt in a large bowl and set aside.

4 • Whisk the eggs, butter, sour cream, and rum in a separate bowl until well blended. Fold in the peaches.

5 • Add the egg mixture to the flour mixture and stir just until moist and blended. Do not overmix.

6 • Scoop the batter into the prepared muffin pan with a large ice cream scoop (1/3-cup scoop). The batter will come to the top of the paper liner or pan. Sprinkle with Brown Sugar–Walnut Streusel Topping and lightly press the topping into the muffin batter.

7 • Bake 30 to 35 minutes, until the tops of the muffins spring back when pressed lightly and a toothpick inserted in the center of a muffin comes out clean.

8 • Remove from the oven and cool for 5 minutes. Turn the muffins out of the pan and serve immediately.

variations: Almost any fresh or frozen fruit (except for very soft fruits like bananas, papaya, or mango) can be substituted for the peaches. Try blackberries, raspberries, blueberries, or strawberries. In autumn, try chopped fresh apples or chopped pears.

Muffin Basics

- Be careful not to overmix muffin batter; overmixing will cause the muffins to be tough. The batter can even be slightly lumpy when scooped into the muffin pans as long as all the dry ingredients are moist and blended.
- Using paper liners makes turning out the baked muffins much easier, and cleanup is a breeze.
- Vegetable oil spray distributes oil more evenly than brushing the pans with vegetable oil. When the muffins bake, they rise over the pan. By greasing the tops of the pans, muffins slide out of the pan more easily.
- An ice cream scoop is the perfect tool for filling muffin pans, since it keeps the batter from dripping onto the edges of the pan and it helps create a nice, rounded top. Use a full ⅓-cup scoop, which will fill a large muffin cup to the top of the paper liner, for a large muffin, and one about three-quarters full for a smaller muffin. (A scoop is great for filling bread pans, too.)

Country Muffins with Carrots, Coconut, and Pecans

This very moist, chewy muffin is similar to carrot cake in texture and flavor. You can mix the batter the night before, refrigerate it overnight, and then bake the muffins in the morning.

MAKES 1 DOZEN MUFFINS

2½ cups all-purpose flour

2 teaspoons baking powder

1 teaspoon baking soda

½ teaspoon salt

1 tablespoon ground cinnamon

1⅓ cups sugar

4 large eggs

1¼ cups canola or safflower oil

1 tablespoon pure vanilla extract

3 large carrots, peeled and grated

1 Granny Smith or other tart apple, peeled, cored, and diced

⅓ cup raisins

⅓ cup sweetened flaked coconut

⅓ cup chopped pecans

1 • Preheat the oven to 375 degrees.

2 • Line 12 large muffin cups with paper liners and spray the top part of the pan lightly with vegetable oil spray.

3 • Combine or sift together the flour, baking powder, baking soda, salt, and cinnamon in a large bowl.

4 • Whisk together the sugar, eggs, oil, and vanilla in a separate bowl.

5 • Add the carrots, apple, raisins, coconut, and pecans to the egg mixture and mix well to combine.

6 • Add the flour mixture to the egg-carrot mixture and stir just until the dry ingredients are moist and blended. Do not overmix. The batter should be thick enough to mound slightly above the muffin pan line.

7 • Scoop the batter into the prepared muffin pan with a large ice cream scoop (⅓-cup scoop).

8 • Bake 25 to 30 minutes, until the tops spring back when pressed lightly and a toothpick inserted in the center of a muffin comes out clean.

9 • Remove from the oven and cool for 5 minutes. Turn the muffins out of the pan and serve immediately.

Jalapeño Corn Muffins

These moist, spicy muffins are great with breakfast, but we also serve them with soup and salads. Or we sometimes make tiny ones and fill them with Tarragon Chicken Salad with Granny Smith Apples and Red Grapes (page 137) or Foster's Pimiento Cheese Spread (page 102) to serve as hors d'oeuvres.

MAKES 1 DOZEN MUFFINS

1½ cups yellow cornmeal

1½ cups all-purpose flour

¼ cup sugar

1½ teaspoons baking powder

½ teaspoon baking soda

½ teaspoon salt

1⅔ cups buttermilk

2 large eggs

8 tablespoons (1 stick) unsalted butter, melted

¼ cup sour cream

1 cup (4 ounces) grated Cheddar cheese

Kernels from 1 ear fresh corn (½ cup fresh or frozen corn)

1 jalapeño, seeded and minced

3 scallions, trimmed and minced

1 • Preheat the oven to 375 degrees.

2 • Line 12 large muffin cups with paper liners and spray the top part of the pan lightly with vegetable oil spray.

3 • Toss together the cornmeal, flour, sugar, baking powder, baking soda, and salt in a large bowl and stir to combine.

4 • Mix together the buttermilk, eggs, butter, and sour cream in a separate bowl and blend well.

5 • Add the cornmeal mixture to the egg mixture and stir just until the dry ingredients are moist and blended. Do not overmix.

6 • Fold in the cheese, corn, jalapeño, and scallions.

7 • Scoop the batter into the prepared muffin pan with a large ice cream scoop (⅓-cup scoop). The batter will come to the top of the paper liner or pan.

8 • Bake 25 to 30 minutes, until the muffins have risen, the tops spring back when pressed lightly, and a toothpick inserted in the center of a muffin comes out clean.

9 • Remove from the oven and cool for 5 minutes. Turn the muffins out of the pan and serve immediately.

variations: This muffin is great with a dollop of pepper jelly or cream cheese in the center, creating a tasty surprise when you bite into the muffin. Fill each muffin cup halfway with batter, add 1 teaspoon pepper jelly or cream cheese, and fill the cup with additional batter. Instead of adding corn, you can substitute cooked black-eyed peas or chopped roasted red peppers.

Apple-Walnut Muffins with Maple Syrup

These are particularly delicious in autumn, when the first local apples are in season. Try them warm with maple butter or applesauce.

3 cups all-purpose flour

1 tablespoon baking powder

1 teaspoon baking soda

$1/2$ teaspoon salt

$1/2$ teaspoon ground mace or
  ground nutmeg

$1/2$ teaspoon ground cardamom

$1/2$ teaspoon ground allspice

$1/2$ teaspoon ground cinnamon

8 tablespoons (1 stick) unsalted
  butter, softened

$1/4$ cup canola or safflower oil

2 large eggs

$1/2$ cup sugar

$1/2$ cup maple syrup

1 cup milk

2 Granny Smith or other tart
  apples, peeled, cored, and
  chopped finely or pulsed in a
  food processor

1 cup coarsely chopped walnuts

1 • Preheat the oven to 375 degrees.

2 • Line 12 large muffin cups with paper liners and spray the top part of the pan lightly with vegetable oil spray.

3 • Combine or sift together the flour, baking powder, baking soda, salt, mace, cardamom, allspice, and cinnamon in a large bowl and stir to mix.

4 • Cream together the butter, oil, eggs, sugar, and maple syrup in a separate bowl until well blended. Stir in the milk and apples and set aside.

5 • Add the egg mixture to the flour mixture and stir just until the ingredients are moist and blended. Fold in the walnuts, being careful not to overmix.

6 • Scoop the batter into the prepared muffin pan with a large ice cream scoop ($1/3$-cup scoop). The batter will come to the top of the paper liner or pan.

7 • Bake 30 to 35 minutes, until the muffins spring back when pressed lightly and a toothpick inserted in the center of a muffin comes out clean.

8 • Remove from the oven and cool for 5 minutes. Turn the muffins out of the pan and serve immediately.

variations: Substitute 1 cup rolled oats for 1 cup of the flour for a chewy texture. Or use 1 cup whole-wheat flour or 1 cup bran for 1 cup of the all-purpose flour.

Oatmeal-Banana Muffins with Chocolate Chips

These chunky muffins are worth waking up for; our early-morning customers love them!

MAKES 1 DOZEN MUFFINS

1½ cups rolled oats

2½ cups all-purpose flour

1 tablespoon baking powder

½ teaspoon salt

¾ cup sugar

12 tablespoons (1½ sticks)
   unsalted butter, melted

3 large eggs

2 very ripe bananas, mashed

¾ cup buttermilk

¼ cup canola or safflower oil

1 cup semisweet chocolate chips

1 • Preheat the oven to 375 degrees.

2 • Line 12 large muffin cups with paper liners and spray the top part of the pan lightly with vegetable oil spray.

3 • Place the oats on a baking sheet and toast for 10 minutes or until light golden. Set aside to cool.

4 • Combine or sift together the flour, baking powder, and salt in a large bowl and stir in the oats.

5 • Whisk together the sugar, butter, eggs, bananas, buttermilk, and oil in a separate bowl until well blended.

6 • Add the egg mixture to the flour mixture and stir just until the dry ingredients are moist and blended. Do not overmix. Fold in the chocolate chips until distributed evenly throughout the batter.

7 • Scoop the batter into the prepared muffin pan with a large ice cream scoop (⅓-cup scoop). The batter will come to the top of the paper liner or pan.

8 • Bake 25 to 30 minutes, until the tops of the muffins spring back when pressed lightly and a toothpick inserted in the center of a muffin comes out clean.

9 • Remove from the oven and cool for 5 minutes. Turn the muffins out of the pan and serve immediately.

variations: Instead of the chocolate chips, try 1 cup of the following: peanut butter chips, sweetened flaked coconut, coarsely chopped walnuts, or coarsely chopped pecans.

Blueberriest Muffins

These blueberry muffins are the only ones that we've made every day since Foster's opened over a decade ago. That's over four thousand days of blueberry muffins! Our customers demand them; they're delicious plain or with butter. Adding finely chopped blueberries to the batter—in addition to whole berries—is the key to these moist, flavorful muffins. They freeze well, so make an extra batch for hurried mornings.

3 cups all-purpose flour

1 cup sugar

2 teaspoons baking powder

$\frac{1}{2}$ teaspoon salt

1 teaspoon ground cinnamon

8 tablespoons (1 stick) unsalted
    butter, melted

3 large eggs

$\frac{3}{4}$ cup milk

Grated zest and juice of 1 lemon

$2\frac{1}{2}$ cups fresh or frozen
    blueberries (see Note)

1 • Preheat the oven to 375 degrees.

2 • Line 12 large muffin cups with paper liners and spray the top part of the pan lightly with vegetable oil spray.

3 • Combine or sift together the flour, sugar, baking powder, salt, and cinnamon in a large bowl.

4 • Whisk together the butter, eggs, milk, lemon zest, and lemon juice in a separate bowl until well combined.

5 • Place 1 cup of the blueberries in the bowl of a food processor fitted with the metal blade and pulse several times until coarsely chopped. Stir the chopped berries into the egg mixture.

6 • Add the egg mixture to the flour mixture and stir just until the dry ingredients are moist and blended. Do not overmix. Fold in the remaining whole blueberries.

7 • Scoop the batter into the prepared muffin pan with a large ice cream scoop ($\frac{1}{3}$-cup scoop). The batter will come to the top of the paper liner or pan.

8 • Bake 25 to 30 minutes, until lightly golden brown and a toothpick inserted in the center of a muffin comes out clean.

9 • Remove from the oven and cool for 5 minutes. Turn the muffins out of the pan and serve immediately.

note: If using frozen blueberries, use them while they are still frozen; it helps hold the shape of the muffin (otherwise, the batter will become too watery).

variations: Substitute raspberries, blackberries, or strawberries for some of the blueberries for a mixed-berry muffin.

Foster's Scones

Some scone recipes call for heavy cream or half-and-half, but we've found that butter-milk, which is lower in fat, makes a lighter, flakier scone. This is the most-requested recipe at the Market; we've been making these scones since the day we opened. We've also included some of our favorite variations. Whether you make our basic scones or one of the variations, they're best served warm, right from the oven.

MAKES 1 DOZEN SCONES

Basic Scones

$4^{1}/_{2}$ cups all-purpose flour

$^{1}/_{2}$ cup sugar

2 teaspoons baking powder

$^{1}/_{2}$ teaspoon baking soda

$^{1}/_{2}$ teaspoon salt

$^{3}/_{4}$ pound (3 sticks) cold unsalted
   butter, cut into $^{1}/_{4}$-inch pieces

$1^{1}/_{4}$ cups plus 2 tablespoons
   buttermilk

Egg wash: 1 large egg beaten with
   2 tablespoons milk

1 • Preheat the oven to 400 degrees.

2 • Lightly grease 2 baking sheets and set aside.

3 • Combine the flour, sugar, baking powder, baking soda, and salt in a large bowl.

4 • Add the butter and cut it into the flour mixture using a pastry blender or 2 knives until the mixture resembles coarse meal. (Or use a food processor fitted with the metal blade to cut the butter into the flour mixture by pulsing 10 to 12 times. Transfer the mixture to a large bowl to continue making the dough.) Do not overwork the dough.

5 • Add $1^{1}/_{4}$ cups of the buttermilk and mix until just combined and the dough begins to stick together. Add the remaining buttermilk one tablespoon at a time if the dough is too dry.

6 • Turn the dough out onto a lightly floured surface and roll or pat into two 6-inch rounds, about $1^{1}/_{2}$ inches thick. Cut each round in half, then cut each half into 3 triangles (pie-shaped wedges) and place on the baking sheets. Brush the tops with the egg wash.

7 • Bake 30 to 35 minutes, until golden brown and firm to the touch. Remove from the oven and serve immediately.

The following suggestions are some of our favorite varieties:

Mixed-Berry Scones

Depending on the ripeness of the berries, you may need to add 2 to 3 tablespoons less buttermilk. Add 1½ cups mixed berries (raspberries, blackberries, and/or blueberries) to the flour-butter mixture just before adding the buttermilk.

Strawberry Scones

Depending on the ripeness of the berries, you may need 2 to 3 tablespoons less buttermilk. Add 2 cups hulled and quartered fresh strawberries (or 16 ounces frozen strawberries) to the flour-butter mixture just before adding the buttermilk.

Chocolate Chip–Espresso Scones

Add 1 cup semisweet chocolate chips to the flour-butter mixture, being careful not to overwork the dough. Dissolve ¼ cup instant espresso or coffee into the buttermilk before adding it to the flour mixture.

Cinnamon-Apple Scones

Add 1 tablespoon ground cinnamon and 2 cups peeled and chopped Granny Smith or other tart apples to the flour-butter mixture before adding the buttermilk. After brushing the scones with egg wash, sprinkle the tops with cinnamon sugar (½ cup sugar mixed with 2 tablespoons ground cinnamon).

Zesty Lemon–Almond Scones

Add 1 cup sliced almonds to the flour-butter mixture just before adding the buttermilk. Use only 1 cup buttermilk. Add the grated zest of 4 lemons and ¼ cup lemon juice to the buttermilk.

Peanut Butter–Banana Scones

Whisk ⅔ cup peanut butter into the buttermilk. Add 3 chopped bananas (approximately 2 cups) to the flour-butter mixture just before adding the buttermilk mixture.

Pear-Almond Scones

Add 1 cup sliced almonds and 2 cups peeled and chopped pears (about 2 pears) to the flour-butter mixture just before adding the buttermilk.

Pineapple-Coconut Scones

Add 1½ cups sweetened flaked coconut and 1 cup fresh diced pineapple to the flour-butter mixture just before adding the buttermilk. Use only 1 cup buttermilk.

Pumpkin-Apricot Scones

Use only ¾ cup buttermilk. Add 1 cup canned pumpkin to the buttermilk and whisk to incorporate. Add 1¼ cups chopped dried apricots to the flour mixture before adding the buttermilk mixture.

Pecan-Praline Scones

2 cups firmly packed light brown
    sugar
$^1/_4$ cup milk
3 tablespoons unsalted butter
1 teaspoon pure vanilla extract
$1^1/_4$ cups chopped pecans

1 • Place the brown sugar, milk, butter, and vanilla in a heavy saucepan over medium heat until the sugar has dissolved and the butter is melted. Bring the mixture to a low boil, stirring constantly.

2 • Add the pecans and continue to boil slowly for about 4 minutes. Remove from the heat.

3 • Drop the praline mixture by the teaspoon onto wax paper, making little "patties."

4 • Allow the pralines to cool completely for 20 to 30 minutes before removing from the wax paper. Pralines may be made up to 1 week ahead of time and stored in an airtight container.

5 • Break the praline into chunks and add to the flour-butter mixture just before adding the buttermilk.

Bananas-Foster Scones

$^1/_2$ cup firmly packed light brown
    sugar
2 firm bananas, peeled and cut
    lengthwise
$^1/_4$ cup brandy

1 • Place the brown sugar in a skillet over medium-high heat and add the bananas, cut side down. Cook 2 to 3 minutes, until the sugar starts to dissolve; do not stir.

2 • Add the brandy and cook several minutes more, carefully shaking the skillet occasionally, until all the sugar has dissolved and the mixture thickens. Remove from the heat and cool slightly.

3 • Chop the bananas, and add to the flour-butter mixture just before adding the buttermilk.

Biscuits, Scones, and Pies: Using the Food Processor

The procedures for making biscuits, scones, and pie dough are similar and they are important for a tender, flaky bread or pastry. First, the fat (usually butter, but sometimes butter and shortening) is cut into the dry ingredients, then the liquid ingredients are added and the mixture is blended until just combined. I like to do all of this by hand so that I can feel the dough. A food processor can also be used to cut in the fat, but I believe the liquids should always be mixed in by hand to be sure that the dough is not overworked, which will cause the dough to become tough.

TO USE THE FOOD PROCESSOR:

- Cut the butter into ¼-inch cubes. (Make sure the butter is very cold.)
- Place the dry ingredients in the bowl of a food processor fitted with the metal blade and pulse several times to combine.
- Add the cold butter or shortening and pulse 10 to 12 times or until the mixture resembles coarse meal.
- Transfer the mixture to a large bowl. Add the liquid ingredients and stir until the mixture just holds together when pressed between your fingers.
- Proceed as the recipe directs.

Old-Fashioned Buttermilk Biscuits

These basic biscuits are light and flaky—perfect for breakfast or, made smaller, just right for hors d'oeuvres. The amount of buttermilk that is added will depend on the brand of flour that you use and the weather. We've found that in high humidity, the dough may require less buttermilk. Always start with the minimum amount of buttermilk, then add a little more as needed. You can keep a quantity of the butter-flour mixture on hand in the refrigerator, then just add the buttermilk, roll, cut, and bake. It's a wonderful convenience, whether you're having weekend guests for breakfast or you simply want to save time.

MAKES 1 DOZEN 2½-INCH BISCUITS

3½ cups all-purpose flour

2 teaspoons baking powder

1 teaspoon baking soda

1 teaspoon salt

½ pound (2 sticks) cold unsalted butter, cut into ¼-inch cubes

1¼ to 1½ cups buttermilk

Egg wash: 1 large egg beaten with 2 tablespoons milk

1 • Preheat the oven to 425 degrees.

2 • Lightly grease a baking sheet and set aside.

3 • Sift together the flour, baking powder, baking soda, and salt in a large bowl.

4 • Add the butter and cut it into the flour mixture using a pastry blender or 2 knives until the mixture resembles coarse meal. (Or pulse 10 to 12 times in the bowl of a food processor fitted with the metal blade. Transfer the mixture to a large bowl to continue making the dough.) The dough can be made up to 1 week in advance to this point and stored in an airtight container in the refrigerator.

5 • Add 1¼ cups of the buttermilk and mix lightly just until the dough begins to stick together; do not overmix. Add up to 4 tablespoons more buttermilk, 1 tablespoon at a time, if the dough is dry.

6 • Turn the dough out onto a lightly floured surface and press together lightly just until the dough forms a ball; do not overwork the dough.

7 • Roll or pat the dough out to ¾-inch thickness. Cut with a 2½-inch biscuit or cookie cutter, dipping the cutter into flour as needed to keep the dough from sticking.

8 • Place the biscuits on the baking sheet and brush the tops with egg wash.

9 • Bake 12 to 15 minutes, until golden brown. Remove from the oven and serve immediately.

Herb-Cheese Biscuits

Add 1 cup grated Cheddar cheese; 2 trimmed, minced scallions; and 2 tablespoons chopped fresh parsley to the flour-butter mixture before adding the buttermilk.

Sweet Potato Biscuits

Add 1 cup peeled, cooked, mashed sweet potato to the flour-butter mixture before adding the buttermilk.

Watercress or Herb Biscuits

Add ¼ cup chopped watercress or herb (such as parsley, basil, or dill) to the flour-butter mixture before adding the buttermilk.

Biscuit Basics

- Do not overwork the dough and do not use too much flour on the work surface.
- The kneading for biscuits is very brief—20 seconds at most—and is simply to distribute the fat particles. Overworked biscuit dough will result in tough biscuits instead of light, flaky biscuits.
- We use butter in our biscuits because we like the flavor. Shortening and lard produce a somewhat flakier biscuit, and can be used instead of, or as a partial replacement for, the butter.
- Always bake at a high temperature and serve the biscuits piping hot.

Molasses Brown Bread

Created by my friend Bobbie Edwards, this quick bread is similar to an Irish brown bread. It's savory—not sweet—and incredibly versatile. Try it toasted for breakfast, spread with butter or honey, or with Herbed Cream Cheese (page 96) topped with smoked salmon. Or use it to make open-faced sandwiches.

MAKES TWO 9 BY 5-INCH LOAVES

3½ cups whole-wheat flour

1 cup all-purpose flour

2 teaspoons salt

1 tablespoon baking soda

1 large egg

½ cup sugar

¾ cup molasses

3 cups buttermilk

1 • Preheat the oven to 375 degrees.

2 • Grease and lightly flour two 9 by 5 by 3-inch loaf pans and set aside.

3 • Mix the whole-wheat flour, all-purpose flour, salt, and baking soda in a large bowl.

4 • Whisk the egg, sugar, molasses, and buttermilk in a separate bowl until well blended.

5 • Add the egg mixture to the flour mixture and stir to blend well. Pour the mixture evenly into the prepared pans.

6 • Bake 45 to 50 minutes, until a toothpick inserted in the center of the loaf comes out clean. Let rest for 10 to 15 minutes before removing from the pans. Serve warm or place on a baking rack to cool.

Preparing Pans for Baking

Greasing and flouring a pan keeps the batter or dough from sticking to the pan. Use vegetable shortening, cooking oil, vegetable oil spray, or clarified butter to grease pans, applying a thin, even layer with a pastry brush or paper towel. When a recipe calls for greasing the bottom of the pan only (not the sides), that is because the batter or dough needs to cling to the ungreased sides in order to rise properly.

Apple Rum-Raisin Bread

This sweet, quick bread is moist and rich, and needs no embellishment at all. It keeps up to 5 days, freezes beautifully, and makes a nice holiday gift.

MAKES TWO 9 BY 5-INCH LOAVES

4 cups all-purpose flour

1 tablespoon baking powder

2 teaspoons baking soda

2 teaspoons ground cinnamon

1 teaspoon ground cardamom

$\frac{1}{2}$ teaspoon salt

2 cups sugar

4 large eggs

$1\frac{1}{4}$ cups canola or safflower oil

$\frac{3}{4}$ cup dark rum

1 tablespoon pure vanilla extract

4 Granny Smith or other tart apples, peeled, cored, and roughly chopped

1 cup raisins

1 cup currants

1 • Preheat the oven to 350 degrees.

2 • Grease and lightly flour two 9 by 5 by 3-inch loaf pans and set aside.

3 • Sift together the flour, baking powder, baking soda, cinnamon, cardamom, and salt in a large bowl and stir to mix.

4 • Cream together the sugar, eggs, oil, rum, and vanilla in a separate bowl with an electric mixer.

5 • Add the flour mixture to the egg mixture and stir just until the dry ingredients are moist and blended. Do not overmix.

6 • Put the apples in the bowl of a food processor fitted with the metal blade and pulse several times; you should have 4 to $4\frac{1}{2}$ cups processed apples. Add the apples, raisins, and currants to the batter and stir until just blended. Pour the batter evenly into the prepared pans.

7 • Bake 1 to $1\frac{1}{4}$ hours, until the breads have risen, the tops are slightly cracked, and a toothpick inserted in the center of each loaf comes out clean. (Note: This is a very dense, moist loaf.)

8 • Let rest for 10 to 15 minutes before removing from the pans. Serve warm or place on a baking rack to cool.

variations: Bourbon can be substituted for the dark rum; raisins—dark or golden—can be substituted for the currants.

Granny Foster's Banana-Walnut Bread

This rich, sweet bread is delicious for breakfast or tea, toasted and spread with butter or cream cheese. Be sure to use very ripe bananas for the sweetest flavor and a moist texture.

4 cups all-purpose flour

2 teaspoons baking powder

1/2 teaspoon baking soda

1/2 teaspoon salt

2 teaspoons ground nutmeg

1/2 teaspoon ground cardamom

1/2 pound (2 sticks) unsalted
   butter, softened

2 cups sugar

4 large eggs, lightly beaten

8 very ripe bananas, crushed

2 teaspoons pure vanilla extract

2 cups coarsely chopped walnuts

1 • Preheat the oven to 350 degrees.

2 • Grease and lightly flour two 9 by 5 by 3-inch loaf pans and set aside.

3 • Combine the flour, baking powder, baking soda, salt, nutmeg, and cardamom in a large bowl and stir to mix.

4 • Cream together the butter and sugar in a separate bowl with an electric mixer until well blended. Slowly add the beaten eggs while continuing to beat. Add the bananas and vanilla and stir to mix.

5 • Slowly add the flour mixture to the butter mixture and stir just until all the dry ingredients are moist and well blended. Do not overmix. Fold in the walnuts and stir just to blend.

6 • Pour the batter evenly into the prepared pans and let it settle to the sides; tap the pans on the counter a few times to even out the batter.

7 • Bake 1 to 1¼ hours or until the bread rises and a toothpick inserted in the center of each loaf comes out clean. The bread will be slightly brown and cracked on the top.

8 • Let rest for 10 to 15 minutes before removing from the pans. Serve warm or place on a baking rack to cool.

variations: Golden raisins or chopped pecans can be substituted for the walnuts.

Spiced Pumpkin Bread

Although we make this beautifully colored bread from early fall through the holidays, it's really delicious all year round. Spicy, moist, and slightly sweet, it's made with canned pumpkin, so it's very easy.

3½ cups all-purpose flour

2 teaspoons baking powder

1 teaspoon baking soda

1 teaspoon salt

1 tablespoon ground cinnamon

1 tablespoon ground nutmeg

2½ cups sugar

4 large eggs

1 cup canola or safflower oil

One 15-ounce can pumpkin puree

½ cup water

1 teaspoon pure vanilla extract

1 • Preheat the oven to 350 degrees.

2 • Grease and lightly flour two 9 by 5 by 3-inch loaf pans.

3 • Sift together the flour, baking powder, baking soda, salt, cinnamon, and nutmeg in a large bowl and set aside.

4 • Whisk together the sugar, eggs, and oil in a separate bowl until well blended. Stir in the pumpkin, water, and vanilla and mix well.

5 • Add the flour mixture to the pumpkin mixture and stir just until all the ingredients are moist and blended. Do not overmix.

6 • Pour the batter evenly into the prepared pans and bake about 1 hour or until a toothpick inserted in the center of each loaf comes out clean and the top begins to crack slightly.

7 • Let rest for 10 to 15 minutes before removing from the pans. Serve warm or place on a baking rack to cool.

variations: After combining the flour and pumpkin mixtures, fold in 1 cup coarsely chopped pecans, walnuts, raisins, currants, dried cherries, dried cranberries, or chopped dried apricots if desired.

Sweet and Spicy Gingerbread

This Foster's classic is a variation of a recipe by Dorian Parker, a wonderful cook whom I met when we both worked as caterers for Martha Stewart. The coffee, dry mustard, and black pepper may sound strange, but they add a subtle depth of flavor so that the bread isn't just sweet, it's spicy. We serve it all day long—for breakfast, for tea, and even for dessert topped with warm applesauce, ice cream, or whipped cream.

MAKES TWO 9 BY 5-INCH LOAVES

3½ cups all-purpose flour

1 tablespoon baking powder

½ teaspoon baking soda

½ teaspoon salt

2 teaspoons ground cinnamon

1 teaspoon ground ginger

1 teaspoon ground cloves

1 teaspoon dry mustard

1 teaspoon freshly ground black
    pepper

12 tablespoons (1½ sticks)
    unsalted butter, softened

1½ cups firmly packed light
    brown sugar

3 large eggs

1½ cups molasses

1 cup brewed strong coffee,
    cooled

1 • Preheat the oven to 375 degrees.

2 • Lightly grease and flour two 9 by 5 by 3-inch loaf pans and set aside.

3 • Combine the flour, baking powder, baking soda, salt, cinnamon, ginger, cloves, mustard, and pepper in a large bowl and stir to mix.

4 • Cream together the butter and sugar in a large bowl with an electric mixer until light and fluffy. Slowly add the eggs, one at a time, beating well after each addition.

5 • Add the molasses to the butter mixture in a slow, steady stream while continuing to beat. Add the coffee, and continue to beat until all the ingredients are well blended.

6 • Slowly add the flour mixture to the butter mixture and stir just until all the dry ingredients are moist and blended. Do not overmix.

7 • Pour the batter evenly into the prepared pans and place the pans on the center rack of the oven.

8 • Bake 40 to 45 minutes, until the bread rises and springs back lightly when pressed and a toothpick inserted in the center of each loaf comes out clean.

9 • Let rest for 10 to 15 minutes before removing from the pans. Serve warm or place on a baking rack to cool. (This is great served warm, but it may be more difficult to slice.)

Granny Foster's Refrigerator Rolls

This is my grandmother's recipe for make-ahead yeast rolls. The dough keeps up to 2 weeks in the refrigerator and is extremely versatile. If you love to bake, I highly recommend having this dough on hand for Killer Pecan Sticky Buns (page 27), Sticky Orange-Coconut Pinwheels (page 28), and Hot Cross Buns with Raisins, Apricots, and Cranberries (page 25), as well as for these delicious dinner rolls.

MAKES 2¹⁄₂ TO 3 DOZEN ROLLS

¹⁄₂ cup warm water
(105 to 115 degrees)
One ¹⁄₄-ounce package active dry
yeast
¹⁄₂ cup sugar
8 tablespoons (1 stick) unsalted
butter
2 cups milk
1 teaspoon salt
6¹⁄₂ cups all-purpose flour
4 tablespoons (¹⁄₂ stick) unsalted
butter, melted

1 • Grease a baking sheet and set aside.

2 • Place the warm water, yeast, and about 1 teaspoon of the sugar in a small bowl; stir once or twice just to mix. Let stand in a warm place for 5 or 7 minutes, until small bubbles form on top.

3 • Meanwhile, in a saucepan, combine the butter, milk, salt, and remaining sugar and cook over very low heat, stirring constantly, until the sugar dissolves and the butter melts. Do not let the mixture go over 115 degrees or it will kill the yeast; it should be just warm enough for the sugar to dissolve. Remove from the heat and pour the mixture into a large bowl.

4 • Add the yeast mixture to the milk mixture and stir until combined. Stir in about 6 cups of the flour and mix until the mixture forms a soft dough. Add the remaining flour if the dough is still sticky.

5 • Remove the mixture from the bowl and knead on a lightly floured work surface 5 to 8 times, until the dough forms a ball or comes together.

6 • Lightly oil a large bowl and place the dough in the bowl; cover with a tea towel or plastic wrap and let rise in a warm place for 30 to 45 minutes, until the dough has doubled in bulk.

7 • Punch down the dough and divide it into 2 equal pieces. Place the pieces on a work surface and cover loosely with a tea towel or an inverted bowl and let rest 5 to 10 minutes. (The dough can be refrigerated in an airtight container until ready to use at this point. Remove from the refrigerator and let rest for 15 to 20 minutes, then proceed as the recipe directs.)

8 • Preheat the oven to 375 degrees.

9 • Working with 1 piece of dough at a time, roll out on a lightly floured work surface until ¾ to 1 inch thick. Cut with a 2½-inch round biscuit cutter.

10 • Place the rolls on the prepared baking sheet and let rise 20 to 25 minutes more, until the rolls have doubled in bulk. (It may take 10 to 15 minutes longer for dough to rise if it has been refrigerated.) Brush the tops lightly with melted butter. Repeat with the remaining dough.

11 • Bake 20 to 25 minutes, until golden brown. Remove from the oven and serve immediately.

Hot Cross Buns with Raisins, Apricots, and Cranberries

We make these buns all year, but they're especially popular around Easter. The citrus and dried fruits make these hot cross buns more flavorful than traditional buns. We use basic Granny Foster's Refrigerator Roll (page 23) dough, which can be made in advance. Our hot cross buns are great for breakfast or tea.

MAKES 1 DOZEN BUNS

½ recipe Granny Foster's Refrigerator Rolls (page 23), prepared through step 6

1 teaspoon ground cinnamon

½ teaspoon ground mace or ground nutmeg

½ teaspoon ground cardamom

¼ teaspoon ground allspice

Grated zest of 1 lemon

Grated zest of 1 orange

⅓ cup currants or dark raisins

⅓ cup chopped dried apricots

⅓ cup dried cranberries

⅓ cup golden raisins

Egg wash: 1 large egg beaten with 2 tablespoons milk

1 recipe Lemon Glaze (recipe follows), optional

1 • Preheat the oven to 350 degrees.

2 • Grease a baking sheet and set aside.

3 • Remove the refrigerator roll dough from the refrigerator and punch it down. Cover and set aside to rest at room temperature at least 10 minutes or up to 30 minutes.

4 • Combine the cinnamon, mace, cardamom, allspice, lemon zest, orange zest, currants, apricots, cranberries, and raisins in a bowl and stir to mix.

5 • Place the dough on a lightly floured surface and knead the fruit-and-spice mixture into the dough for 3 to 4 minutes, until it is evenly distributed.

6 • Divide the mixture into 12 pieces, each one about the size of a small orange. Roll and knead each piece of dough into a round by pressing down lightly as you roll.

7 • Place the shaped rolls on the prepared baking sheet about 2 inches apart and allow them to rise, loosely covered, about 30 minutes in a warm place, until the dough has almost doubled in size. Brush the rolls with egg wash and bake 25 to 30 minutes, until the rolls are golden brown and firm to the touch.

8 • Remove the rolls from the oven and allow to cool. Drizzle a crisscross shape across the top of the rolls with the glaze and allow to dry before serving.

Lemon Glaze

¹/₂ cup confectioners' sugar
1 tablespoon fresh lemon juice
Grated zest of 1 lemon

Place the confectioners' sugar in a bowl and whisk in the lemon juice until smooth. You will have a thin icing. Add the lemon zest and stir to mix. Store in an airtight container until ready to use.

Killer Pecan Sticky Buns

2 tablespoons unsalted butter, softened

$\frac{1}{2}$ recipe Granny Foster's Refrigerator Rolls (page 23), prepared through step 6

$\frac{3}{4}$ cup raisins

$\frac{1}{4}$ cup bourbon

1 teaspoon ground cinnamon

$1\frac{1}{4}$ cups firmly packed light brown sugar

8 tablespoons (1 stick) unsalted butter, melted

$\frac{1}{2}$ cup honey

$\frac{3}{4}$ cup coarsely chopped pecans

1 • Preheat the oven to 350 degrees.

2 • Grease a deep 9-inch round glass baking dish with the softened butter and set aside.

3 • Remove the refrigerator roll dough from the refrigerator, punch it down, cover loosely with a tea towel or plastic wrap, and set aside to rest for 15 to 20 minutes.

4 • Combine the raisins and bourbon in a bowl and set aside to soak 20 to 30 minutes, until plumped.

5 • Stir together the cinnamon, $\frac{1}{2}$ cup of the brown sugar, and the butter in a separate bowl and set aside.

6 • Stir together the remaining brown sugar, the honey, and the pecans in a separate bowl. Spread this mixture evenly in the bottom of the glass baking dish and set aside.

7 • Roll the dough out on a lightly floured surface into a 12 by 6-inch rectangle about $\frac{1}{8}$ inch thick. Spread the brown sugar–butter mixture evenly over the center of the dough, leaving about 1 inch of exposed dough all the way around. Drain the raisins and sprinkle them over the brown sugar–butter mixture.

8 • Roll up the dough lengthwise into a 12-inch log.

9 • Place the log, seam side down, on the work surface and use a sharp knife to cut the log crosswise into twelve 1-inch slices. Place the slices in the baking dish, cut side down, on top of the pecan mixture. (The slices should touch one another, and should fit snugly in the dish.) Set aside in a warm place and allow to rise 15 to 20 minutes, until slightly puffy.

10 • Place the dish on a baking sheet and bake 50 minutes to 1 hour, until the buns are golden brown and a toothpick inserted in the center comes out clean.

11 • Remove from the oven and cool 5 to 10 minutes. Run a knife around the edge of the dish to loosen the buns. While still warm, place a platter or plate on top of the baking dish. Turn the dish over to unmold the sticky buns onto the platter. Serve immediately.

Sticky Orange-Coconut Pinwheels

A treat with breakfast or at tea, this coconut- and orange-flavored yeast bread is topped with a rich, gooey glaze that melts right into the bread.

MAKES 2 DOZEN PINWHEELS

Glaze

½ cup sugar
½ cup sour cream
¼ cup fresh orange juice
4 tablespoons (½ stick) unsalted butter

Combine the sugar, sour cream, orange juice, and butter in a medium saucepan. Stir over medium heat until the sugar dissolves. Bring to a low boil and boil about 3 minutes, stirring constantly.

Pinwheels

½ recipe Granny Foster's Refrigerator Rolls (page 23), prepared through step 6
2 tablespoons unsalted butter, melted
¾ cup sugar
1 cup sweetened flaked coconut
Grated zest of 1 orange

1 • Lightly butter two 9-inch glass pie plates and set aside.

2 • Remove the refrigerator roll dough from the refrigerator, punch it down, cover loosely with a tea towel or plastic wrap, and set aside to rest for 15 to 20 minutes. Divide the dough into 2 even pieces and form into rounds. Using a rolling pin, roll each round of dough into a 12-inch circle about ¼ inch thick. Brush each with 1 tablespoon of the butter; set aside.

3 • Combine the sugar, ¾ cup of the coconut, and the orange zest in a small bowl and stir to mix. Sprinkle the mixture over the dough rounds. Cut each round into 12 pie-shaped wedges. Roll up the wedges, starting at the wide end, to form a crescent shape.

4 • Arrange the rolled wedges in pinwheel fashion in the prepared pie plates. Cover with a tea towel and let rise 30 minutes, until doubled in bulk.

5 • Preheat the oven to 350 degrees.

6 • Bake 25 to 30 minutes, until golden brown and firm to the touch in the center.

7 • Cool slightly (about 5 minutes) before drizzling the glaze over the warm pinwheels. Sprinkle the pinwheels with the remaining coconut and serve warm.

New York–Style Crumb Cake

We've served this rich breakfast cake since we opened, for all the New York transplants and homesick Duke students. It's great with morning coffee. As you make this, you'll think you have too much topping and not enough crust. Don't worry: that is how the cake should look.

MAKES 2 DOZEN 2$\frac{1}{2}$ BY 3-INCH PIECES

Topping

5 cups all-purpose flour

2 cups firmly packed light brown sugar

1 tablespoon plus 1$\frac{1}{2}$ teaspoons ground cinnamon

1 pound (4 sticks) unsalted butter, melted

Combine the flour, brown sugar, and cinnamon in a bowl and stir to blend well. Stir in the butter and set aside.

Cake

3 cups all-purpose flour

1 cup sugar

1 tablespoon plus 1$\frac{1}{2}$ teaspoons baking powder

$\frac{1}{2}$ teaspoon salt

2 large eggs

1$\frac{1}{4}$ cups milk

$\frac{1}{4}$ cup canola or safflower oil

1 tablespoon plus 2 teaspoons pure vanilla extract

$\frac{1}{3}$ cup confectioners' sugar, to garnish

1 • Preheat the oven to 325 degrees.

2 • Grease and lightly flour a 12 by 17 by 1-inch jelly roll pan.

3 • Sift together the flour, sugar, baking powder, and salt in a large bowl.

4 • Combine the eggs, milk, oil, and vanilla in a separate bowl and whisk until well blended.

5 • Add the flour mixture to the egg mixture and stir just until the dry ingredients are moist and blended. Do not overmix.

6 • Spread the cake batter evenly in the bottom of the jelly roll pan and set aside. The batter will barely cover the bottom of the pan. It should look sparse.

7 • Sprinkle all the crumb topping evenly over the dough and press lightly into the batter.

8 • Bake 35 to 40 minutes, until the cake rises and the topping bakes into the dough.

9 • Remove from the oven and cool slightly in the pan. Trim the edges and cut into 2$\frac{1}{2}$ by 3-inch pieces. (For a smaller slice, cut the piece in half down the center or on the diagonal.) Sprinkle with confectioners' sugar and serve immediately.

Classic Sour Cream Coffee Cake

This classic cake is one of our most popular breakfast breads. It keeps well (up to 2 or 3 days) and is delicious warm or at room temperature. The Brown Sugar–Pecan Filling can be made ahead; the cake freezes beautifully and is wonderful for brunch or tea.

MAKES ONE 10-INCH BUNDT CAKE

Brown Sugar–Pecan Filling

$1/3$ cup firmly packed light brown
    sugar
2 teaspoons ground cinnamon
2 teaspoons all-purpose flour
1 cup coarsely chopped pecans

Combine the brown sugar, cinnamon, flour, and pecans in a bowl and stir until well mixed. Set aside or refrigerate in an airtight container until ready to use.

Cake

$3^{1}/_{2}$ cups all-purpose flour
2 teaspoons baking powder
$1/2$ teaspoon baking soda
$1/2$ teaspoon salt
10 tablespoons ($1^{1}/_{4}$ sticks)
    unsalted butter, softened
1 cup sugar
3 large eggs
$1^{3}/_{4}$ cups sour cream

1 • Preheat the oven to 350 degrees.

2 • Grease and lightly flour a 10-inch bundt pan and set aside.

3 • Sift together the flour, baking powder, baking soda, and salt in a large bowl and set aside.

4 • Cream together the butter and sugar in a separate bowl with an electric mixer until light and fluffy, starting on low speed, then increasing to medium.

5 • Add the eggs one at a time, beating well after each addition, scraping down the sides of the bowl after each addition.

6 • Add the flour mixture, alternating with the sour cream, to the egg mixture, beating slowly, beginning and ending with the flour mixture. Scrape the sides of the bowl several times. Beat just until all the ingredients are well combined. Do not overmix.

7 • Spoon half the batter into the prepared pan. Sprinkle evenly with the Brown Sugar–Pecan Filling. Spoon the remaining batter on top of the filling.

8 • Bake 50 minutes to 1 hour, until golden brown and a toothpick inserted in the center of the cake comes out clean.

9 • Remove from the oven and cool in the pan for 10 to 15 minutes. Turn the cake out onto a baking rack to cool completely.

variations: Substitute $1/2$ cup chocolate chips or $1/2$ cup fresh berries for the pecans. Other spices—such as 1 teaspoon ground nutmeg and 1 teaspoon ground cardamom—can be used instead of the cinnamon. Add 1 tablespoon grated lemon zest or orange zest with 1 cup chopped almonds in place of the pecans.

Foster's Omelets

An omelet can be as delicious plain as filled with an almost endless array of cooked vegeta-bles, cheeses, herbs, smoked meats, fish, and more. Look in your refrigerator and utilize left-overs such as grilled asparagus, cooked broccoli, or spinach. I always garnish the omelet with a sauce, salsa, or herb that complements the filling. If you're short on time, Foster's Salsa (page 90) is a tasty alternative to just about any of the garnishes mentioned here.

Basic Omelet

SERVES 1

3 large eggs
Salt and freshly ground black
    pepper to taste
1¹/₂ tablespoons unsalted butter

1 • Heat an 8-inch nonstick omelet pan over medium heat.

2 • Beat the eggs with the salt and pepper in a small bowl with a whisk or fork.

3 • Place the butter in the pan and swirl it around in the pan to distribute evenly. When the butter has melted and the foam subsides, pour the eggs into the pan.

4 • Let the eggs sit for a few seconds to begin cooking, then push the outer edges of the eggs toward the center of the pan with a spatula. As they cook, con-tinue pushing the edges toward the center, allowing uncooked egg to flow to the outer edges of the pan.

5 • When the eggs are still moist but no longer runny, place the desired filling on one side of the omelet.

6 • Fold the omelet over the filling with a spatula. Slide the omelet onto a warm plate and serve immediately or keep warm while you make the remaining ome-lets. Garnish as desired.

The following suggestions are some of our favorite combinations:

Asparagus, Corn, and Spinach with Chèvre
Fill each omelet with cooked asparagus tips, cooked corn kernels, fresh spinach leaves, and crumbled chèvre. Fold the omelet over the filling, top with additional chèvre if desired, and serve immediately.

Roasted Tomatoes, Fresh Mozzarella, and Pesto
Fill each omelet with Oven-Roasted Tomatoes (page 235), thinly sliced fresh mozzarella, and fresh basil chiffonade (page 34). Fold the omelet over the filling, top with Foster's Pesto (page 90), and serve immediately.

Spinach, Tomato, and Feta

Fill each omelet with wilted spinach (page 213), crumbled drained feta, and sautéed chopped tomatoes. Fold the omelet over the filling. Top with a dollop of Artichoke Aïoli (page 93) or Cajun Rémoulade (page 40) and serve immediately.

Mushrooms, Swiss, and Caramelized Onions

Fill each omelet with sautéed sliced mushrooms, grated Swiss cheese, and caramelized onions (page 142). Fold the omelet over the filling, top with caramelized onions and fresh chopped herbs, and serve immediately.

Grilled Vegetable Ratatouille

Fill each omelet with Grilled Vegetable Ratatouille (page 124), crumbled chèvre or grated mozzarella, and fresh basil chiffonade (see below). Fold the omelet over the filling, top with Grilled Vegetable Ratatouille or chopped tomatoes, and serve immediately.

Smoked Salmon and Herbed Cream Cheese

Fill each omelet with thinly sliced smoked salmon, Herbed Cream Cheese (page 96), and caramelized onions (page 142). Fold the omelet over the filling, top with Foster's Arugula Pesto (page 236), and serve immediately.

Lump Crabmeat with Farmer Cheese and Crunchy Corn Relish

Fill the omelet with lump crabmeat and farmer cheese (or cream cheese). Fold the omelet over the filling, top with Crunchy Corn Relish (page 193), and serve immediately.

Bacon, Tomato, Arugula, and Chèvre with Croutons

Fill each omelet with crumbled cooked bacon, diced tomato, crumbled chèvre, croutons, and fresh basil chiffonade (see below). Fold the omelet over the filling, top with croutons and Foster's Pesto (page 90), and serve immediately.

Chiffonade

The culinary term "chiffonade" means to slice very thinly into fine strips. The term is used for lettuces and other greens, as well as fresh herbs. The resulting delicate, thin ribbons of lettuce or herbs are usually used as a garnish, but are occasionally used to make salads. To "chiffonade," either stack or roll up the greens or herb leaves and slice crosswise very thinly. The purpose of this technique is to keep the delicate leaf from bruising, as it would if you chopped it.

Grits Soufflé

Heartier, creamier, and more custardlike than a classic soufflé, this dish is also easier and less temperamental. It's especially good for people who think they don't like grits; we find they always come back for seconds! With the added spiciness from the peppers and texture from the corn, this dish is also delicious as a side to Balsamic-Roasted Chicken (page 154) or Salmon Cakes with Crunchy Corn Relish (page 192), or Foster's Salsa (page 90). If you don't have a soufflé dish, you can use a shallow baking dish, but adjust the cooking time accordingly, since it will cook faster.

SERVES 8 TO 10

8 tablespoons (1 stick) unsalted butter

3 cups water

1 teaspoon salt

2 cups yellow grits (do not use quick-cooking grits)

3 cups milk

1 tablespoon sugar

2 cups (8 ounces) grated pepper Jack cheese

1 red bell pepper, cored, seeded, and diced

1 jalapeño, seeded and diced

Kernels from 2 ears fresh corn (1 cup fresh or frozen corn)

4 eggs, lightly beaten

1 tablespoon fresh thyme or 1 teaspoon dried thyme

2 teaspoons salt

½ teaspoon freshly ground black pepper

1 • Preheat the oven to 350 degrees.

2 • Butter a 3-quart soufflé dish or 9 by 13-inch baking dish with 2 tablespoons of the butter and set aside.

3 • Bring the water and salt to a boil in a medium saucepan. Reduce heat to medium and gradually add the grits in a slow, steady stream while whisking constantly. Cook and stir about 10 minutes, until the grits have thickened.

4 • Add 1½ cups of the milk and cook and stir about 5 minutes more, until the milk is absorbed.

5 • Remove from the heat and stir in the remaining milk, the remaining butter, and the sugar until well blended.

6 • Add the cheese, red bell pepper, jalapeño, corn, eggs, thyme, and salt and pepper and mix well. Pour the mixture into the prepared soufflé dish and bake 45 to 55 minutes, until the soufflé has risen and is firm around the edges. The center should be slightly soft. Remove from the oven and let stand 5 minutes before serving. Serve warm.

variations: Try using different types of cheese, such as Cheddar, chèvre, or Swiss. Chopped scallions, onions, or fresh basil can also be added for a little extra flavor if desired.

Mushroom-Risotto Hash with Fried Eggs and Grilled Ham

Our mushroom risotto serves double duty: it can be enjoyed as a starter, a side, or a main dish for lunch or supper, then leftovers can be turned into a delicious hash for brunch later in the week. The ham can be grilled in advance and kept warm while you cook the eggs and heat the hash.

SERVES 4

4 slices Grilled Ham (page 37)

4 cups Mushroom-Risotto Hash (recipe follows)

8 fried eggs

4 fresh basil leaves, cut into very thin strips (chiffonade), to garnish

1 • Place a slice of Grilled Ham on each of 4 plates.

2 • Top the ham with 1 cup Mushroom-Risotto Hash.

3 • Top the hash with 2 fried eggs.

Mushroom-Risotto Hash

5 cups chicken broth (page 57)

3 tablespoons unsalted butter

3 tablespoons olive oil

8 ounces fresh mushrooms, such as button, crimini, and/or shiitakes, wiped clean, stems removed, and sliced

1 yellow onion, diced

2 ribs celery, diced

1 cup Arborio rice

½ cup dry white wine

3 tablespoons fresh thyme or 1 tablespoon dried thyme

Salt and freshly ground black pepper to taste

1 • Bring the chicken broth to a simmer in a medium saucepan over medium-high heat. Reduce heat to low and keep the broth warm.

2 • Melt 1 tablespoon of the butter with 1 tablespoon of the olive oil in a large skillet over medium-high heat and add the mushrooms. Turn heat to high and cook 2 to 3 minutes, stirring occasionally, until the mushrooms are lightly brown. Remove from the pan and set aside.

3 • Add 1 tablespoon of the butter and 1 tablespoon of the olive oil to the same pan and reduce heat to medium. Add the onion and celery. Cook, stirring often, for about 5 minutes, until the onions are soft.

4 • Add the rice and stir about 1 minute, until you see a white dot in each grain of rice (the rest of the rice grain will be slightly translucent). Add the wine and stir the rice with a wooden spoon until the wine is absorbed.

5 • Ladle in 1 cup of the hot chicken broth and simmer, stirring constantly, until all the broth is absorbed.

Add another cup of broth and continue to cook, stirring constantly.

6 • Continue adding broth, 1 cup at a time, stirring constantly, until all of the broth has been absorbed. The entire process will take 20 to 25 minutes. When done, the rice will be creamy and tender, but not mushy. Stir in the mushrooms and thyme and season with salt and pepper. (Note: Risotto can be served as a starter or side dish at this point; sprinkle with grated Parmesan cheese and serve immediately.)

7 • Spread the risotto in a greased 9 by 9-inch baking dish and allow it to cool to room temperature. Cover and refrigerate the risotto until it is firm, 1 to 2 hours, or up to 2 days.

8 • To make the hash, add the remaining olive oil and butter to a large cast-iron or nonstick skillet and heat over medium-high heat.

9 • Cut the risotto into quarters (4 equal squares) and place them in the pan. (Note: Don't worry if the risotto squares break up a bit.) Let the risotto cook until it is brown and crispy, about 3 to 4 minutes per side. Place in the oven to keep warm until ready to serve.

Grilled Ham

4 large, 1/4-inch-thick slices baked ham

1 • Heat a grill, grill pan, or skillet over medium-high heat until a drop of water sizzles.

2 • Add the ham and cook about 2 minutes per side until heated through and grill marks are visible.

Corn Pancakes with Crispy Fried Oysters and Cajun Rémoulade

Great for breakfast, brunch, or supper, this dish can also be served as a first course. Oysters are at their best during the "r" months (they spawn in June, July, and August and aren't quite as tasty), so enjoy this dish when they're in season. The corn cakes—which are similar to johnnycakes—are also great topped with caviar, smoked fish, or chicken and served as an hors d'oeuvre. Serve with mixed greens or fried, poached, or scrambled eggs.

SERVES 4 TO 6

Corn Pancakes

1 cup all-purpose flour

$^1\!/_2$ cup yellow cornmeal

2 tablespoons sugar

2 teaspoons baking powder

1 teaspoon salt

$^1\!/_2$ teaspoon freshly ground black
  pepper

Pinch of ground red pepper
  (cayenne)

3 large eggs

$^3\!/_4$ cup buttermilk

6 tablespoons ($^3\!/_4$ stick) unsalted
  butter, melted

Kernels from 4 ears fresh corn
  (2 cups fresh or frozen corn)

1 tablespoon chopped fresh basil

1 tablespoon chopped fresh chives

1 cup Cajun Rémoulade (page 40)
  or 1 cup Foster's Salsa (page
  90)

1 • Preheat the oven to 200 degrees.

2 • Mix together the flour, cornmeal, sugar, baking powder, salt, black pepper, and ground red pepper in a bowl and stir to blend.

3 • Combine the eggs, buttermilk, 3 tablespoons of the butter, corn, basil, and chives in a separate bowl and stir to mix.

4 • Add the flour mixture to the egg mixture and stir just until the dry ingredients are moist and blended. Do not overmix.

5 • Brush a hot griddle or skillet with the remaining melted butter and heat over medium-high heat. Spoon 1 heaping tablespoon of the mixture onto the griddle or skillet and cook about 2 minutes per side, until the cakes are golden brown and fluffy. This will make 15 or 16 small cakes. Place on a baking sheet and keep warm in the oven while you prepare the remaining cakes. Serve with oysters (recipe follows) and Cajun Rémoulade (page 40) or Foster's Salsa (page 90).

Crispy Fried Oysters

These can also be served without the corn cakes. They make a tasty supper served with Asian Cole Slaw with Corn and Frisée (page 111) and Corn and Roasted Red Pepper Chowder (page 72).

16 to 18 large oysters, shucked
  (10 to 12 ounces)
½ cup all-purpose flour
¼ cup yellow cornmeal
2 large eggs
¼ cup milk
3 tablespoons unsalted butter
3 tablespoons canola or
  safflower oil
Salt and freshly ground black
  pepper to taste

1 • Drain the oysters and place on a paper towel to dry slightly.

2 • Mix together ¼ cup of the flour and the cornmeal in a shallow bowl and set aside. Place the remaining flour in a small shallow bowl and set aside.

3 • Whisk together the eggs and milk in a separate bowl and set aside.

4 • Dredge the oysters one at a time in the flour, then in the egg mixture. Dredge the oysters lightly in the flour-cornmeal mixture and place them on a baking sheet. Repeat until all the oysters have been dipped. Place the baking sheet with the oysters in the freezer or refrigerator for about 1 hour, until the crust has set.

5 • Heat the butter and oil in a large, heavy skillet (preferably cast iron) over medium-high heat until hot but not smoking. Add the oysters, a few at a time, and cook until golden brown on both sides, 2 to 3 minutes total time. Remove the oysters from the oil and drain on a paper towel. Keep warm in the oven until all the oysters are cooked. (Note: You may need to add additional butter and oil to the skillet as you cook the oysters.) Sprinkle with salt and pepper and serve immediately on top of the corn cakes with wedges of fresh lemon and 1 heaping tablespoon of Cajun Rémoulade (page 40) or Foster's Salsa (page 90).

Cajun Rémoulade

Serve with Salmon Cakes (page 192), Crispy Fried Oysters (page 39), or Sautéed Soft-Shell Crabs (page 197).

1 cup good-quality mayonnaise

1 hard-boiled egg, peeled and chopped

¼ cup chopped roasted red bell pepper (see sidebar)

¼ cup chopped celery

Juice of 1 lemon

1 scallion, trimmed and minced

1 tablespoon chopped fresh parsley

1 tablespoon drained capers

1 teaspoon spicy mustard (try Dijon, whole-grain, or Cajun mustard)

1 garlic clove, chopped

½ teaspoon hot sauce (such as Tabasco or Texas Pete)

¼ teaspoon ground red pepper (cayenne)

¼ teaspoon ground paprika

¼ teaspoon red pepper flakes

1 • Place the mayonnaise, egg, roasted red bell pepper, celery, lemon juice, scallion, parsley, capers, mustard, garlic, hot sauce, ground red pepper, paprika, and red pepper flakes in the bowl of a food processor fitted with the metal blade. Pulse several times until well blended. Do not overmix; this should be chunky, not smooth.

2 • Serve immediately or refrigerate in an airtight container up to 5 days or until ready to use.

Roasted Peppers

We roast peppers two ways: in the oven or over a gas flame on a stovetop. To roast peppers in the oven, rub whole peppers with olive oil, place on a baking sheet, and roast in a preheated 450-degree oven, turning twice, until the skin is charred, about 20 minutes. Remove the peppers from the oven and cool, then remove the charred skin, stem, core, and seeds, leaving as much of the flesh as possible. To roast peppers over a gas flame, use tongs to hold the peppers—one at a time—over a high flame, rotating the pepper until all sides are charred and blackened. Place in a paper bag and fold to close (or place in a bowl and cover with plastic wrap) and let cool. Remove the charred skin, stem, core, and seeds, leaving as much of the flesh as possible.

Huevos Rancheros with Granny Foster's Chili Sauce

If you're short on time, use good-quality purchased salsa instead of Granny Foster's Chili Sauce and use tortilla chips instead of frying your own tortillas. Except for the eggs, all the components of this robust breakfast dish can be made in advance.

SERVES 4

8 Crispy Corn Tortillas (page 42)

4 cups Spicy Black Beans (recipe follows)

8 fried eggs

1 cup (4 ounces) grated pepper Jack cheese

1 cup Granny Foster's Chili Sauce (page 43) or Foster's Salsa (page 90)

1 avocado, to garnish, optional

Sour cream, to garnish, optional

1 • Place 2 Crispy Corn Tortillas on each of 4 plates, slightly overlapping the tortillas.

2 • Spoon 1 cup of the Spicy Black Beans over the tortillas.

3 • Place 2 fried eggs over the beans.

4 • Sprinkle ¼ cup of the pepper Jack cheese over the eggs.

5 • Drizzle ¼ cup Granny Foster's Chili Sauce or Foster's Salsa over the entire dish.

6 • Peel, pit, and thinly slice the avocado. Garnish each serving with avocado and a dollop of sour cream and serve.

Spicy Black Beans

These spicy beans are also delicious served with quesadillas. They can be prepared up to 5 days in advance.

MAKES 2½ TO 3 CUPS COOKED BEANS

1 cup dried black beans, rinsed and picked over, or canned beans (see Variation)

2 teaspoons salt

2 tablespoons canola or safflower oil

1 onion, finely diced

1½ teaspoons ground cumin

2 teaspoons dried oregano (preferably Mexican oregano)

1 canned chipotle in adobo sauce, minced

1 • Place the beans in a large pot with water to cover by 3 inches and bring to a boil. Reduce heat and simmer uncovered 45 minutes. Remove from the heat, drain, rinse, and return to the pot.

2 • Add fresh water to cover the beans by 2 inches. Bring the beans to a boil over high heat. Reduce heat to medium and cook the beans at a low boil until they are completely tender, about 1 hour.

3 • Stir in the salt, then let the beans cool in the cooking water at least 15 minutes. Drain the beans, reserving 1 cup of the cooking liquid.

4 • Heat the oil in a large, heavy skillet over medium-high heat.

5 • Add the onion, cumin, and oregano. Cook and stir about 4 minutes, until the onion begins to soften.

6 • Stir in the chipotle and black beans, along with the reserved cooking liquid. Reduce heat to low and cook until the beans are warm. (Note: This can be prepared in advance up to 5 days up to this point. Refrigerate the beans in an airtight container and reheat before serving.)

variation: You can substitute two 15-ounce cans of black beans and proceed as follows: Rinse and drain the beans into a bowl to reserve 1 cup of the liquid and proceed directly to step 4.

Crispy Corn Tortillas

MAKES 8 CRISPY TORTILLAS

1 cup canola or safflower oil
Eight 6-inch corn tortillas

1 • Preheat the oven to 200 degrees.

2 • Pour enough oil in a small skillet to reach a depth of ½ inch. Heat the oil over medium-high heat until it is very hot but not smoking, about 375 degrees.

3 • When the oil is hot, use tongs to place a tortilla carefully in the oil. The oil should sizzle vigorously around the edges of the tortilla. If it does not, the oil is not hot enough and the tortillas will be soggy.

4 • Fry each tortilla 15 seconds on one side, then turn the tortilla and fry 45 seconds longer. Transfer the fried tortilla to a baking sheet lined with paper towels to drain. The tortillas will become crisp as they cool.

5 • Repeat with remaining tortillas, adding more oil if necessary to maintain a depth of at least ½ inch. Place in the oven to keep warm until ready to serve.

Granny Foster's Chili Sauce

My father makes this tasty sauce every summer, when tomatoes are plentiful. Made from a recipe handed down from his mother, it's delicious with eggs and just about any garden-fresh vegetable.

MAKES ABOUT 1 QUART (4 CUPS) CHILI SAUCE

3 tomatoes, blanched, peeled, cored, and chopped

$\frac{1}{2}$ cup distilled white vinegar

$\frac{1}{2}$ cup sugar

1 yellow onion, chopped

1 green bell pepper, cored, seeded, and diced

1 jalapeño, stem removed, diced, with seeds, or other fresh hot pepper such as cayenne or serrano

2 teaspoons salt

$\frac{1}{2}$ teaspoon ground cloves

$\frac{1}{2}$ teaspoon ground ginger

$\frac{1}{4}$ teaspoon ground cinnamon

1 Granny Smith or other tart apple, peeled, cored, and chopped

1 • Place the tomatoes, vinegar, sugar, onion, green bell pepper, jalapeño, salt, cloves, ginger, and cinnamon in a saucepan over medium heat and cook for 35 to 40 minutes, stirring occasionally.

2 • Add the apple and cook, stirring frequently, 25 to 30 minutes more, or until mixture has thickened. Cool completely. Refrigerate in an airtight container until ready to use or up to 1 week.

Panama Buttermilk Pancakes

We call these "Panama" pancakes because of the banana and coconut in the fruit topping. The dry ingredients can be mixed up to 5 days in advance, so when you're ready, simply add the liquid ingredients and fire up the griddle.

2 cups all-purpose flour

$1/4$ cup granulated sugar

2 tablespoons firmly packed light
  brown sugar

1 tablespoon baking powder

1 teaspoon baking soda

$1/2$ teaspoon salt

3 large eggs, separated

2 cups buttermilk

12 tablespoons ($1^1/2$ sticks)
  unsalted butter, melted

1 tablespoon dark rum
  or 2 teaspoons pure vanilla
  extract

1 pint fresh strawberries,
  hulled and sliced

2 bananas, peeled and sliced
  $1/4$ inch thick on the diagonal

$1/2$ cup sweetened flaked coconut

1 • Mix the flour, granulated sugar, brown sugar, baking powder, baking soda, and salt together in a large bowl and set aside. (May be kept in an airtight container up to 5 days.)

2 • Whisk the egg yolks, buttermilk, 6 tablespoons of the butter, and rum in a separate bowl and set aside.

3 • Whisk the egg whites in a separate bowl until soft peaks form and set aside.

4 • Heat a skillet or griddle over medium-high heat until a drop of batter sizzles. Spread about 1 tablespoon of the butter evenly over the griddle.

5 • Add the flour mixture to the egg-buttermilk mixture and stir just until well blended. Gently fold in the egg whites just until combined. Do not overmix.

6 • Scoop about $1/4$ cup of the batter, using an ice cream scoop or measuring cup with a handle, into the hot skillet. Allow the batter to spread, or spread it with the bottom of the scoop or measuring cup before you add another pancake. They should be about 2 to 3 inches apart.

7 • Cook the pancakes 2 to 3 minutes, until they start to bubble on top. Flip the cakes and cook about 2 minutes more. Continue the process, adding additional butter as needed, until all the pancakes are cooked. Remove from the skillet and serve immediately, topped with the strawberries, bananas, and coconut.

variations: Instead of the banana, coconut, and strawberry topping, sprinkle fresh berries, chopped mango, chopped papaya, chopped pineapple, or chopped kiwi into the pancake batter just after it is poured into the skillet, before flipping the pancakes.

buttermilk pancakes

Another variation is to omit the brown sugar from the batter, and sprinkle it into the pancake batter just after it has been poured into the skillet. The sugar melts and is a nice surprise when you bite into the pancake.

Garden Vegetable Frittata

Great for make-ahead brunch, tailgate lunches, and picnics of any kind, frittatas can be made in advance and served at room temperature.

SERVES 4 TO 6

1 tablespoon olive oil

1 tablespoon unsalted butter

3 red potatoes, sliced $1/4$ inch thick

1 red onion, thinly sliced

1 zucchini, cut into $1/4$-inch rounds

1 red bell pepper, cored, seeded, and diced

1 cup firmly packed spinach, washed, drained, and stems removed

10 large eggs, lightly beaten

1 cup (4 ounces) grated Gruyère or Swiss cheese

Salt and freshly ground black pepper to taste

$1/4$ cup cream cheese

1 tablespoon fresh rosemary

1 • Preheat the oven to 400 degrees.

2 • Heat the olive oil and butter in a 12-inch, ovenproof, nonstick skillet over medium-high heat. Add the potatoes and onion and cook 10 to 12 minutes, stirring occasionally, until light brown and crispy.

3 • Add the zucchini and red bell pepper and stir and cook 3 to 4 minutes more, until the zucchini is lightly cooked but still crunchy. Add the spinach and stir and cook about 1 minute longer, until the spinach wilts.

4 • Whisk together the eggs, Gruyère, salt, and pepper in a bowl and pour over the vegetables. Remove the skillet from the heat and gently shake the skillet to distribute the eggs evenly through the mixture. Divide the cream cheese into $1/4$-inch pieces and distribute evenly on top of the egg mixture. Sprinkle with rosemary.

5 • Bake 12 to 15 minutes, uncovered, just until the eggs set. Remove from the oven, cut into wedges, and serve immediately, or let cool and serve at room temperature. Frittata can be made up to 2 hours in advance.

variations: Like omelets, frittatas can be flavored with an almost unlimited list of ingredients, from herbs to cheeses to smoked meats and more. Check the refrigerator for leftovers, see what's fresh in the garden, and then decide what to add to your frittata.

Turkey–Sweet Potato Hash

This lighter, more healthful variation on traditional hash is a delicious way to use up left-over turkey.

SERVES 4

1 sweet potato, peeled and diced

1 tablespoon unsalted butter

2 tablespoons olive oil

1 red onion, chopped

1 red bell pepper, cored, seeded, and diced

1 pound skinless cooked turkey breast, chopped

Salt and freshly ground black pepper to taste

4 large eggs

1 tablespoon chopped fresh chives

1 tablespoon chopped fresh parsley

1 • Place the diced potatoes in a saucepan and add enough water to cover by 1 inch. Bring to a boil and cook 3 to 4 minutes, until the potatoes are just barely tender; they should still be firm and hold their shape. Drain well and set aside.

2 • Heat the butter and 1 tablespoon of the olive oil in a large skillet over medium-high heat. Add the onion and red bell pepper and cook, stirring occasionally, 4 to 5 minutes, until light brown.

3 • Add the potatoes and cook 6 to 7 minutes, stirring occasionally, until potatoes are crispy. Add the remaining olive oil and the turkey. Season with salt and pepper and cook 1 to 2 minutes more, stirring occasionally.

4 • Make four 3-inch holes in the hash and break an egg into each hole. Reduce heat to low, cover, and cook 4 to 5 minutes, until the eggs are cooked to the desired degree of doneness. Sprinkle with the chives, parsley, and additional salt and pepper, if desired. Use a spatula to divide into portions and serve immediately.

variations: Use chicken, smoked turkey, smoked trout, smoked salmon, or andouille sausage instead of turkey. Substitute red new potatoes, Yukon gold, or other potatoes for the sweet potatoes and try other peppers—such as Italian sweet peppers or banana peppers—instead of the bell peppers. This is also great topped with Granny Foster's Chili Sauce (page 43) or Foster's Salsa (page 90).

Quick Broth   •   Chicken, Leek, and Fennel Soup   •

Succotash Soup with Chicken and Oven-Roasted Tomatoes

•   Italian-Style Chicken and Mushroom Soup with Orecchiette   •

Chicken Chili with Navy Beans   •   Chicken Gumbo with Chicken-

Apple Sausage   •   Chicken and Sweet Potato Soup   •

Old-Fashioned Turkey Noodle Soup   •   Provençal-Style Beef and

Bean Soup   •   Split Pea Soup with Country Ham   •   Corn and

Roasted Red Pepper Chowder   •   Creamy Spinach and Chèvre

Soup   •   Fiery Three-Bean Chili   •   Four-Onion Soup   •   Roasted

Butternut Squash Soup with Tomatoes, Thyme, and Corn Bread

Croutons   •   Roasted Eggplant and Red Pepper Soup   •

Jamaican Black Bean Soup

Hints for Successful Soups

THE SOUP PANTRY: *Having some (or all) of the ingredients below on hand means that making soup doesn't necessarily require a trip to the grocery store.*

broth or stock	*Canned broth or homemade stock is the foundation of soups and stews. Although some homemade stocks take only 30 to 40 minutes to make, having the cans on hand is a timesaving bonus.*
beans	*Dried, frozen, or canned, legumes add body, flavor, and protein to soups, stews, and chilies. Some frozen legumes are just as good in soups as fresh, so take advantage of the convenience!*
grains and pasta	*Rice and small pasta shapes such as orzo, orecchiette, and bow ties can be added to almost any soup. Also, thick soups can be served over rice or pasta as a main dish.*
in the refrigerator	*Carrots, parsley, celery, parsnips, fennel, apples.*
in the pantry	*Onions, garlic, potatoes, acorn or butternut squash.*
in the freezer	*Chicken (cooked or uncooked); mussels; shrimp; frozen stock; cooked, leftover, or uncooked beef or pork; leftover mashed potatoes.*
spices and dried herbs	*Cumin, chili powder, filé powder, ground red pepper (cayenne), red pepper flakes, oregano, marjoram, rosemary, basil, thyme, sage, bay leaves, saffron, salt, black pepper.*
miscellaneous	*Canned tomatoes, dried mushrooms, canned green chilies, canned roasted red peppers, canned beans, tomato paste.*

The Frugal Cook: Using Vegetable Trimmings

When making just about any soup or broth, instead of or in addition to whole vegetables, you can use the trimmings from the vegetables that go into the soup. Some vegetables to consider are carrot and onion peels, fennel core and fronds, and herb stems. Almost any vegetable can be added except for those that are naturally bitter, like eggplant, or those that are very strong in flavor, like broccoli, Brussels sprouts, turnip or mustard greens. At the Market, we even make fruit broths for chilled summer soups, using pineapple, apple, and pear cores, and orange, lemon, and lime peels. Just about any fruit trimmings will do except bananas, since the peel is so thick.

Mirepoix: A Flavorful Foundation

Mirepoix is a French term for a mixture of diced carrots, onions, and celery cooked in a skillet in butter. A mirepoix traditionally is used to flavor soups, stews, and sauces, and although the final dish won't taste like the mirepoix, it is one of the most important "layers" of flavoring in the finished dish. The longer you cook the mirepoix (and the lower the temperature), the more intense it becomes and the more flavor it will add to the soup. The intensity of the mirepoix is more important in some soups than in others. In vegetable-based soups— like Four-Onion Soup (page 76)—the flavor of the mirepoix adds depth to the final dish. In other soups—like Jamaican Black Bean Soup (page 82)—the flavor of the onions is not as important, so the mirepoix doesn't need to cook as long.

Dried Herbs Versus Fresh for Soup

Since dried herbs are more concentrated in flavor than fresh herbs, they are often preferable when it comes to making soups and stews. Despite their convenience, however, dried herbs lose their potency over time, especially if exposed to heat and light. Give dried herbs a whiff after six to twelve months; if they are no longer fragrant, discard them. Most soup and stew recipes will call for adding dried herbs early in the cooking process to help develop flavors and fresh herbs toward the end, for added freshness and flavor.

Pureeing Soups with a Handheld Immersion Blender

We think this little appliance—which looks something like an electric toothbrush—is a must in the kitchen. We prefer the cordless, rechargeable models because you never have to worry if the cord will reach from the power outlet to the pot. We use immersion blenders at the Market for pureeing soups, making smoothies, milkshakes, hollandaise sauce, whipped cream, and for mixing salad dressings right in the container. They'll do almost everything that a countertop blender or food processor will do, but they're less expensive and easier to use and clean. They're also smaller, so they don't take up much storage space.

Ways to Thicken Soups

- **roux:** A blend of flour and fat (usually butter or cooking oil, but lard is sometimes used in making classic gumbo) that is cooked until the mixture thickens and turns to the desired shade of brown. When a roux is just barely cooked, it is called a white roux. Cooked longer, it becomes a dark roux. Generally speaking, the darker the roux, the deeper the flavor of the roux and of the finished dish.

- **puree:** Thickening a soup with a puree adds flavor and a creamy texture without adding fat or many calories. You can thicken just about any soup with a puree, since the technique is simple: Pour a portion of the cooked soup into the bowl of a food processor or blender and puree until smooth. Add the puree back to the soup, and stir until blended. If the recipe calls for meat, chicken, or fish, do not puree those ingredients; instead, add them to the soup after you've stirred in the puree. Leftover pureed vegetables—such as potatoes, carrots, squash, or onions—are great for thickening soups.

- **heavy cream:** Heavy cream will not "break" when added to a hot liquid; it can even be boiled. Heavy cream can be swirled into soups, or it can be lightly whipped (unsweetened) and used to garnish a soup just before serving. However, heavy cream does break down when frozen.

- **milk and half-and-half:** Milk and half-and-half will add extra body to soups (heat them at a low boil) but will break down when frozen.

- **sour cream:** Sour cream—swirled into or spooned on top of hot or cold soup just before serving—adds body and a mildly tangy flavor. Like heavy cream, however, sour cream breaks down when frozen.

- **yogurt and buttermilk:** These tangy liquids are best added to cold soups, since they tend to separate when added to hot liquids.

- **okra:** This naturally viscous vegetable is used to thicken gumbo.

- **filé powder:** Made from the dried, ground leaves of the sassafras tree, filé powder is used to thicken gumbo in addition to or instead of okra. It should be stirred in after the gumbo has been removed from the heat, since longer cooking can make the filé stringy. Look for filé powder in the spice section at the supermarket, and store it in a cool, dark place for up to 6 months.

- **potatoes:** Mashed potatoes add body to soups without adding much flavor. You can even use frozen mashed potatoes; simply thaw before adding to the soup. Other purees, such as carrot, turnip, parsnip, celeriac, and even apple—are also good. They add texture as well as a certain amount of flavor to the soup.

Freezing Soups

Since soup usually is made in large quantities, some, or all, of it is likely to be frozen for later use. Here are some tips for freezing soup:

- Before putting soup into the freezer, let the mixture cool to room temperature, then chill it uncovered in the refrigerator and skim the fat off the top before freezing.
- Always store soups in tightly sealed containers, leaving a little space at the top for the soup to expand as it freezes.
- Soups with heavy cream, sour cream, milk, half-and-half, yogurt, and buttermilk break down when frozen. If the recipe calls for these ingredients, do not add them until the frozen soup has been thawed. Heavy cream and sour cream can be added to reheated soups and even brought to a boil. Milk and half-and-half can be added to soups and reheated, but only at a low boil. Yogurt and buttermilk should be added only to cold soups, since they break down when heated.
- Soups calling for pasta or rice are best if made up to the point of adding the pasta or rice. Freeze as directed above. When ready to serve, thaw the soup and bring it to a boil. Add the pasta or rice and cook until the pasta is al dente or until the rice is just tender.

Ways to Finish Soups

Garnishes add flavor and texture to soups; they look pretty, too. Consider the following toppings:

- Chopped fresh herbs
- Croutons
- Toasted nuts
- Sour cream
- Unsweetened whipped cream
- Crème fraîche
- Crumbled bacon
- Julienned prosciutto
- Sautéed or grilled vegetables

Quick Broth

With Vegetable, Chicken, Beef, and Seafood Variations

Homemade broth is really very easy, and it's tastier and more healthful than canned broth. When making broth, it's important to start with cold water, as opposed to hot water. This quick broth differs from traditional stock in that we use less meat, chicken, or fish and more vegetables and it cooks in less time.

Vegetable Broth

MAKES ABOUT 4 QUARTS BROTH

5 to 6 pounds fresh vegetables or vegetable or fruit trimmings, such as a combination of onions, carrots, celery, leeks, parsnips, tomatoes, garlic, shallots, fennel, sweet potatoes, lettuce, mushrooms, spinach, ginger, lemongrass, apples, peaches, or pears

5 quarts cold water

4 bay leaves

4 sprigs fresh rosemary

4 sprigs fresh thyme

4 sprigs fresh parsley

1 tablespoon kosher salt

1 teaspoon coarsely ground black pepper

1 • Combine the vegetables and/or fruit and/or trimmings with the water, bay leaves, rosemary, thyme, parsley, salt, and pepper in a large saucepan or stockpot and place over medium-high heat. Bring to a boil and reduce to a simmer. Cook uncovered, 45 minutes to 1 hour, skimming the surface occasionally to remove any foam that forms on the top while cooking.

2 • Strain the broth through a colander or strainer, discarding vegetables and herbs.

3 • Cool to room temperature, then refrigerate in an airtight container for up to 4 days or until ready to use.

Chicken or Beef Broth

MAKES ABOUT 4 QUARTS BROTH

6 pounds chicken and/or chicken
   bones or beef and/or beef
   bones
5 quarts cold water
1 yellow onion, quartered
2 carrots, cut into large chunks
2 ribs celery, peeled and cut into
   large chunks
4 bay leaves
4 sprigs fresh rosemary
4 sprigs fresh thyme
4 sprigs fresh parsley
1 tablespoon kosher salt
1 teaspoon coarsely ground black
   pepper

1 • Combine the chicken or beef, water, onion, carrots, celery, bay leaves, rosemary, thyme, parsley, salt, and pepper in a large saucepan or stockpot and place over medium-high heat. Bring to a boil and reduce to a simmer. Cook uncovered, 45 minutes to 1 hour, skimming the surface occasionally to remove any foam that forms on the top while cooking.

2 • Strain the broth through a colander or strainer, discarding the meat, bones, and vegetables.

3 • Cool to room temperature, then refrigerate in an airtight container for up to 4 days or until ready to use.

Fish Broth

MAKES ABOUT 4 QUARTS BROTH

6 to 8 pounds bones and head
   from snapper or any mild-
   flavored fish
4 quarts cold water
2 cups dry white wine
1 yellow onion, quartered
2 carrots, peeled and cut into large
   chunks
2 ribs celery, cut into large chunks
3 bay leaves
1 lemon, cut in half
Salt and freshly ground black
   pepper to taste

1 • Combine the fish bones and head, water, wine, onion, carrots, celery, bay leaves, lemon, salt, and pepper in a large saucepan or stockpot and place over high heat. Bring to a boil and reduce heat to a simmer. Cook uncovered, 45 minutes to 1 hour, skimming the surface occasionally to remove any foam that forms on the top while cooking.

2 • Strain the broth through a colander or strainer, discarding vegetables and fish bones.

3 • Cool to room temperature, then refrigerate in an airtight container up to 4 days or until ready to use.

Poached Whole Chicken

Poached chicken is low in fat and calories. Vegetable trimmings add flavor to the broth; just about any vegetable will do except very assertive ones such as eggplant or cruciferous vegetables like cabbage, Brussels sprouts, and broccoli. An added plus to poaching chicken is the delicious broth that results, which can be used for soups, stews, and sauces.

MAKES ABOUT 4 CUPS SHREDDED COOKED CHICKEN

One 3- to 4-pound chicken with skin
2 teaspoons salt
6 ribs celery
1 onion, cut in half
8 to 10 fresh herb stems with leaves
2 carrots, peeled and cut in half

1 • Rinse the chicken and pat dry. Place the chicken in a stockpot over medium-high heat and add enough cold water to cover the chicken by 2 inches. Add the salt, celery, onion, herbs, and carrots.

2 • Bring to a simmer and cook, covered, 40 to 45 minutes if using chicken for soups (the chicken will continue to cook in the soup) or 50 minutes to 1 hour for salads and sandwiches. The juices should run clear when the chicken is pierced with the tip of a sharp knife in the thickest part.

3 • Remove the chicken from the broth (strain, discard solids, and reserve the broth for another use) and place in a colander set over a bowl until cool enough to handle. Any juice that collects in the bowl can be added back to the strained broth.

Quick-Cooked Chicken for Soups, Salads, and Sandwiches

There are three basic methods for preparing quick-cooked chicken: poaching (either a whole chicken or breasts only), roasting, and grilling. All the methods are fast and easy and result in simply flavored chicken that can be added to soups, stews, salads, and sandwiches. If you are short on time, for most recipes in this book calling for cooked chicken you can substitute leftover cooked chicken or cooked chicken from the deli or supermarket.

Poached Chicken Breasts

2 whole bone-in chicken breasts
    (about 2 pounds) or 4 chicken
    breast halves, bone-in, skin on
Salt and freshly ground black
    pepper to taste

1 • Rinse the chicken. Season the chicken with salt and pepper and place in a large saucepan. Add enough cold water to cover the chicken by 2 inches. Bring to a boil, lower heat so the liquid simmers, and cook 30 to 35 minutes or until just cooked through. The juices should run clear when the chicken is pierced with the tip of a sharp knife in the thickest part.

2 • Remove the chicken from the water and cool until easy to handle. Remove the skin and discard. Pull the meat from the bones and shred into bite-sized pieces.

Roasted Chicken Breasts

2 whole bone-in chicken breasts
    (about 2 pounds) or 4 chicken
    breast halves, bone-in, skin on
Salt and freshly ground black
    pepper to taste

1 • Preheat the oven to 400 degrees.

2 • Rinse the chicken and pat dry. Season the chicken with salt and pepper and place skin side down in a roasting pan.

3 • Cook 30 to 35 minutes or until just done. The juices should run clear when the chicken is pierced with the tip of a sharp knife in the thickest part.

4 • Remove the chicken from the pan and cool until easy to handle. Remove the skin and discard. Pull the meat from the bones and shred into bite-sized pieces.

Grilled Chicken Breasts

Safflower oil or canola oil, for oiling the grill

4 boneless, skinless chicken breast halves

2 tablespoons olive oil

Salt and freshly ground black pepper to taste

1 • Brush the grill grates lightly with the safflower oil. Prepare a hot fire in a gas or charcoal grill.

2 • Rinse the chicken and pat dry. Brush the chicken on all sides with olive oil and season with salt and pepper.

3 • Place the chicken breasts on grill grates and cook 6 to 8 minutes per side or until they are firm to the touch and the juices run clear when the chicken is pierced with the tip of a sharp knife in the thickest part. Cool 5 minutes before slicing or shredding.

Chicken, Leek, and Fennel Soup

This soup can be made several days in advance and refrigerated or frozen. It's full of flavor, but since it's thickened with a vegetable puree, it's relatively low in fat. Try it with a thick slice of grilled Italian bread or warm focaccia. Be sure to save some of the feathery fennel fronds to use as a garnish.

MAKES 2½ TO 3 QUARTS SOUP; SERVES 6 TO 8

4 leeks, trimmed and split
   lengthwise

2 tablespoons unsalted butter

3 tablespoons olive oil

1 fennel bulb, trimmed (reserve
   some of the fronds for garnish),
   halved, cored, and sliced
   ⅛ inch thick

3 ribs celery, chopped

1 Granny Smith or other tart apple,
   peeled, cored, and chopped

4 garlic cloves, minced

1 russet potato, peeled and
   chopped

8 cups chicken broth (page 57)

2 teaspoons salt

1 teaspoon freshly ground black
   pepper

4 cups shredded cooked chicken
   (page 58)

1 tablespoon fresh chopped sage
   or 1 teaspoon dried sage

1 tablespoon fresh thyme or
   1 teaspoon dried thyme

1 • Clean the leeks by soaking them in a bowl of water for 10 to 15 minutes; remove the leeks from the water, rinse and drain. Slice into ¼-inch half rounds.

2 • Melt the butter and olive oil in a large saucepan over medium-low heat. Add the leeks; cook and stir about 10 minutes, until the leeks have softened. Add the fennel and celery and continue to cook and stir 10 minutes longer. Add the apple and garlic and cook and stir 2 to 3 minutes more.

3 • Add the potato, broth, salt, and pepper and bring to a slow boil over medium-high heat. Reduce heat to low and cook, uncovered, 25 to 30 minutes, stirring occasionally, until the potato is tender.

4 • Remove about 3 cups of the mixture from the pot and allow to cool slightly. Place the cooled soup mixture in the bowl of a food processor fitted with the metal blade and puree until smooth. Return this mixture back to the soup pot, stir to mix thoroughly, and return to medium heat.

5 • Add the chicken, sage, thyme, and additional salt and pepper if needed and simmer 15 to 20 minutes longer. Serve immediately or refrigerate up to 3 days in an airtight container, then reheat and serve.

variations: Add lima beans for a heartier soup; use both dark and white chicken meat for a richer flavor.

Succotash Soup with Chicken and Oven-Roasted Tomatoes

The classic combination of corn and lima beans becomes a summertime feast with the addition of garden-fresh tomatoes and basil. The tomatoes can be roasted ahead of time, and the chicken can be cooked several days in advance. Serve this with Granny Foster's Refrigerator Rolls (page 23) or, for a southern touch, Old-Fashioned Buttermilk Biscuits (page 16). This soup is also delicious ladled into a shallow bowl and topped with Pan-Seared Sea Scallops (page 194) or Sautéed Soft-Shell Crabs (page 197).

MAKES 2 ½ TO 3 QUARTS SOUP; SERVES 6 TO 8

12 plum tomatoes, cored and cut
   into quarters
¼ cup olive oil
2 tablespoons unsalted butter
1 large yellow onion, chopped
4 ribs celery, chopped
8 cups chicken broth (page 57)
Kernels from 3 ears fresh corn
   (1½ cups fresh or frozen corn)
2 cups fresh or frozen lima beans
4 cups shredded cooked chicken
   (page 58)
1 tablespoon dried marjoram
1 teaspoon dried basil
1 tablespoon salt
1 teaspoon freshly ground black
   pepper
3 tablespoons chopped fresh
   marjoram or fresh basil,
   to garnish, optional
2 tablespoons chopped fresh
   chives or fresh parsley, to
   garnish, optional

1 • Preheat the oven to 400 degrees.

2 • Toss the tomatoes with 2 tablespoons of the olive oil in a baking dish and roast 30 minutes, until the skin begins to shrivel and the tomatoes are slightly brown. Remove from the oven and set aside.

3 • Heat the remaining olive oil with the butter in a large saucepan over medium-low heat, add the onion, and cook 15 minutes, stirring occasionally, until the onion has softened. Add the celery and cook an additional 10 minutes, stirring frequently.

4 • Add the broth, corn, lima beans, roasted tomatoes, chicken, dried marjoram, dried basil, salt, and pepper and simmer uncovered for about 45 minutes. Remove from the heat, add fresh marjoram and chives, and stir to combine all the ingredients. Serve immediately, or let cool and refrigerate in an airtight container until ready to serve. As with most soups, this is better the next day, after the flavors have had time to develop.

variations: Although roasted tomatoes give this soup extra flavor, if you're short on time, you can use chopped fresh tomatoes or even chopped canned tomatoes. Chopped fresh spinach can be added during the last few minutes of cooking for extra flavor, color, and texture.

Italian-Style Chicken and Mushroom Soup with Orecchiette

Pasta, rosemary, garlic, and Tuscan white beans give this hearty soup a distinct Italian flair. Despite the long list of ingredients, the soup is easy to make and freezes well, too. You can also leave out the pasta, then ladle the thick, meaty soup over cooked fettuccine or other pasta for a more substantial meal. To make this soup ahead and freeze, proceed as the recipe directs but omit the pasta. When ready to serve, thaw the soup, reheat it, and then add the pasta and cook until it is al dente.

MAKES ABOUT 2½ QUARTS SOUP; SERVES 6 TO 8

6 tablespoons olive oil

1 yellow onion, diced

4 ribs celery, chopped

8 cups chicken broth (page 57)

4 cups shredded cooked chicken
(page 58)

4 bay leaves

2 teaspoons salt

1 teaspoon freshly ground black
pepper

2 whole heads garlic

8 ounces button mushrooms,
cleaned

1 cup orecchiette pasta, or other
small pasta shapes such as
bow ties or elbow macaroni

1 cup canned cannellini or navy
beans, rinsed and drained

2 tablespoons chopped fresh
rosemary or 2 teaspoons dried
rosemary

2 tablespoons chopped fresh
parsley

8 cups firmly packed spinach,
washed, drained, and stems
removed

Grated Parmesan cheese,
to garnish

1 • Preheat the oven to 450 degrees.

2 • Heat 4 tablespoons of the olive oil in a large saucepan over medium heat. Add the onion, reduce the heat to low, and cook, stirring occasionally, about 15 minutes. Add the celery and cook about 5 minutes longer, stirring constantly.

3 • Add the broth, chicken, bay leaves, salt, and pepper. Reduce heat and simmer about 1 hour, stirring occasionally.

4 • Place both heads of garlic on a small sheet of aluminum foil and drizzle with 1 tablespoon of the olive oil. Wrap tightly and place in the oven to roast, about 35 to 40 minutes, or until the garlic is soft. Meanwhile, toss the mushrooms with the remaining olive oil in a baking dish, place in the oven, and roast 15 to 20 minutes, until golden brown, stirring once or twice during cooking to coat evenly.

5 • Remove the mushrooms from the oven and add to the soup. Remove the garlic from the oven, peel the cloves, and add to the soup, leaving them whole.

6 • Add the orecchiette to the soup and cook, stirring occasionally, 10 to 12 minutes longer, just until the pasta is al dente. Add the beans and heat through. Add the rosemary and parsley and stir to mix; remove from the heat.

7 • Place a handful of spinach in each bowl and ladle the soup over the spinach. Top with Parmesan and serve immediately.

Chicken Chili with Navy Beans

This chili is lighter than classic chili but flavorful. It's a great way to use up leftover chicken; try it with Jalapeño Corn Muffins (page 7) or on a soft tortilla topped with baby greens and Foster's Salsa (page 90).

MAKES 2½ TO 3 QUARTS SOUP; SERVES 6 TO 8

1 cup dried navy beans, picked over and rinsed, or about 2 cups canned navy beans

¼ cup olive oil

1 yellow onion, chopped

1 red or green bell pepper, cored, seeded, and chopped

1 jalapeño, diced, with seeds

6 garlic cloves, minced

1 tablespoon chili powder

2 teaspoons ground cumin

2 teaspoons dried basil

8 cups chicken broth (page 57)

One 14-ounce can chopped tomatoes

12 ounces beer

¼ cup Worcestershire sauce

4 cups shredded cooked chicken (page 58)

¼ cup cornmeal

2 teaspoons salt

1 teaspoon freshly ground black pepper

¼ cup chopped fresh cilantro

4 scallions, trimmed and chopped

1 • If using dried beans, quick-cook them: Place the beans in a large pot with water to cover by 3 inches and bring to a boil. Reduce heat and simmer uncovered 45 minutes. Remove from the heat, drain, rinse, and set aside.

2 • Heat the olive oil over medium heat in a large saucepan. Add the onion and cook about 15 minutes, stirring constantly, until the onion has softened. Add the bell pepper, jalapeño, and garlic and cook about 5 minutes more, stirring constantly.

3 • Stir in the chili powder, cumin, and basil and cook 2 to 3 minutes, stirring constantly.

4 • Add the broth, tomatoes, beer, Worcestershire sauce, chicken, beans (if using canned beans, see note in step 5), and cornmeal and stir to mix well.

5 • Add the salt and pepper, reduce heat to low, and simmer about 1½ hours, uncovered, until the beans are tender and the flavors have developed. (Note: If using canned beans, add them at this point and cook about 30 minutes, stirring occasionally.) Serve immediately, garnished with cilantro and scallions.

variations: Turkey can be substituted for the chicken. Or use leftover beef or pork or a combination of the two. Make this a "green chili" by using chopped tomatillos (fresh or canned) instead of chopped tomatoes. Any kind of bean can be used; at Foster's, we often make this with pinto, kidney, or lima beans. Roasted jalapeños or chipotles (for a smoky flavor) can be used instead of fresh jalapeños.

Chicken Gumbo with Chicken-Apple Sausage

Because we use chicken-apple sausage instead of the traditional andouille, this gumbo is lighter than the New Orleans classic but no less flavorful. It makes a terrific main course with crusty French bread. This soup can also be served as a "sauce": make the gumbo without the cooked chicken, then ladle it over grilled, broiled, or pan-cooked chicken breasts served on a bed of steamy rice. Although this dish is easy to make, it does call for a lot of ingredients, so have all the ingredients prepped and ready ahead of time.

MAKES 2½ TO 3 QUARTS GUMBO; SERVES 6 TO 8

One 3- to 4-pound chicken, cut into quarters

¼ cup canola or safflower oil

2 tablespoons bacon drippings or unsalted butter

½ cup all-purpose flour

1 yellow onion, diced

1 green bell pepper, cored, seeded, and diced

1 red bell pepper, cored, seeded, and diced

3 ribs celery, diced

4 garlic cloves, minced

8 cups chicken broth (page 57)

3 bay leaves

2 tablespoons Worcestershire sauce

2 teaspoons salt

1 teaspoon freshly ground black pepper

1 teaspoon red pepper flakes

2 cups chopped fresh or frozen okra

6 plum tomatoes, cored and cut in half lengthwise

4 chicken-apple sausages (about 1 pound)

2 tablespoons olive oil

1 • Preheat the oven to 400 degrees.

2 • Rinse the chicken and pat dry.

3 • Heat the canola oil over medium-high heat in a Dutch oven or a large, heavy saucepan. Add the chicken; cook about 4 to 5 minutes per side (8 to 10 minutes total), until crispy and brown. Remove the chicken from the Dutch oven; place it in a roasting pan or baking dish and cook it in the oven 30 to 40 minutes or until the juices run clear when the chicken is pierced in the thickest part with the tip of a sharp knife.

4 • While the chicken is roasting, make a roux in the Dutch oven in which the chicken was cooked. Add the bacon drippings and heat to the smoking point, about 3 minutes. Add flour slowly while whisking constantly and cook 4 to 5 minutes, reducing the heat to medium if the roux is browning too quickly. Continue to cook and whisk until the roux turns a dark brownish-orange color.

5 • Reduce heat to low and add the onion, green bell pepper, red bell pepper, and celery and continue to cook and stir 3 to 4 minutes longer, until the vegetables have softened. Add the garlic and cook and stir 2 minutes more.

6 • Remove the chicken from the oven and set aside until cool enough to handle. Leave the oven on at 400 degrees. Remove the meat from the chicken, discarding the skin and bones. Tear the chicken into

1 tablespoon chopped fresh
  marjoram or oregano,
  to garnish, optional
¼ cup dry sherry
2 tablespoons filé powder
  (gumbo filé) (see page 54)
2 tablespoons chopped fresh
  parsley

bite-sized chunks and add to the roux and vegetables.

7 • Add the chicken broth, bay leaves, Worcestershire sauce, salt, black pepper, and red pepper flakes to the chicken mixture and stir to mix well. Reduce heat to low and cook, uncovered, about 40 minutes, stirring occasionally. Add the okra and continue to cook about 20 minutes longer, stirring occasionally, until the gumbo is thick and flavors have developed.

8 • Meanwhile, toss the tomatoes and sausages with the olive oil in a baking dish and bake in the oven 15 to 20 minutes, turning once, or until lightly brown. Remove from the oven, chop the sausages into ½-inch pieces, and add to the gumbo along with the tomatoes.

9 • Remove the gumbo from the heat and stir in the marjoram, sherry, filé powder, and parsley. Discard the bay leaves. Season with additional salt and pepper if desired and serve immediately, over a bowl of steamed rice if desired.

Chicken and Sweet Potato Soup

Light but full of flavor, this wintry soup can be made several days in advance. Try it for lunch or dinner, with Jalapeño Corn Muffins (page 7) or a Grilled Pimiento Cheese Sandwich with Grilled Ham (page 88).

2 tablespoons unsalted butter

1 tablespoon olive oil

1 red onion, diced

2 shallots, thinly sliced

1 red bell pepper, cored, seeded, and diced

3 ribs celery, diced

6 garlic cloves, minced

8 cups chicken broth (page 57)

4 cups shredded cooked chicken (page 58)

2 sweet potatoes, peeled and chopped into ½-inch chunks

One 14½-ounce can chopped tomatoes

½ teaspoon red pepper flakes

1 teaspoon dried marjoram

3 bay leaves

2 teaspoons salt

1 teaspoon freshly ground black pepper

1 tablespoon chopped fresh marjoram, to garnish, optional

1 tablespoon chopped fresh thyme, to garnish, optional

Salt and freshly ground pepper to taste

1 • Melt the butter and olive oil over medium-low heat in a large saucepan and add the onion and shallots. Cook and stir about 15 minutes, or until softened. Add the bell pepper and celery and continue to cook and stir about 5 minutes longer. Add the garlic and cook and stir 2 to 3 minutes longer.

2 • Add the broth, chicken, sweet potatoes, tomatoes, red pepper flakes, dried marjoram, bay leaves, salt, and pepper and stir until combined. Bring to a low boil, reduce heat, and simmer, uncovered, about 1 hour, until the potatoes are tender and flavors have developed. Skim the top of the soup as it cooks if necessary to remove foam or fat.

3 • Discard the bay leaves. Add the fresh marjoram, thyme, and additional salt and pepper if desired. Serve immediately.

variations: Try different kinds of peppers (sweet Italian or banana peppers, for example) to see what you like best. Turkey can be substituted for the chicken; chopped spinach can be added to the soup when the soup is done (it will cook in 1 to 2 minutes in the hot soup). Or add roughly chopped fresh kale and simmer about 3 to 4 minutes in the soup, until the kale is tender.

Old-Fashioned Turkey Noodle Soup

After the Thanksgiving feast, try this easy, comforting soup with some of the leftover turkey. It appeals to all ages, so if you have a house full of holiday guests, this is a real winner. Of course, you don't have to wait until you have leftovers to make this soup; you can grill or braise a turkey breast specifically for this dish or buy cooked turkey. I also like to make this soup with drumsticks, since the rich dark meat makes a very flavorful soup. To use drumsticks, simply poach them in lightly salted water 50 minutes to 1 hour, then reserve the cooking liquid to use as broth for the soup.

MAKES 2½ TO 3 QUARTS SOUP; SERVES 6 TO 8

3 tablespoons unsalted butter

2 tablespoons olive oil

1 yellow onion, chopped

6 ribs celery, chopped

2 carrots, peeled and chopped

2 parsnips, peeled and chopped

4 garlic cloves, minced

¼ cup all-purpose flour

8 cups turkey or chicken broth
   (page 57)

4 cups shredded cooked turkey

4 bay leaves

1 tablespoon dried marjoram

2 teaspoons salt

1 teaspoon freshly ground black
   pepper

2 cups small pasta (bow ties or
   short egg noodles)

2 tablespoons chopped fresh
   marjoram or 2 teaspoons dried
   marjoram

2 tablespoons chopped fresh sage
   or 2 teaspoons dried sage

1 • Heat the butter and olive oil in a large saucepan over medium-low heat. Add the onion and cook 15 minutes or until softened, stirring occasionally. Add the celery, carrots, and parsnips and cook 10 minutes longer or until softened, stirring occasionally. Add the garlic and cook 2 to 3 minutes more, stirring constantly.

2 • Sprinkle the flour over the cooked vegetables. Cook 3 to 4 minutes, stirring constantly while scraping up the flavorful bits on the bottom of the pan.

3 • Slowly add the broth and stir to mix thoroughly. Add the turkey, bay leaves, dried marjoram, salt, and pepper. Reduce heat and simmer 1 hour, uncovered, stirring occasionally.

4 • Add the pasta, fresh marjoram, and sage and stir to mix thoroughly. Simmer 15 minutes longer, stirring occasionally, until the pasta is al dente. Discard the bay leaves and serve immediately.

variations: Chicken can be substituted for the turkey; diced new potatoes can be used instead of pasta. Try other vegetables, such as cabbage, spinach, or kale. Celeriac or winter squash can also be added.

Provençal-Style Beef and Bean Soup

This is a hearty, chunky soup that's perfect for using leftover cooked beef or steak. Sundried tomatoes, garlic, rosemary, and basil give this soup a South of France flavor. It freezes beautifully, too. It's also great served with Crostini (page 104) spread with Artichoke Aïoli (page 93).

MAKES 2½ TO 3 QUARTS SOUP; SERVES 6 TO 8

1½ cups dried navy beans, picked over and rinsed

1 tablespoon unsalted butter

2 tablespoons olive oil

1 red onion, cut in half lengthwise and thinly sliced

2 ribs celery, sliced ⅛ inch thick

1 head garlic, roasted and peeled (page 63)

2 pounds chuck roast, cut into 1-inch cubes

6 plum tomatoes, cored and chopped

8 cups beef broth (page 57)

3 bay leaves

2 teaspoons salt

1 teaspoon freshly ground black pepper

½ cup sun-dried tomatoes

3 tablespoons chopped fresh rosemary or 1 tablespoon dried rosemary

6 fresh basil leaves, cut into very thin strips (chiffonade)

1 • Quick-cook the beans: Place the beans in a large pot with water to cover by 3 inches and bring to a boil. Reduce heat and simmer uncovered 45 minutes. Remove from the heat, drain, rinse, and set aside.

2 • Heat the butter and olive oil in a large, heavy saucepan over low heat. Add the onions and cook and stir 15 minutes or until light brown. Add the celery and cook and stir 10 minutes longer.

3 • Add the garlic and the beef and cook and stir until the beef is brown on all sides, 8 to 10 minutes. Add the tomatoes, broth, bay leaves, salt, pepper, and beans and simmer 1½ to 1¾ hours, uncovered, until the beans are soft and the beef is fork-tender.

4 • Add the sun-dried tomatoes and rosemary and simmer about 10 minutes longer. Discard the bay leaves. Add the fresh basil and serve immediately.

variations: Cooked, leftover roast beef, chicken, or lamb (about 3 cups cubed meat) can be used instead of the chuck roast; add it during the final 30 to 40 minutes of cooking. (Note: If using chicken, substitute chicken broth for the beef broth.) Whether you use beef or chicken, pasta can be added for a more filling soup: add it after the beans have cooked and boil 3 to 7 minutes, depending on the size and shape of the pasta, just until the pasta is al dente. Serve immediately.

Legumes in Soups and Stews

Heart-healthy and high in fiber, most legumes can be substituted for one another, since their tastes and textures are fairly similar. The exceptions are lentils and split peas, which cook in less time than other legumes, since they're smaller. Frozen or canned legumes are a great time-saver and are perfectly fine in most soups or stews. Just remember to cut back on the cooking time, since canned and frozen legumes are already cooked and just need to be heated through.

Split Pea Soup with Country Ham

This comforting, old-fashioned soup freezes well, so double the recipe and freeze half for an easy dinner. Just thaw and reheat.

2 tablespoons unsalted butter

2 tablespoons olive oil

1 yellow onion, chopped

2 ribs celery, chopped

2 carrots, peeled and chopped

2 thin slices country ham, chopped (about 4 to 5 ounces, bone and rind removed)

6 garlic cloves, minced

½ cup dry white wine

10 cups chicken broth (page 57)

1 cup dried green split peas, picked over and rinsed

½ teaspoon salt

½ teaspoon freshly ground black pepper

2 teaspoons dried marjoram or basil

2 bay leaves

⅓ cup chopped fresh parsley

1 • Melt the butter and olive oil in a large saucepan. Add the onion and cook over medium-low heat about 15 minutes, stirring occasionally, until softened. Add the celery and carrots. Cook 10 minutes more, stirring occasionally, until the vegetables are soft.

2 • Add the ham and garlic and cook 5 minutes longer, stirring constantly.

3 • Add the wine, broth, split peas, salt, pepper, marjoram, and bay leaves; bring to a low boil. Reduce heat and simmer, uncovered, stirring occasionally, 1 to 1¼ hours, until the peas are soft and the soup is creamy and thick. (Note: If you prefer an even thicker, creamier soup, cook up to 15 to 20 minutes longer.)

4 • Add the parsley and stir to mix. Discard the bay leaves. Serve immediately.

variations: Use baked or smoked ham or shredded cooked chicken or turkey instead of country ham. Or eliminate the meat altogether—and use vegetable broth instead of chicken broth—for a vegetarian soup. Yellow split peas can be used instead of green. Garnish with diced fresh tomatoes or crunchy Corn Bread Croutons (page 79), if desired.

Corn and Roasted Red Pepper Chowder

This vegetable soup is a treat any time of year, but especially in summer, when corn is sweet and tender. It can be made partially in advance and reheated with the cream just before serving. (For a lower-calorie soup, omit the heavy cream.) Try this hearty summer chowder with Jalapeño Corn Muffins (page 7) or Sweet Potato Biscuits (page 17) and Roasted Chicken, Sweet Potato, and Arugula Salad (page 131).

MAKES 2½ TO 3 QUARTS CHOWDER;
SERVES 6 TO 8

2 tablespoons olive oil

2 leeks, trimmed and split
    lengthwise

4 tablespoons (½ stick) unsalted
    butter

1 yellow onion, diced

4 ribs celery, diced

6 garlic cloves, minced

8 cups vegetable broth (page 56)
    or chicken broth (page 57)

2 Yukon gold or russet potatoes,
    peeled and chopped

Kernels from 4 ears fresh corn
    (2 cups fresh or frozen corn)

3 roasted red bell peppers,
    peeled, cored, seeded, and
    chopped (page 40)

2 teaspoons salt

1 teaspoon freshly ground black
    pepper

2 tablespoons fresh thyme or
    2 teaspoons dried thyme

2 tablespoons chopped fresh
    chives or chopped fresh parsley

1 cup heavy cream

Fresh chives, to garnish, optional

1 • Soak the leeks in a bowl filled with cold water for 10 minutes. Rinse and drain. Slice into ¼-inch rounds and set aside.

2 • Melt the butter in a large saucepan over medium-low heat and add the onion. Cook and stir about 15 minutes, until softened. Add the leeks and celery and cook and stir about 10 minutes longer, until the leeks and celery have softened. Add the garlic and cook and stir about 2 minutes more.

3 • Add the broth and potatoes and bring to a low boil, reduce heat, and simmer, uncovered, about 30 minutes, until the potatoes are tender. Add the corn, roasted red peppers, salt, black pepper, and thyme and simmer about 15 minutes longer. Remove the pot from the heat and add the chives.

4 • Remove about 4 cups of the mixture from the pot and cool slightly. Place the cooled soup in the bowl of a food processor fitted with the metal blade and puree until smooth. Return this mixture to the soup and stir until well blended.

5 • Stir in the cream and reheat over low heat, stirring constantly, until heated through. Serve immediately, garnished with chives if desired.

variations: This soup is great with the addition of clams, lump crabmeat, shrimp, mussels, or firm-fleshed fish such as haddock. Add the fish or shellfish after adding the puree to the soup; you can then eliminate or add the cream, as desired. If you decide to omit the cream, I recommend using chicken broth instead of vegetable broth for added flavor. Try other vegetables—such as summer squash, sweet Italian peppers, or roasted poblano peppers (for a spicier flavor)—in place of the red bell peppers and the potatoes.

Creamy Spinach and Chèvre Soup

Chèvre gives this soup a creamy taste without much added fat.

MAKES 2½ TO 3 QUARTS SOUP; SERVES 6 TO 8

3 leeks, trimmed and split lengthwise

3 tablespoons unsalted butter

2 tablespoons olive oil

1 yellow onion, chopped

4 ribs celery, chopped

½ fennel bulb, trimmed, halved, cored, and sliced ⅛ inch thick

3 garlic cloves, minced

8 cups chicken (page 57) or vegetable broth (page 56)

1 russet potato, peeled and chopped

1 teaspoon dried basil

1 teaspoon dried tarragon

2 teaspoons salt

1 teaspoon freshly ground black pepper

8 cups firmly packed spinach, washed, drained, and stems removed

1 cup (4 ounces) crumbled creamy chèvre

8 to 10 fresh spinach leaves, cut into very thin strips (chiffonade), to garnish, optional

1 • Soak the leeks in a large bowl filled with cold water about 10 minutes. Rinse, drain, and slice into ¼-inch half-rounds.

2 • Heat the butter and olive oil over medium-low heat in a large saucepan and add the onion and leeks. Cook and stir about 10 minutes until the onion and leeks are soft.

3 • Add the celery and fennel and cook and stir about 5 minutes longer. Add the garlic and cook and stir about 2 minutes more.

4 • Add the broth, potato, basil, tarragon, salt, and pepper and bring to a low boil. Reduce heat to low and simmer 35 to 40 minutes, uncovered, until the potato is tender and the flavors have developed.

5 • Add the spinach and cook and stir 3 to 4 minutes, until the spinach has wilted. Remove the soup from the heat and allow it to cool slightly.

6 • Working in batches, place some of the soup in the bowl of a food processor fitted with the metal blade and puree until smooth.

7 • Add the chèvre and puree about 1 minute more, until the chèvre is well blended and the soup is smooth.

8 • Return the mixture to the pot. Reheat if necessary, over low heat, stirring constantly. Serve immediately or let cool and refrigerate until ready to reheat and serve. This soup can also be served chilled. Garnish with the spinach chiffonade and/or remaining crumbled chèvre, if desired.

Fiery Three-Bean Chili

We get lots of requests for recipes at Foster's Market, including this one, which is a year-round favorite with our customers. Dark beer adds to the deep, heady flavors of this vegetarian chili.

½ cup dried black beans, picked over and rinsed

½ cup dried navy beans, picked over and rinsed

½ cup dried kidney or pinto beans, picked over and rinsed

3 tablespoons olive oil

1 yellow onion, chopped

1 red bell pepper, cored, seeded, and chopped

1 green bell pepper, cored, seeded, and chopped

1 jalapeño, seeded and diced

1 sweet potato, peeled and diced

6 garlic cloves, minced

2 tablespoons chili powder

1 tablespoon prepared mustard

1 tablespoon ground cumin

2 teaspoons dried basil

1 teaspoon dried marjoram

1 teaspoon red pepper flakes

3 bay leaves

1 tablespoon salt

1 teaspoon freshly ground black pepper

One 14½-ounce can chopped tomatoes

¼ cup Worcestershire sauce

12 ounces dark beer

10 cups vegetable broth (page 56) or chicken broth (page 57)

Chopped fresh cilantro and scallions, to garnish, optional

1 • Quick-soak the black beans, navy beans, and kidney beans by placing all of the beans in a large pot with water to cover by 3 inches. Bring to a boil. Reduce heat and simmer uncovered 45 minutes. Remove from the heat, drain, rinse, and set aside.

2 • Heat the olive oil in a stockpot or a large, heavy saucepan over medium-low heat and add the onion. Cook the onion 15 minutes, stirring occasionally. Add the red bell pepper, green bell pepper, jalapeño, sweet potato, and garlic and cook about 5 minutes more, stirring occasionally.

3 • Add the chili powder, mustard, cumin, basil, marjoram, red pepper flakes, bay leaves, salt, and pepper. Cook, stirring frequently, 2 to 3 minutes.

4 • Add the tomatoes, Worcestershire sauce, beer, broth, and beans and simmer uncovered 1¼ to 1½ hours, until the beans are tender. Remove the soup from the heat, discard the bay leaves, and serve immediately, garnished with cilantro and scallions.

variations: Shredded cooked chicken or leftover shredded pork or beef can be added for a meaty chili. Try other types of beans, such as lima, adzuki, or cranberry beans.

Four-Onion Soup

Leeks, shallots, scallions, and sweet Vidalias take the idea of "onion soup" to a higher level. Tart apples and earthy parsnips add a hint of sweetness.

4 leeks, trimmed and split
   lengthwise

3 tablespoons unsalted butter

2 tablespoons olive oil

2 Vidalia onions (or Maui or Walla
   Walla or any other mild onion),
   diced

6 shallots, thinly sliced

4 garlic cloves, minced

2 parsnips, peeled and chopped

1 Granny Smith or other tart apple,
   peeled, cored, and chopped

1 cup dry white wine

6 cups vegetable broth (page 56)
   or chicken broth (page 57)

2 teaspoons salt

1 teaspoon freshly ground black
   pepper

1 tablespoon chopped fresh
   marjoram or fresh basil or
   fresh oregano

1 tablespoon chopped fresh chives
   or fresh parsley

4 scallions, trimmed and chopped

1 • Soak the leeks in a large bowl filled with cold water about 10 minutes. Rinse, drain, and slice into ¼-inch half-rounds.

2 • Heat the butter and olive oil in a large saucepan over medium-low heat. Add the leeks, onions, and shallots; cook and stir 15 minutes.

3 • Add the garlic, parsnips, and apple and cook 5 minutes more, stirring occasionally. Add the wine and simmer several minutes. Add the broth, salt, and pepper and bring to a low boil. Reduce heat and simmer, uncovered, 30 to 40 minutes, stirring occasionally.

4 • Remove about 2 cups of the soup from the pan and let cool slightly. Place the cooled soup in the bowl of a food processor fitted with the metal blade and puree until smooth. Return this mixture to the pan and stir to blend thoroughly. Season with additional salt and pepper if necessary.

5 • Stir in the marjoram and chives, ladle into individual bowls, garnish with the scallions, and serve immediately.

variations: Make this a springtime soup by adding parboiled fresh green peas, tender asparagus tips, or watercress after step 4. Heat through, then proceed as the recipe directs through step 5.

Roasted Butternut Squash Soup with Tomatoes, Thyme, and Corn Bread Croutons

This intensely flavored soup makes a terrific first course for Thanksgiving or Christmas dinner. It's delicious chilled, so it can also be served as a starter for an Indian summer harvest meal. It freezes well, so make plenty.

MAKES ABOUT 2½ QUARTS SOUP; SERVES 6 TO 8

1 butternut squash, cut in half lengthwise and seeds removed

¼ cup olive oil

6 plum tomatoes, cored and halved

4 garlic cloves

1 tablespoon balsamic vinegar

4 tablespoons (½ stick) unsalted butter

1 red onion, diced

1 carrot, peeled and chopped

2 ribs celery, chopped

6 cups chicken broth (page 57) or vegetable broth (page 56)

2 teaspoons salt

1 teaspoon freshly ground black pepper

¼ cup fresh thyme leaves or 4 teaspoons dried thyme

2 tablespoons chopped fresh chives or fresh parsley, optional

1 tablespoon chopped fresh sage or 1 teaspoon dried sage

Juice of 2 oranges

2 cups Corn Bread Croutons (page 79), optional

Additional fresh sage and thyme, to garnish, optional

1 • Preheat the oven to 450 degrees.

2 • Place the squash cut side down in a large baking dish. Add 1 cup water and 1 tablespoon of the olive oil to the dish and roast 35 to 40 minutes, until the squash is soft and tender to the touch.

3 • Meanwhile, toss the tomatoes and garlic with 2 tablespoons of the olive oil and the vinegar in a baking dish. Roast 30 to 35 minutes or until soft and the skin is slightly shriveled. Let stand until cool enough to handle, and then lightly crush the tomatoes with your hands or a potato masher into small pieces, reserving the liquid. Set aside until ready to use.

4 • Heat the remaining olive oil and the butter over medium heat in a large saucepan. Add the onion and cook and stir about 10 minutes, until onion is soft and translucent. Add the carrot and celery and cook 10 to 15 minutes longer, stirring constantly, until the vegetables are soft.

5 • Add the broth, salt, and pepper and reduce heat to low; simmer, uncovered, 20 to 25 minutes.

6 • Remove the squash from its skin by scooping out the flesh with a spoon. Discard the skin and add the flesh to the soup. Simmer about 20 minutes longer, stirring occasionally.

7 • Remove from the heat and add the thyme, chives, and sage. Cool slightly, then, working in batches, pour the soup into the bowl of a food processor fitted with the metal blade and puree until smooth. Return the soup to the pot and add the tomatoes and their liquid and the orange juice; stir to mix. Season with additional salt and pepper if desired. Reheat the soup on low if necessary. Serve immediately,

topped with Corn Bread Croutons, garnished with fresh sage and thyme.

variations: Any type of winter squash can be used instead of butternut squash. For added richness, swirl in a little heavy cream or top each serving with jalapeño cream (combine minced jalapeños and fresh lime juice with sour cream or unsweetened whipped cream). Or float Crostini (page 104) topped with lump crabmeat on each serving. For a heartier soup, add cooked ravioli (pumpkin ravioli is great) to each serving. You can also use this soup to flavor risotto, by alternating broth and some of this soup instead of just using broth.

Winter Squash

Butternut, acorn, hubbard, turban, kabocha, sweet dumpling, gold nugget, delicata, buttercup, and pumpkin are all fairly similar in taste and texture and can be substituted for one another in most recipes, including soups. (Spaghetti squash—which is also a winter squash—is similar to the others in taste, but has a naturally stringy texture, and therefore is not recommended for most soups.) Winter squash—which are very decorative and make great centerpieces—can also be substituted for sweet potatoes in most recipes.

Corn Bread Croutons

If you have leftover corn bread, try these croutons; they're delicious on soups and salads, or with Black Bean and Yellow Rice Salad (page 115). They keep up to 2 weeks in an airtight container.

MAKES ABOUT 4 CUPS CROUTONS

4 cups day-old or dry corn bread, cut into ½-inch cubes

4 tablespoons (½ stick) unsalted butter, melted

2 tablespoons olive oil

1 teaspoon salt

½ teaspoon freshly ground black pepper

1 • Preheat the oven to 400 degrees.

2 • Mix the corn bread gently with the butter, olive oil, salt, and pepper in a bowl.

3 • Spread out the corn bread cubes in one layer on a baking dish and bake, uncovered, 15 to 20 minutes, turning several times, until golden brown and crispy. Remove from the oven and cool. Use immediately or store in an airtight container until ready to use.

variations: Add 2 teaspoons ground chili powder or ground cumin or 2 to 3 tablespoons chopped fresh herbs (such as thyme, rosemary, or parsley) when you toss the corn bread in the butter and olive oil.

Roasted Eggplant and Red Pepper Soup

The gentle flavor of this pureed soup comes from the roasted vegetables: roasting makes the eggplant milder and the peppers sweeter. For a tasty garnish, top each serving with Crostini (page 104) spread with mild chèvre or a dollop of Rouille (page 200). This soup is also delicious chilled.

MAKES ABOUT 2½ QUARTS SOUP; SERVES 6 TO 8

1 red bell pepper

6 shallots, cut in half, or 1 onion, cut into eighths

6 tablespoons olive oil

2 eggplants, cut in half lengthwise

8 garlic cloves

2 tablespoons unsalted butter

1 red onion, chopped

2 ribs celery, chopped

1 carrot, peeled and chopped

8 cups vegetable broth (page 56) or chicken broth (page 57)

1 teaspoon dried marjoram

½ teaspoon dried oregano

2 teaspoons salt

1 teaspoon freshly ground black pepper

1 tablespoon chopped fresh marjoram, to garnish, optional

1 • Preheat the oven to 400 degrees.

2 • Toss the red bell pepper and shallots with 2 tablespoons of the olive oil in a large baking pan. Move this mixture to one side of the pan to make room for the eggplant.

3 • Drizzle the cut side of the eggplant with 1 tablespoon of the olive oil and place, cut side down, in the baking pan. Add ¼ cup water to the pan. Bake 25 to 30 minutes, until the eggplant is soft to the touch and the bell peppers are lightly brown. Add the garlic and cook 10 minutes longer, turning the pepper, shallots, and garlic several times during the cooking process.

4 • Meanwhile, heat the remaining olive oil and the butter in a saucepan over medium heat. Add the onion and cook and stir about 10 minutes, until the onion is soft and translucent. Add the celery and carrot and cook and stir about 5 minutes more.

5 • Add the broth, marjoram, oregano, salt, and pepper and reduce heat to a simmer.

6 • Remove the eggplant, bell pepper, shallots, and garlic from the oven. Add the shallots and garlic to the soup.

7 • Scoop out the inside of the eggplant and add to the soup. Peel, core, and seed the pepper and add it to the soup. Let the soup simmer 30 to 40 minutes. Remove from the heat and cool slightly.

8 • Working in batches, add the soup to the bowl of a food processor fitted with the metal blade and puree until smooth. Stir in the fresh marjoram and additional salt and pepper if desired. Reheat if necessary and serve immediately.

variations: Add 1 cup of half-and-half or heavy cream after step 7 for a richer flavor and creamier texture.

Roasted Vegetables and Garlic

When vegetables are roasted, their flavors intensify or—in the case of garlic and eggplant—become sweeter. The reason for this is that natural moisture evaporates and the vegetables' natural sugars caramelize slightly. Make sure the vegetables are placed in one layer, so they brown evenly. (If they're piled up, they'll steam instead of roast.) Always coat the vegetables and garlic with a little oil to seal in moisture and to help them brown. Roast 30 to 40 minutes at 350 degrees until tender. There's no need to peel tender vegetables or those with soft skins, such as zucchini or summer squash; however, garlic should be squeezed out of its skin. At Foster's, we like to add roasted vegetables to many of our soups, since they provide extra flavor and it's a great way to use leftover roasted vegetables.

Jamaican Black Bean Soup

Delicious hot or cold, this hearty soup can be served over cooked rice for a vegetarian main course or as a sauce for enchiladas, huevos rancheros, or grilled fish or chicken.

2 cups dried black beans, picked
   over and rinsed

¼ cup olive oil

1 red onion, diced

1 red bell pepper, cored, seeded,
   and diced

2 carrots, peeled and diced

4 ribs celery, diced

2 jalapeños, diced, with seeds

8 garlic cloves, minced

1 Granny Smith or other tart apple,
   peeled, cored, and diced

1 tablespoon dried basil

8 cups chicken broth (page 57) or
   vegetable broth (page 56)

4 bay leaves

2 teaspoons salt

1 teaspoon freshly ground black
   pepper

Juice of 4 limes

3 tablespoons chopped fresh
   cilantro, to garnish, optional

6 scallions, trimmed and minced,
   to garnish, optional

1 • Quick-soak the beans: Place the beans in a large pot with water to cover by 3 inches and bring to a boil. Reduce heat and simmer uncovered 45 minutes. Remove from the heat, drain, rinse, and set aside.

2 • While the beans are cooking, heat the olive oil in a large saucepan over medium-low heat, add the onion, and cook and stir 10 to 12 minutes, until softened.

3 • Add the red bell pepper, carrots, celery, and jalapeños and cook and stir about 10 minutes more. Add the garlic and cook and stir 2 minutes longer.

4 • Add the apple, basil, broth, bay leaves, salt, pepper, and drained beans and stir to blend. Bring to a low boil. Reduce heat and simmer, uncovered, 1 to 1¼ hours, until the beans are tender.

5 • Remove half of the soup mixture and allow to cool slightly. Discard the bay leaves. Place the cooled soup in the bowl of a food processor fitted with the metal blade and puree until smooth. Return the pureed mixture to the soup and cook an additional 15 minutes.

6 • Remove the pot from the heat and stir in the lime juice. Ladle into bowls, garnish with the cilantro and scallions, and serve immediately.

variations: Instead of garnishing with the cilantro and scallions, serve with cilantro cream, made by mixing sour cream, fresh lime juice, and chopped fresh cilantro to taste. Sweet Italian peppers or banana peppers can be substituted for the bell peppers for a slightly different flavor.

sandwiches, spreads, and snacks

Foster's Sandwich Sensations • Foster's Pesto • Foster's Salsa

• Horseradish Mustard • Honey Mustard • Beet-Horseradish

Mustard • Basil Mayonnaise • Artichoke Aïoli • Caesar

Dressing • Ginger-Sesame Vinaigrette • Herbed Cream Cheese

• Mediterranean Dip • Hummus • Provençal White Bean Dip

• Fat-Free Black Bean Dip • Southwestern Cheese Dip •

Foster's Pimiento Cheese Spread • Potato Crisps with Herbs •

Crostini • Bruschetta a Dozen Ways • Rosemary Focaccia

Foster's Sandwich Sensations

Like salads and soups, the variations and permutations for sandwiches are seemingly endless. Try to think "outside the box," and consider sandwich fillings (or toppings for open-faced sandwiches) that are a little unexpected. Try different breads, including soft wheat tortillas (to make "wraps"), bagels, Crostini (page 104) or Bruschetta (page 106), and rolls. Use spreads other than mayonnaise and mustard (try chutney, salsa, salad dressings, pesto sauce, aïolis, oils, and vinegars, for example). Perhaps the greatest inspiration for a sandwich comes from leftovers: last night's meat loaf, grilled tuna, roast chicken, or grilled or roasted vegetables can have a second life as a tasty sandwich.

Roasted Chicken Salad on Toasted Baguette

Slice a baguette open lengthwise and brush the cut sides of the bread with olive oil. Broil or grill until lightly toasted. Fill with Roasted Chicken, Sweet Potato, and Arugula Salad (page 131) or Pesto Chicken Salad (page 127) and top with mixed greens or arugula, or serve open-faced.

Grilled Chicken Fajita on Syrian Bread

Lightly toast or grill Syrian bread so it becomes soft. Spread evenly with Basil Mayonnaise (page 92). Top with slices of grilled or roasted chicken, grilled onion and bell peppers, Foster's Salsa (page 90), sliced avocado, and lettuce. (Note: Syrian bread is like pita bread without the pocket. It is flat, easy to roll, and great grilled or toasted.)

Grilled Chicken Caesar on Sourdough Bread

Toast slices of sourdough bread and spread Caesar Dressing (page 94) evenly on each slice. Top with slices of grilled or roasted chicken, freshly shaved Parmesan, crisp romaine, and freshly ground black pepper. Grill the sandwich, if desired, by placing it in a skillet or grill pan with a small amount of olive oil and grilling lightly on both sides until bread is toasted and cheese has melted.

Turkey Barbecue on Sweet Potato Biscuit

Slice open a Sweet Potato Biscuit (page 17) or a whole-wheat roll and toast lightly. Top with Laura's Spicy Turkey Barbecue (page 166), Foster's Sweet and Tangy Barbecue Sauce (page 167), and Asian Cole Slaw with Corn and Frisée (page 111).

Grilled Turkey Club on Focaccia

Slice focaccia through the center to make 2 thin slices. Spread the cut side of each slice with Basil Mayonnaise (page 92). Top with roasted turkey, crispy bacon, fresh spinach, and several slices of Brie. Place the sandwich in a skillet or grill pan with a small amount of olive oil and grill lightly on both sides until bread is toasted and cheese has melted.

Meat Loaf Sandwich

Slice open a focaccia and grill or lightly toast. Spread the cut sides evenly with Dijon mustard. Top with a thick slice of Ratatouille Meat Loaf (page 223), sliced pickles or cornichons, thinly sliced red onions, arugula, or sprouts.

Bagel with Smoked Salmon

Split the bagel in half lengthwise and lightly toast both sides. Spread the cut sides evenly with Herbed Cream Cheese (page 96), top with slices of smoked salmon, thinly sliced red onions, capers, and sprouts. (This is delicious as an open-faced sandwich; it's one of our bestsellers at brunch.)

Roast Beef with Beet-Horseradish Mustard

Use a hearty rye or pumpernickel roll or bread and slice open. Spread both sides with Beet-Horseradish Mustard (page 92). Top with slices of rare roast beef, red onion slices, and fresh watercress.

Cobb Sandwich

Use a hearty whole-grain bread and spread one side of each slice with Basil Mayonnaise (page 92). Top with slices of roasted turkey or chicken, crispy bacon, sliced avocado, crumbled blue cheese or slices of Swiss cheese, cucumbers, and crisp lettuce leaves.

Curried Chicken Salad

This is a great open-faced sandwich. Use a hearty whole-grain or pumpernickel bread. Top with a scoop of Curried Chicken Salad (page 114) and radish sprouts, alfalfa sprouts, or pea sprouts.

Bacon, Avocado, Cucumber, and Sprouts

Spread Herbed Cream Cheese (page 96) on one side of a slice of whole-grain bread. Top the Herbed Cream Cheese with crispy bacon, sliced tomato, sliced cucumber, sliced avocado, and alfalfa sprouts (or use mustard, radish, sunflower, or pea sprouts). Spread 1 side of a second slice of bread with Basil Mayonnaise (page 92) and place on top of the sprouts.

Grilled Pimiento Cheese Sandwich with Grilled Ham

Spread Foster's Pimiento Cheese Spread (page 102) on 1 side of a slice of pumpernickel bread. Top with a few slices of grilled ham, several slices of tomato, and 5 or 6 watercress leaves. Top with a second slice of pumpernickel bread. Brush both sides of the sandwich with melted butter and grill in a skillet or grill pan over medium-high heat until the bread is toasty and the cheese is slightly melted.

Tomato and Mozzarella with Pesto

Slice a baguette open lengthwise and brush the cut side of the bread with olive oil. Broil or grill until lightly toasted. Spread the inside of the baguette with Foster's Pesto (page 90), then layer sliced tomatoes, sliced fresh mozzarella, mixed greens or arugula, and salt and pepper to taste.

Mediterranean Vegetarian Sandwich

Lightly toast or grill Syrian bread so it becomes soft. Spread with Mediterranean Dip (page 97). Top with artichoke hearts, thinly sliced cucumbers, sliced tomatoes, spinach leaves, grilled onions, pickled pepperoncini peppers, and provolone. Fold in half and serve.

Greek Turkey Wrap

Warm a spinach-flavored flour tortilla in the oven or microwave oven to soften it. Lay the tortilla on a flat work surface. Spread 1 side of the tortilla evenly with Mediterranean Dip (page 97). Place several slices of shredded roast turkey in the center of the tortilla. Top the turkey with artichoke hearts, roasted red peppers, pickled pepperoncini peppers, cucumbers, thinly sliced red onions, and fresh spinach leaves. Fold the sides of the tortilla toward the center over the filling. Starting at the bottom, roll away from you, like a log, pressing the rolled portion firmly while rolling and tucking in the sides as you go. Cut in half and serve.

Thai Chicken Wrap

Warm a spinach-flavored flour tortilla in the oven or microwave oven to soften it. Lay the tortilla on a flat work surface. Place several slices of shredded cooked chicken (pages 58–59) on the bottom half of the tortilla. Top the chicken with grated carrots, cucumbers, and baby greens or arugula, and drizzle with Ginger-Sesame Vinaigrette (page 95). Fold the sides of the tortilla toward the center over the filling. Then, starting at the bottom, roll away from you, like a log, pressing the rolled portion firmly while rolling and tucking in the sides as you go. Cut in half and serve.

Foster's Pesto

We plant rows and rows of basil every spring so that we can make this pesto all summer long. To keep the pesto bright green, you can add one vitamin C tablet to the mixture when you add the pine nuts and Parmesan.

2 cups firmly packed basil leaves, washed and dried

10 garlic cloves

¾ cup extra-virgin olive oil

One 2-ounce jar (¼ cup) pine nuts

1 cup (4 ounces) grated Parmesan cheese

1 teaspoon salt

1 teaspoon freshly ground black pepper

1 • Place the basil in the bowl of a food processor fitted with the metal blade. Add the garlic and pulse several times to make a roughly chopped mixture.

2 • Add the olive oil in a slow, steady stream down the feed tube, with the motor running. Stop the machine and scrape down the sides of the bowl several times.

3 • Add the pine nuts, Parmesan, salt, and pepper and puree about 1 minute longer, until the mixture is well blended and smooth. (Note: If adding vitamin C, add it along with the pine nuts.) Refrigerate in an airtight container until ready to use or up to 2 weeks.

Foster's Salsa

Fresh, homemade salsa is infinitely better than packaged salsa. This recipe is quick and easy, and keeps 3 to 4 days in the refrigerator. Try Foster's Salsa with grilled fish or chicken, poached or fried eggs, enchiladas, burritos, or huevos rancheros.

7 tomatoes, cored and chopped

One 14½-ounce can chopped tomatoes with juice (see Note)

One 4½-ounce can mild green chili peppers, diced

1 red bell pepper, cored, seeded, and diced

1 red onion, diced

1 jalapeño, seeded and diced

3 garlic cloves, minced

Combine the fresh tomatoes, canned tomatoes, green chilies, red bell pepper, onion, jalapeño, garlic, olive oil, cilantro, lemon juice, lime juice, cumin, salt, black pepper, and red pepper flakes in a large bowl and stir to mix well. Adjust seasonings, depending on how hot you like your salsa.

¼ cup olive oil

½ cup chopped fresh
     cilantro

Juice of 1 lemon

Juice of 1 lime

2 teaspoons ground cumin

2 teaspoons salt

1 teaspoon freshly ground black
     pepper

1 teaspoon red pepper
     flakes

note: If tomatoes are in season, you can omit canned tomatoes entirely and add 3 more large, chopped fresh tomatoes.

Horseradish Mustard

½ cup mayonnaise

½ cup sour cream or yogurt

⅓ cup Dijon mustard

¼ cup drained prepared
     horseradish

Juice of ½ lemon

1 teaspoon salt

Freshly ground black pepper to
     taste

Combine the mayonnaise, sour cream, mustard, horseradish, lemon juice, salt, and pepper in a bowl and stir until well blended. Refrigerate in an airtight container until ready to use or up to 1 week.

serving suggestions: Great on grilled beef, lamb, or steaks or on roast beef or turkey sandwiches.

Honey Mustard

1½ cups whole-grain mustard
     or stone-ground mustard

¼ cup honey

1 tablespoon cider vinegar

1 teaspoon salt

Freshly ground black pepper to
     taste

Combine the mustard, honey, vinegar, salt, and pepper in a bowl and stir to blend well. Refrigerate in an airtight container until ready to use or up to 2 weeks.

serving suggestions: Spread on biscuits with grilled ham or on turkey sandwiches. Or use to glaze ham before baking or for marinating chicken for the grill.

Beet-Horseradish Mustard

MAKES ABOUT 2 CUPS MUSTARD

1½ cups Dijon mustard

½ cup drained, prepared beet
horseradish (available in
kosher or gourmet delis)

2 tablespoons honey

Freshly ground black pepper to
taste

Combine the mustard, beet horseradish, honey, and pepper in a bowl and stir until well blended. Refrigerate in an airtight container until ready to use or up to 1 week. (Note: If you cannot find beet horseradish, proceed as follows: Combine mustard, honey, pepper, and ½ cup drained, sliced, canned or cooked beets in the bowl of a food processor fitted with the metal blade and puree until smooth. Stir in ¼ cup prepared horseradish.)

serving suggestions: Try this with grilled steak or lamb. It's also good with pot roast or short ribs, as well as spread on turkey or roast beef sandwiches.

Basil Mayonnaise

This herbed mayonnaise is delicious as a sandwich spread, drizzled on sliced tomatoes and crisp salad greens, or as a sauce for poached chicken, fish, or shellfish. It can be made up to 5 days in advance and refrigerated until ready to use. Leave out the basil for plain mayonnaise.

MAKES ABOUT 2½ CUPS MAYONNAISE

1 large egg or ¼ cup pasteurized
eggs or 2 cups good-quality
mayonnaise

2 tablespoons white wine vinegar

Juice of 1 lemon

1 teaspoon Dijon mustard

2 garlic cloves, chopped

2 cups canola or safflower oil
(omit if using mayonnaise)

10 fresh basil leaves, cut into very
thin strips (chiffonade)

2 tablespoons chopped fresh parsley

Salt and freshly ground black pepper
to taste

1 • Place the egg or the mayonnaise, vinegar, and lemon juice in the bowl of a food processor fitted with the metal blade and pulse to blend. With the motor running, add the mustard and garlic.

2 • Add the oil in a slow, steady stream down the feed tube, with the motor running, until the mixture becomes thick and is the consistency of mayonnaise. (Omit the oil if using mayonnaise.)

3 • Add the basil and parsley and puree until well combined and the mixture is bright green. Season with salt and pepper and refrigerate in an airtight container until ready to use.

Artichoke Aïoli

This variation on the classic South of France garlic mayonnaise has artichokes, capers, horseradish, and spicy red pepper for added flavor. It can be made 3 to 4 days in advance. At the Market, we use artichoke aïoli on sandwiches and in salads or spread it on Crostini (page 104) or pita chips.

MAKES ABOUT 2½ CUPS AÏOLI

One 14-ounce can water-packed artichoke hearts, drained and chopped

1 large egg or ¼ cup pasteurized eggs or 1 cup good-quality mayonnaise

3 garlic cloves

Juice of 1 lemon

2 tablespoons Dijon mustard

2 tablespoons drained capers

1 teaspoon drained prepared horseradish

½ teaspoon salt

½ teaspoon freshly ground black pepper

¼ teaspoon ground red pepper (cayenne)

¾ cup canola or safflower oil (omit if using mayonnaise)

1 • Place the artichokes, egg or mayonnaise, garlic, lemon juice, mustard, capers, horseradish, salt, black pepper, and red pepper in the bowl of a food processor fitted with the metal blade and pulse to mix.

2 • Add the oil in a slow, steady stream down the feed tube, with the motor running, until the mixture thickens. (Omit the oil if using mayonnaise.)

3 • Refrigerate in an airtight container until ready to use or up to 4 days.

Pasteurized Eggs for Dips, Dressings, and Mayonnaise

Pasteurized eggs are a safe and healthful substitute for raw eggs when making uncooked sauces and dips. One-fourth cup pasteurized eggs is equivalent to 1 large egg. If you can't find pasteurized eggs and don't want to use raw eggs, omit the eggs entirely and substitute 1 cup good-quality mayonnaise for every cup of oil in the recipe. Whenever we use pasteurized eggs or mayonnaise in an uncooked sauce, we always puree in a food processor or blender rather than whisking by hand. And if herbs are added, pureeing gives the final sauce a more intense flavor.

Caesar Dressing

This creamy dressing is quick and easy, and it keeps in the refrigerator up to 1 week. We make it with pasteurized eggs at the Market, but if you can't find pasteurized eggs where you live, you can substitute mayonnaise. Caesar dressing is not only delicious on Caesar salads; it's terrific as a sandwich spread, or to sauce grilled or poached chicken breasts or boiled or roasted new potatoes, or as a dip for crudités.

MAKES ABOUT 2½ CUPS DRESSING

2 large eggs or ½ cup pasteurized eggs or 2 cups good-quality mayonnaise

4 garlic cloves, minced

2 tablespoons cider vinegar

Juice of 1 lemon

½ teaspoon hot sauce (such as Tabasco or Texas Pete)

1 teaspoon salt

1 teaspoon freshly ground black pepper

½ teaspoon dry mustard

1 cup canola or safflower oil (omit if using mayonnaise)

½ cup olive oil (omit if using mayonnaise)

¾ cup freshly grated Parmesan cheese

1 • Combine the eggs or the mayonnaise, garlic, vinegar, lemon juice, hot sauce, salt, pepper, and mustard in the bowl of a food processor fitted with the metal blade and pulse until well blended.

2 • Add the canola oil and olive oil in a slow, steady stream down the feed tube, with the motor running, until the dressing is thick and smooth. (Omit the oils if using mayonnaise.) Add the Parmesan and pulse several times until well blended. Refrigerate in an airtight container until ready to use or up to 1 week.

Ginger-Sesame Vinaigrette

This rich, nutty dressing has a hint of citrus and the zing of fresh ginger. Try it on salads, cold buckwheat noodles, and steamed vegetables, as well as on sandwiches.

Grated zest and juice of 1 orange
Grated zest and juice of 1 lime
$\frac{1}{4}$ cup light soy sauce
$\frac{1}{4}$ cup cider vinegar
$\frac{1}{4}$ cup white distilled vinegar
2 tablespoons honey
2 tablespoons peeled, grated
    fresh ginger
5 garlic cloves, minced
3 scallions, trimmed and chopped
1 tablespoon red pepper flakes
$\frac{1}{4}$ cup dark sesame oil
1 cup canola or safflower oil
$\frac{1}{4}$ cup toasted sesame seeds
Salt and freshly ground black
    pepper to taste

1 • Place the orange zest and juice and lime zest and juice, soy sauce, cider vinegar, white distilled vinegar, honey, ginger, garlic, scallions, and red pepper flakes in a bowl and whisk to mix thoroughly.

2 • Slowly whisk in the sesame oil, canola oil, and sesame seeds and whisk until well blended. Season with salt and pepper. Refrigerate in an airtight container until ready to use or up to 1 week.

Herbed Cream Cheese

This versatile spread is easy to make, and keeps well, too. It's great on a sandwich, as a dip for crudités or Crostini (page 104), or as a filling for omelets, burritos, or frittatas.

Two 8-ounce packages cream
   cheese, softened
Juice of 1 lemon
2 scallions, trimmed and minced
1 tablespoon chopped fresh
   parsley
1 teaspoon chopped fresh dill
1 teaspoon freshly ground black
   pepper

1 • Cream together the cream cheese and lemon juice in a bowl.

2 • Stir in the scallions, parsley, dill, and pepper and mix until smooth and well blended. Refrigerate in an airtight container until ready to use or up to 6 days.

variations: Substitute ricotta, mild chèvre, or plain, unsweetened yogurt for half of the cream cheese for a lower-calorie spread. You can also flavor the spread with smoked salmon (puree 1 ounce of salmon with the cream cheese in a food processor until smooth), or fold in finely chopped sun-dried tomatoes.

Mediterranean Dip

We not only serve this as a dip, but also as a salad dressing and a sandwich spread. I particularly love it on our Greek Turkey Wrap (page 89), which is loaded with vegetables.

MAKES ABOUT 2 1/2 CUPS DIP

1 cup good-quality mayonnaise

1/2 pound drained, crumbled feta cheese

1/2 cup sour cream

10 pickled pepperoncini peppers, stems removed, chopped

8 garlic cloves, chopped

3 tablespoons drained capers

1 teaspoon dried oregano

1 teaspoon dried marjoram

1 teaspoon hot sauce (such as Tabasco or Texas Pete)

1 teaspoon freshly ground black pepper

2 tablespoons freshly chopped parsley

Place the mayonnaise, feta, sour cream, pepperoncini peppers, garlic, capers, oregano, marjoram, hot sauce, pepper, and parsley in the bowl of a food processor fitted with the metal blade. Process about 1 minute, until all the ingredients are thoroughly mixed. (Note: The mixture will not be completely smooth because of the feta.) Refrigerate in an airtight container until ready to use or up to 1 week.

Hummus

This Middle Eastern classic is delicious as a dip for toasted pita triangles or crudités. It also makes a tasty spread for sandwiches. At the Market, we spread hummus inside a toasted pita, then fill the pocket with grated carrots, sliced cucumbers, sprouts, and tomatoes.

One 15½-ounce can chickpeas

¾ cup tahini

6 garlic cloves

2 teaspoons salt

1 teaspoon freshly ground black
    pepper

½ teaspoon red pepper flakes

Juice of 3 lemons

¼ cup olive oil

2 tablespoons chopped fresh
    parsley

1 • Drain the chickpeas, reserving the liquid. Place the chickpeas in the bowl of a food processor fitted with the metal blade.

2 • Add the tahini, garlic, salt, black pepper, and red pepper flakes and pulse several times. Add the lemon juice and olive oil in a slow, steady stream down the feed tube with the machine running and puree until smooth. Add ¼ to ⅓ cup of the reserved liquid from the can if necessary to make a smooth paste.

3 • Add the parsley, and additional salt and pepper if desired. Pulse several times just until blended. Refrigerate in an airtight container until ready to use or up to 5 days.

Provençal White Bean Dip

We've added sun-dried tomatoes and capers to this classic Mediterranean dip. It's easy, versatile, and high in protein, too. Although this is best made with dried beans that you cook yourself, canned beans are fine if you're short on time.

¾ cup dried navy beans

4 garlic cloves, chopped

1 jalapeño

½ cup olive oil

¼ cup sun-dried tomatoes

2 tablespoons drained capers

Juice of 1 lime

1 teaspoon hot sauce (such as
Tabasco or Texas Pete)

2 tablespoons chopped fresh
oregano or fresh marjoram

1 teaspoon salt

½ teaspoon freshly ground
black pepper

1 • Place the beans in a large, heavy saucepan and add enough water to cover the beans by about 4 inches. Bring to a boil, lower heat to medium, and simmer, uncovered, about 1½ hours, until the beans are soft. Rinse and drain the beans and set aside.

2 • Preheat the oven to 400 degrees.

3 • While the beans are cooking, toss the garlic and jalapeño with 2 tablespoons of the olive oil in a small baking dish. Roast 15 to 20 minutes, or until soft and light golden brown. (Note: The garlic may be ready before the jalapeño.) Discard the jalapeño skin. Cut the jalapeño in half, and discard the seeds.

4 • Place the beans, sun-dried tomatoes, garlic, jalapeño, capers, remaining olive oil, lime juice, hot sauce, oregano, salt, and pepper in the bowl of a food processor fitted with the metal blade and process until smooth. Refrigerate in an airtight container until ready to use or up to 6 days.

serving suggestions

• Spread on Crostini (page 104) or Bruschetta (page 106) and serve alongside soups or salads.

• Use as a vegetarian sandwich filling, topped with tomatoes, onions, olives, and arugula.

• Serve as a dip for crudités or tortilla chips.

• Spread on top of warm tortillas filled with sliced chicken breast.

• Serve alongside or on top of grilled vegetables.

Fat-Free Black Bean Dip

When we created this recipe, our goal was to have a really flavorful, healthful dip—one that could accompany tortilla chips as well as fill burritos, enchiladas, and omelets. We achieved that, and more.

MAKES ABOUT 2 CUPS DIP

1 cup dried black beans

1 green bell pepper, cut in half, cored and seeded

3 bay leaves

$\frac{1}{2}$ cup tomato juice

Juice of 2 limes

1 tablespoon cider vinegar

3 garlic cloves, chopped

1 jalapeño, seeded and chopped

$\frac{1}{2}$ red onion, chopped

4 scallions, trimmed and chopped

1 teaspoon ground cumin

1 teaspoon chili powder

2 teaspoons salt

$\frac{1}{2}$ teaspoon red pepper flakes

$\frac{1}{3}$ cup fresh cilantro

1 • Place the beans in a large pot and add water to cover the beans by about 4 inches. Add the green bell pepper and bay leaves, bring to a boil, and cook 1 to $1\frac{1}{4}$ hours, uncovered, until the beans are tender. Remove from the heat, rinse, and set aside to drain. Discard the bell pepper and bay leaves.

2 • Place the beans in the bowl of a food processor fitted with the metal blade and add the tomato juice, lime juice, vinegar, garlic, jalapeño, onion, scallions, cumin, chili powder, salt, and red pepper flakes and process until smooth. Add the cilantro and pulse several times until the cilantro is roughly chopped. Refrigerate in an airtight container until ready to use or up to 5 days.

Southwestern Cheese Dip

This rich, spicy dip is great served with crudités or tortilla or pita chips, accompanied by cold beer or margaritas. It's also delicious spread on soft flour tortillas filled with chicken, or as a spread for vegetarian sandwiches or wraps.

MAKES ABOUT 3½ CUPS DIP

1 cup good-quality mayonnaise

3 cups (12 ounces) grated sharp
　　Cheddar cheese

¾ cup sour cream or yogurt

Grated zest and juice of 1 lemon

1 jalapeño, roasted, seeded, and
　　chopped

One 4½-ounce can green chili
　　peppers, diced

1 roasted red bell pepper, peeled,
　　cored, seeded, and diced
　　(page 40)

4 scallions, trimmed and chopped

½ teaspoon salt

½ teaspoon freshly ground black
　　pepper

½ teaspoon ground red pepper
　　(cayenne)

½ teaspoon ground cumin

½ teaspoon ground coriander

Combine the mayonnaise, Cheddar, sour cream, lemon zest, lemon juice, jalapeño, green chilies, roasted red bell pepper, scallions, salt, black pepper, red pepper, cumin, and coriander in a bowl and stir until well blended. Refrigerate in an airtight container until ready to use or up to 5 days.

Foster's Pimiento Cheese Spread

We've tweaked a southern classic by adding Parmesan, smoked Gouda, and homemade mayonnaise. The result is a sophisticated spread that can be used for party hors d'oeuvres as well as for sandwiches.

MAKES ABOUT 4 CUPS SPREAD

1 cup (4 ounces) grated sharp
  Cheddar cheese
1½ cups (6 ounces) grated
  Parmesan cheese
1 cup (4 ounces) grated smoked
  Gouda cheese
1 roasted red bell pepper, peeled,
  cored, seeded, and chopped
  (page 40)
1 roasted green bell pepper,
  peeled, cored, seeded, and
  chopped (page 40)
1 cup good-quality mayonnaise
1 jalapeño, seeded and minced
1 tablespoon cider vinegar
1 tablespoon honey
1 teaspoon salt
1 teaspoon freshly ground black
  pepper

1 • Mix together the Cheddar, Parmesan, Gouda, roasted red bell pepper, and roasted green bell pepper in a large bowl.

2 • In a separate bowl, combine the mayonnaise, jalapeño, vinegar, honey, salt, and pepper and stir to blend well.

3 • Stir the mayonnaise mixture into the cheese mixture and mix well. Season with additional salt and pepper if desired. Refrigerate in an airtight container until ready to use or up to 1 week.

serving suggestions

• Spread on Crostini (page 104) or Bruschetta (page 106) and top with sliced or chopped tomatoes and fresh basil or arugula.

• Serve as a dip with tortilla chips, bagel chips, pita chips, or crostini.

• Use as a sandwich spread for hot or cold sandwiches, with tomatoes, bacon, or ham added if desired.

• Use as a topping for baked potatoes.

• Use as an omelet filling.

• Spread on crostini and float on soups.

• Spread on toast in the morning for a quick breakfast (it's a yummy variation on cheese toast).

Potato Crisps with Herbs

These are great with dips and salsa or served alongside sandwiches or salads.

SERVES 8 TO 10

¼ cup olive oil

3 russet potatoes, peeled and thinly sliced lengthwise into ⅛-inch slices

1 tablespoon kosher salt or coarse sea salt

2 teaspoons freshly ground black pepper

1 tablespoon chopped fresh rosemary

1 tablespoon chopped fresh thyme

1 • Preheat the oven to 450 degrees.

2 • Brush a large baking pan with 2 tablespoons of the olive oil and place the potatoes on it in a single layer.

3 • Brush the tops of the potatoes lightly with the remaining olive oil and sprinkle lightly with the salt, pepper, rosemary, and thyme.

4 • Bake 15 to 18 minutes until golden brown and crispy. Let the potatoes cool on the baking sheet so they stay crisp, then serve.

Crostini

Crostini are toasted slices of bread—usually Italian or French bread—used for snacking, dipping, or to float on soups as a crunchy garnish. Crostini are also delicious as an accompaniment to salads or topped with various spreads and cheeses and served as hors d'oeuvres. When making crostini, use the best-quality bread you can find; day-old bread works well, too.

MAKES 25 TO 30 CROSTINI

1 long, thin, good-quality baguette

¼ cup olive oil

2 tablespoons unsalted butter, melted

2 tablespoons chopped fresh parsley

1 tablespoon chopped fresh dill

1 teaspoon freshly ground black pepper

Kosher salt or coarse sea salt to taste

1 • Preheat the oven to 400 degrees.

2 • Slice the bread on a slight angle into ¼-inch-thick slices and place on a baking pan in a single layer.

3 • Mix together the olive oil, butter, parsley, dill, and pepper in a small bowl.

4 • Brush one side of each piece of bread with the butter mixture and sprinkle with the salt. Toast in the oven 10 to 15 minutes, until golden brown and crunchy.

5 • Let cool completely, then serve or store in an airtight container up to 1 week.

variations: We use a mixture of butter and olive oil for our crostini, but they're equally good with either one alone. Or try Asian chili oil for added spiciness or lemon- or lime-flavored olive oil for a mild citrus flavor. You also can drizzle or brush a little balsamic vinegar on the crostini before baking for a bit of tartness. Experiment with other herbs, such as rosemary, thyme, oregano, and marjoram.

serving suggestions for crostini

• A vehicle for dipping

• A base for spreads

• Instead of croutons on soups or salads

• An hors d'oeuvre, spread with any of the following:

*Herbed Cream Cheese (page 96), with or without a
slice of smoked salmon and a few watercress
leaves*

*Soft chèvre or Brie topped with
fruit chutney or Foster's Salsa (page 90)*

Curried Chicken Salad (page 114)

Scrambled eggs with cheese and crumbled bacon

*Cream cheese and Foster's Seven-Pepper Jelly with
Fresh Mint (page 178)*

*Chopped Caesar salad topped with
freshly grated Parmesan*

Roasted or grilled vegetables and fresh basil

Grilled Vegetable Ratatouille (page 124)

Foster's Pimiento Cheese Spread (page 102)

Hummus (page 98)

Bruschetta a Dozen Ways

Bruschetta—grilled Italian bread—is as delicious as it is versatile, since it can be served as a vehicle for an almost limitless number of toppings. It's also good just as is, to accompany soups and salads. Since bruschetta is so simple, the quality of ingredients really matters. Choose a fruity, extra-virgin cold-pressed olive oil and the best country bread you can find. Although I think bruschetta is best grilled, it can also be toasted under the broiler.

MAKES 6 SLICES

Safflower oil or canola oil, for oiling the grill

¼ cup olive oil, preferably a very fruity extra-virgin cold-pressed olive oil

2 garlic cloves, minced

½ teaspoon freshly ground black pepper

1 tablespoon chopped fresh rosemary

6 slices rustic country bread (slices should be about ¾ inch thick)

Kosher salt or coarse sea salt to taste

1 • Brush the grill grates lightly with the safflower oil. Prepare a hot fire on a gas or charcoal grill.

2 • Mix together the olive oil, garlic, pepper, and rosemary in a bowl. Brush both sides of each slice of bread with the olive oil mixture.

3 • Place on the hot grill and grill about 2 minutes per side, depending on how hot the fire is. Season with the salt and serve immediately.

serving suggestions: Prepare bruschetta as directed, then top with one of the following:

- Crumbled blue cheese
- Crumbled or creamy, spreadable chèvre
- Chopped fresh tomatoes mixed with fresh basil, olive oil, lemon juice, salt and pepper
- Mediterranean Dip (page 97), topped with crunchy pickles or carrots
- Foster's Pesto (page 90) and fresh mozzarella cheese
- Sautéed wild mushrooms with wilted spinach (page 213)
- Provençal White Bean Dip (page 99)
- Foster's Pimiento Cheese Spread (page 102)
- Sliced prosciutto or salami with Basil Mayonnaise (page 92)
- Tuna salad
- Curried Chicken Salad (page 114)
- Olive tapenade

Rosemary Focaccia

This bread is great for sandwiches or with soup or salads, or for dinner instead of a traditional roll. For tailgating or picnics, you can use the entire focaccia to make festive sandwiches as follows: Using a serrated knife, slice the entire focaccia through the center to form two rounds. Place sandwich fillings on the cut side of the bottom half of the focaccia, then top with the remaining focaccia round. Slice the entire round into pie-shaped wedges.

MAKES TWO 9-INCH ROUND LOAVES

2^1/$_4$ cups warm water

^{1}/$_4$ teaspoon sugar

One ^{1}/$_4$-ounce package active dry yeast

5^1/$_2$ to 6 cups all-purpose flour

1 teaspoon salt

5 tablespoons olive oil

2 tablespoons fresh rosemary or 2 teaspoons dried rosemary

^{1}/$_2$ teaspoon kosher salt or coarse sea salt

^{1}/$_4$ teaspoon freshly ground black pepper

1 • Preheat the oven to 400 degrees.

2 • Place the water, sugar, and yeast in a small bowl; stir once or twice just to mix. Let stand in a warm place 5 to 7 minutes, until small bubbles form on top.

3 • Mix 5^1/$_2$ cups of the flour and the salt in a large bowl and stir to blend. Make a well in the center of the flour and add 2 tablespoons of the olive oil and the yeast mixture. Stir to combine until the dough begins to stick together. Add remaining flour as needed.

4 • Remove the dough from the bowl and transfer to a lightly floured work surface. Knead for about 10 minutes, until the dough forms a smooth ball. Lightly oil a large bowl with 1 tablespoon of the olive oil and place the dough in the bowl, turning to coat the dough lightly with the oil. Cover and let rise in a warm place 30 to 45 minutes, until dough has almost doubled in size.

5 • Remove the dough from the bowl, punch down, and divide into 2 pieces. Set aside to rest 10 to 15 minutes. Roll the dough into two 9-inch rounds, about ^{1}/$_2$ to 1 inch thick, and place on a baking sheet. Brush lightly with the remaining olive oil. Sprinkle with the rosemary, salt, and pepper and bake 25 to 30 minutes, until the focaccia is golden brown. Remove from the oven and serve immediately.

variations: Try herbs other than rosemary, or top the dough with thinly sliced red onion or bell peppers or a sprinkling of grated Parmesan cheese before baking.

Mixed Greens with Baby Beets, Chèvre, and Walnuts • Asian Cole Slaw with Corn and Frisée • Balsamic-Roasted Vegetables • Curried Chicken Salad • Black Bean and Yellow Rice Salad • Pesto Green Beans with Three Types of Tomatoes • Sesame Noodles with Baby Greens and Cucumbers • Lentil, Spinach, and Feta Salad with Sour Cherry Vinaigrette • Grilled Vegetable Antipasto with Herbed Chèvre and Crostini • Grilled Vegetable Ratatouille • Old-Fashioned Chicken Salad • Orzo with Grilled Zucchini and Sun-Dried Tomatoes • Pesto Chicken Salad • Grilled Chicken Salad with Provençal Vinaigrette • Roasted Chicken, Sweet Potato, and Arugula Salad • Grilled Asparagus with Roasted Shallots and Cranberry Vinaigrette • Roasted New Potato Salad with Dijon Vinaigrette • Southwestern Fried Chicken Salad • Tarragon Chicken Salad with Granny Smith Apples and Red Grapes • Grilled Chicken Salad with Tomatoes, Spinach, and Dijon Vinaigrette • Turkey Waldorf Salad with Dried Apricots and Chèvre Dressing • Bow-Tie Pasta with Eggplant, Caramelized Onions, and Pine Nuts • Shrimp Salad with Lemon-Dill Vinaigrette • Cucumber, Avocado, and Tomato Salad • Asian-Style Roasted Vegetables with Bok Choy and Hoisin Sauce • Lemon-Roasted Asparagus with Teriyaki Orange Salsa • Succotash Salad with Garden Tomatoes • Tuscan White Bean Salad with Spinach, Olives, and Sun-Dried Tomatoes

Mixed Greens with Baby Beets, Chèvre, and Walnuts

Baby beets are so tender they don't need to be peeled. Their natural sweetness is the perfect foil to the tangy cheese and the earthy nuts.

SERVES 4

8 ounces (about 6 cups firmly
   packed) mesclun mix salad
   greens
1 bunch of baby beets (8 to 10
   very small beets)
1 cup (4 ounces) crumbled creamy
   chèvre
1/2 cup toasted walnut halves
1/2 cup Herbed Balsamic
   Vinaigrette (page 131)
Salt and freshly ground black
   pepper to taste

1 • Wash the greens thoroughly and set aside to drain.
2 • Scrub and trim the beets, leaving about 1 inch of the stem end with some of the small leaves attached. Place in a pot of boiling water, reduce heat to a simmer, and cook, uncovered, 10 to 15 minutes, until the beets are tender when pierced with a fork. Drain and set aside to cool. Slice the beets in half lengthwise.
3 • Combine the greens with the beets, chèvre, walnuts, and vinaigrette in a large bowl and toss gently to mix. Season with salt and pepper and serve immediately.

Asian Cole Slaw with Corn and Frisée

At Foster's, we serve this on our Turkey Barbecue or Sweet Potato Biscuit sandwich (page 86), but it also stands alone as an unusual and tasty side to dishes such as Grilled Tuna with Scallions and Wasabi Mustard (page 188). Crisp and full of flavor, it can be served as a first course when topped with crispy calamari or grilled shrimp.

SERVES 8 TO 10 AS A SIDE DISH (ENOUGH TO TOP
10 TO 12 TURKEY BARBECUE ON SWEET POTATO
BISCUIT SANDWICHES, PAGE 86)

1 head green cabbage, cored and
   thinly sliced

2 heads frisée

Kernels from 2 ears fresh corn
   (1 cup fresh or frozen corn)

1 red bell pepper, cored, seeded,
   and julienned

$\frac{1}{2}$ cup chopped fresh cilantro

$\frac{1}{2}$ cup chopped fresh parsley

2 tablespoons peeled, julienned
   fresh ginger

$\frac{1}{2}$ teaspoon red pepper flakes

1 cup Cider Vinegar–Honey
   Dressing (recipe follows)

$\frac{1}{4}$ cup sesame seeds, toasted
   (see Note)

Salt and freshly ground black
   pepper to taste

Toasted sesame seeds, to garnish,
   optional

Cilantro and parsley, to garnish,
   optional

1 • Place the cabbage in a large bowl of ice water for 20 to 30 minutes to crisp it. Drain thoroughly and pat dry. (You can refrigerate it at this point up to 1 day ahead of time to make it extra crispy.)

2 • Remove the stem end of the frisée and tear into separate leaves; wash and drain thoroughly.

3 • Place the corn kernels in a skillet and add just enough water to cover the kernels. Simmer over medium heat about 1 minute or until crisp-tender. Remove immediately and drain well.

4 • Combine the cabbage, frisée, corn, red bell pepper, cilantro, parsley, ginger, and red pepper flakes in a large bowl and toss with the Cider Vinegar–Honey Dressing and 3 tablespoons of the sesame seeds. Season with salt and pepper. Garnish with the remaining sesame seeds, cilantro, and parsley and serve immediately.

note: To toast the sesame seeds, place in a dry skillet, uncovered, over medium heat for 3 to 4 minutes, stirring constantly, or until all the seeds are evenly browned. Remove from the pan immediately or they will continue to brown.

variation: Cucumbers, snow peas, or sugar snap peas can be added to the salad; diced red bell peppers can be sprinkled on top for a colorful garnish.

Cider Vinegar–Honey Dressing

This tangy-sweet dressing is also delicious on mixed greens or marinated vegetables.

MAKES ABOUT 1 CUP DRESSING

⅓ cup cider vinegar

2 tablespoons honey

Grated zest and juice of 1 orange

1 teaspoon red pepper flakes

1 teaspoon freshly ground black
   pepper

1 tablespoon peeled, grated fresh
   ginger

½ cup canola or safflower oil

1 • Combine the vinegar, honey, orange zest, orange juice, red pepper flakes, black pepper, and ginger in a bowl.

2 • Add the oil in a slow, steady stream while whisking constantly until well blended. Refrigerate in an airtight container until ready to serve or up to 1 week.

Frisée

Frisée—a member of the chicory family—is a nice addition to salads because the light, feathery leaves add an interesting texture and slightly bitter taste similar to Belgian endive. If frisée is not available, substitute curly endive, which has larger leaves but resembles frisée in taste and texture. Or try julienned Belgian endive, which would give you a similar taste as frisée, although not the same texture. If none of the above is available, use mixed baby greens, watercress, or spinach.

Olive Oil for Salads

At Foster's, we feel that the flavor of olive oil is too strong to use alone in most dressings. For a milder, less assertive flavor, we usually combine olive oil with a neutral oil like canola, safflower, or grapeseed oil. We also tend to use more vinegar, citrus, and fruit juices than most vinaigrette recipes, so our salad dressings are lower in fat and the salad has more of a "bite."

THE FOSTER'S MARKET COOKBOOK | 112

Balsamic-Roasted Vegetables

This dish can be made with almost any vegetable, but I try to choose those that require approximately the same amount of cooking, so they can go into and out of the oven at the same time. And, of course, choose your vegetables with the seasons in mind. Balsamic-roasted vegetables can be made several hours in advance and served at room temperature. Try them as a delicious side dish to accompany Roast Pork Tenderloin with Dried Cherries and Rosemary (page 185) or Braised Chicken Thighs with Chèvre Stuffing (page 155). They're also great as an entrée, served on top of a large platter of rice, couscous, or orzo.

SERVES 8 TO 10 AS A SIDE DISH

1/2 cup balsamic vinegar

3/4 cup olive oil

1/4 cup mixed chopped fresh
herbs, such as thyme,
rosemary, and parsley, or
1 heaping tablespoon
dried herbs

2 sweet potatoes, peeled and cut
into 2-inch wedges

1 butternut squash, peeled,
seeded, and cut into 2-inch
wedges

1 red onion, cut into 2-inch
wedges

1 pint cherry tomatoes, stems
removed

2 red bell peppers, cored, seeded,
and cut into 2-inch pieces

1 head broccoli, stem removed,
cut into florets

1 pound green beans, trimmed

Salt and freshly ground black
pepper to taste

Fresh herbs, to garnish, optional

1 • Preheat the oven to 400 degrees.

2 • Whisk the vinegar, olive oil, and herbs together in a large bowl. Add the sweet potatoes, squash, and onion and toss until the vegetables are well coated.

3 • Transfer the vegetables with a slotted spoon (reserve the liquid in the bowl) to a baking dish and spread them out in 1 even layer. Roast them in the oven for 40 to 45 minutes, until the potatoes are tender and slightly brown and the vinegar mixture has evaporated to a thick glaze. Stir several times during the cooking.

4 • Meanwhile, toss tomatoes, red bell peppers, broccoli, and green beans with the reserved liquid, and spread them in 1 even layer in a separate baking dish. Roast them in the oven for 25 to 30 minutes, until the skin on the tomatoes starts to shrivel.

5 • Gently toss all of the vegetables together in a bowl with any remaining cooking liquid until just mixed. Season with salt and pepper; garnish with fresh herb leaves if desired. Serve immediately or at room temperature.

variations: Cauliflower or Brussels sprouts can be used instead of broccoli, substitute any kind of potato for the sweet potatoes, and try sweet Italian peppers or banana peppers instead of the bell pepper. Acorn squash or pumpkin can be used in place of the butternut squash. Carrots, garlic, and onions are a delicious addition any time of year.

Curried Chicken Salad

Whitney Aichner, one of Foster's cooks, created this spicy salad, and it has become a favorite in the Market and on our catering menu. It's delicious as a side dish or piled on whole-grain bread topped with sprouts or baby greens.

SERVES 8 TO 10

1½ cups sweetened flaked coconut

4 cups shredded cooked chicken (page 58)

1 red bell pepper, cored, seeded, and diced

1 green bell pepper, cored, seeded, and diced

7 scallions, trimmed and chopped

1 Granny Smith or other tart apple, cored and thinly sliced

½ cup currants

¼ cup chopped parsley

2 cups Curried Dressing (recipe follows)

Salt and freshly ground black pepper to taste

Additional parsley and scallions, to garnish, optional

1 • Preheat the oven to 400 degrees.

2 • Spread the coconut evenly on a baking sheet and toast in the oven 5 to 7 minutes or until light brown around the edges. Remove from the oven and cool.

3 • Mix the chicken, red bell pepper, green bell pepper, scallions, apple, currants, parsley, and 1 cup of the coconut in a bowl. Add the dressing, season with salt and pepper, and toss to mix. Serve immediately or refrigerate until ready to serve. Garnish with the remaining coconut and additional parsley and scallions just before serving.

Curried Dressing

MAKES ABOUT 2 CUPS DRESSING

1¼ cups good-quality mayonnaise

½ cup chopped parsley

¼ cup curry powder

¼ cup honey

Juice of 1 lemon

2 teaspoons salt

1 teaspoon freshly ground black pepper

Combine the mayonnaise with the parsley, curry powder, honey, lemon juice, salt, and pepper in a bowl and whisk to mix until thoroughly blended. Refrigerate in an airtight container until ready to use or up to 5 days.

Black Bean and Yellow Rice Salad

This colorful dish makes a great addition to a buffet or a tasty vegetarian main course.

2 cups dried black beans, picked over and rinsed

2 garlic cloves

1 cup long-grain white rice

$\frac{1}{2}$ cup olive oil

1 yellow onion, diced

$\frac{1}{2}$ teaspoon turmeric

2 scallions, trimmed and minced

1 red bell pepper, cored, seeded, and chopped

1 jalapeño, seeded and minced

Juice of 1 lime

1 teaspoon red pepper flakes

Salt and freshly ground black pepper to taste

1 ripe avocado

1 cup Foster's Salsa (page 90)

1 cup Corn Bread Croutons (page 79), optional

$\frac{1}{4}$ cup fresh cilantro

1 • Quick-soak the beans: Place the beans and garlic in a large pot with water to cover by 3 inches and bring to a boil. Reduce heat and simmer, uncovered, for 45 minutes. Remove from the heat, drain, rinse, and set aside. Discard the garlic.

2 • Rinse the rice in a sieve under running water until the water runs clear, and set aside to drain.

3 • Heat 2 tablespoons of the olive oil in a saucepan over medium heat. Add the onion and cook and stir 4 to 5 minutes, until the onion is soft and translucent.

4 • Add the rice and stir to mix. Add the turmeric and just enough water to cover the rice by $\frac{1}{4}$ inch. Reduce heat to low. Cover and simmer 20 to 25 minutes, until all the water is absorbed and the rice is flaky and tender. Remove from the heat and set aside to cool.

5 • Combine the scallions, red bell pepper, jalapeño, lime juice, red pepper flakes, and remaining olive oil in a bowl and stir until mixed. Add half of this mixture to the beans and stir gently to mix. Add the remaining scallion mixture to the rice and stir gently to mix. Season with salt and pepper.

6 • Just before serving, peel and pit the avocado, and cut into 1-inch slices.

7 • Put the rice mixture on a platter and top with the bean mixture. Place the salsa on top of the beans, top with the avocado, croutons, and cilantro. Serve immediately or refrigerate until ready to serve. (If you are refrigerating, do not add the salsa, avocado, croutons, or cilantro until ready to serve.)

Pesto Green Beans with Three Types of Tomatoes

This summer salad is great for buffets, picnics, potlucks, and tailgates. It's easy, too: if you don't have time to make your own pesto, use a good-quality, store-bought fresh pesto from the deli case.

SERVES 6 TO 8

2 plum tomatoes, cored and quartered

1 cup yellow pear tomatoes, cut in half, or cherry tomatoes or grape tomatoes

1/2 cup red cherry tomatoes, cut in half

1/4 cup olive oil

3 garlic cloves, minced

1 1/2 pounds green beans, stem ends removed

1 cup Foster's Pesto (page 90)

1 cup (4 ounces) grated Parmesan cheese

Salt and freshly ground black pepper to taste

One 2-ounce jar (1/4 cup) pine nuts, toasted (page 141), to garnish, optional

1/2 cup grated Parmesan cheese, to garnish, optional

1 • Preheat the oven to 400 degrees.

2 • Toss the plum tomatoes, yellow pear tomatoes, and cherry tomatoes with the olive oil and garlic in a baking dish. Roast 20 to 25 minutes, until the tomatoes start to release their juices and begin to shrivel. Set aside to cool.

3 • Meanwhile, bring a large saucepan of water to a boil, add the beans, and cook 1 to 2 minutes or until the beans are bright green and crisp-tender.

4 • Drain the beans immediately and immerse them in a large bowl of cold water to stop the cooking process. (Note: This helps the beans retain their color and keep their crisp texture.) Remove the beans from the water and set aside to drain thoroughly.

5 • Toss the beans with the pesto, Parmesan, and salt and pepper in a large bowl. Place the beans on a platter or individual serving plates, top with tomatoes, garnish with toasted pine nuts and Parmesan if desired, and serve immediately.

variation: Any type of tomato can be used instead of the plum and cherry tomatoes. Or if tomatoes are not in season, eliminate them entirely and substitute roasted or sautéed red or yellow bell peppers. This is great with the addition of grilled chicken.

Sesame Noodles with Baby Greens and Cucumbers

This cool salad has a light, nutty dressing, crunchy cucumbers, and the zing of fresh ginger. It's a refreshing dish anytime, but especially in summer. By adding the sesame oil to the pasta—and not to the vinaigrette—the dish has a much milder sesame flavor than most sesame noodle salads. The finished dish can sit up to 4 hours in the refrigerator before serving. Add the greens just before serving.

SERVES 6 TO 8

8 ounces soba noodles or whole-wheat linguine or spaghetti

1 tablespoon dark sesame oil

1 cup Peanut-Ginger Dressing (recipe follows)

2 tablespoons chopped fresh chives or fresh parsley

Grated zest of 1 orange

Grated zest of 1 lime

Salt and freshly ground black pepper to taste

3 cucumbers, peeled, seeded, and cut into 1/4-inch half-rounds

4 scallions, trimmed and julienned

4 ounces (about 5 cups, loosely packed) mixed baby greens

Fresh chives or parsley to garnish, optional

Julienned red bell peppers to garnish, optional

1 • Bring a large pot of lightly salted water to a boil. Add the noodles and cook, stirring occasionally, until just tender, 3 to 4 minutes. (Note: Soba noodles cook much faster than whole-wheat spaghetti, which takes 6 to 7 minutes.) Drain, rinse with cold water, and set aside to drain thoroughly. Toss with the sesame oil in a colander and set aside.

2 • Mix together the noodles, the dressing, chives, orange zest, and lime zest in a large bowl and toss to mix. Season with salt and pepper.

3 • Add the cucumbers, scallions, and greens and toss gently. Garnish with the chives and red bell peppers if desired.

variations: Snow peas, sugar snap peas, julienned yellow bell peppers, sprouts, or julienned carrots can be added to this dish. This salad is also great with Ginger-Sesame Vinaigrette (page 95) instead of the Peanut-Ginger Dressing. When choosing the mixed baby greens, try several of the following: red mustard, mizuna, kale, arugula, dandelion, watercress, or Napa cabbage.

Peanut-Ginger Dressing

¹/₄ cup creamy peanut butter, at
    room temperature
Juice of 1 orange
Juice of 1 lime
¹/₄ cup rice wine vinegar
2 tablespoons soy sauce
1 teaspoon red pepper flakes
2 tablespoons peeled, grated
    fresh ginger
3 garlic cloves, minced
¹/₂ cup canola or safflower oil

Mix the peanut butter, orange juice, lime juice, vinegar, soy sauce, red pepper flakes, ginger, and garlic in a bowl and whisk to combine the ingredients to a smooth paste. Slowly add the oil and whisk until all the oil is incorporated. Use immediately or refrigerate in an airtight container until ready to use or up to 6 days.

Lentil, Spinach, and Feta Salad with Sour Cherry Vinaigrette

Delicious as a vegetarian lunch, this hearty salad is also good as a side dish with Balsamic-Roasted Chicken (page 154).

1½ cups dried green lentils (preferably dark green Du Puy lentils from France), picked over and rinsed

4 cups lightly packed fresh spinach, washed, drained, and stems removed

1 red onion, halved through root end and thinly sliced

6 ounces drained feta cheese, cut into ½-inch cubes

¾ cup Sour Cherry Vinaigrette (recipe follows)

Salt and freshly ground black pepper to taste

1 • Place the lentils in a saucepan, add enough water to cover by 3 inches, and bring to a boil. Reduce heat to low, and simmer, stirring occasionally, about 15 minutes for Du Puy French lentils, 20 minutes for regular green lentils. The lentils will be just tender and still holding their shape. (Note: French lentils cook much faster than regular lentils; do not overcook.) Drain and rinse the lentils and set aside to cool slightly.

2 • Place the spinach, lentils, onion, feta, and vinaigrette in a large bowl. Season with salt and pepper and toss gently to blend. Do not overmix because the spinach may bruise and the feta will crumble. Serve at room temperature.

Sour Cherry Vinaigrette

This tart, fruity dressing is also good on mixed greens or Grilled Chicken Breasts (page 60).

¼ cup red wine vinegar

¼ cup balsamic vinegar

1 shallot, minced

½ cup dried tart cherries or dried
    cranberries

1 tablespoon chopped fresh chives

Juice of 2 limes

¼ cup olive oil

¼ cup canola or safflower oil

¼ teaspoon salt

¼ teaspoon freshly ground black
    pepper

Mix together the red wine vinegar, balsamic vinegar, shallot, cherries, chives, and lime juice in a bowl. Slowly add the olive oil and canola oil while whisking constantly until well blended. Season with salt and pepper. Refrigerate in an airtight container until ready to use or up to 6 days.

Dried Cherries

Dried cherries are tangy-sweet, and just a little larger than raisins. They're available at most supermarkets and specialty food stores nationwide. Try dried cherries in place of other dried fruits—apricots, raisins, currants, cranberries, prunes, etc.—for a slightly different flavor and appealing burgundy red color.

Grilled Vegetable Antipasto with Herbed Chèvre and Crostini

This dish is particularly delicious in summer, when zucchini, peppers, and summer squash are farm-fresh. You can also pile the grilled vegetables onto crusty French bread that's been slathered with creamy chèvre. Or make hors d'oeuvres by topping Crostini (page 104) with slices of grilled vegetable and some crumbled chèvre. The vegetables can be grilled up to 1 hour in advance; assemble just before serving.

SERVES 6 TO 8

Safflower oil or canola oil, for oiling the grill

$\frac{1}{2}$ cup olive oil

$\frac{1}{4}$ cup balsamic vinegar

5 fresh basil leaves, cut into very thin strips (chiffonade)

2 zucchini, cut into $\frac{1}{2}$-inch slices lengthwise

2 yellow squash, cut into $\frac{1}{2}$-inch slices lengthwise

1 red onion, cut into $\frac{1}{2}$-inch-thick rounds

2 red bell peppers, cored, seeded, and cut into 2-inch strips

7 scallions, trimmed

Salt and freshly ground black pepper to taste

$\frac{1}{4}$ cup sun-dried tomatoes

2 ripe tomatoes, cut into $\frac{1}{2}$-inch slices

1 recipe Herbed Chèvre (recipe follows)

1 recipe Herbed Balsamic Vinaigrette (page 131)

Fresh parsley and fresh basil, to garnish, optional

Crostini (page 104)

1 • Brush the grill grates lightly with the safflower oil. Prepare a hot fire on a gas or charcoal grill.

2 • Whisk together the olive oil, vinegar, and basil in a small bowl until well blended. Brush the zucchini, yellow squash, onion, red bell peppers, and scallions with the olive oil mixture. Place the vegetables on the hot grill and cook 3 to 4 minutes per side until crisp-tender. Season with salt and pepper.

3 • Soak the sun-dried tomatoes in 1 cup hot water, covered, about 5 minutes or until softened. Drain and set aside. (Note: Eliminate this step if you are using sun-dried tomatoes packed in oil.)

4 • Arrange the grilled vegetables, sun-dried tomatoes, and sliced tomatoes on individual plates or a serving platter. Add a slice of chèvre on the side of the vegetables. Drizzle the vegetables with the vinaigrette, and drizzle a little more vinaigrette around the plate. Garnish with the parsley and basil. Season with additional salt and pepper, if desired, and serve with crostini.

Herbed Chèvre

¼ cup fresh parsley, chopped, or
  mixed fresh herbs, such as
  thyme, rosemary, and dill
1 tablespoon freshly ground black
  pepper
One 8-ounce mild, creamy chèvre
  log

1 • Mix the parsley and pepper together on a plate. Roll
the chèvre log in the mixture, pressing lightly so the
seasonings adhere. Wrap in plastic wrap and chill 1
to 2 hours.

2 • Remove the log from the refrigerator and unwrap.
Cut into 1-inch slices with string, dental floss, or
wire. Keep refrigerated until ready to serve.

Chèvre

Chèvre is the French word for goat, but it has
become the generic name for all cheeses made
from goat's milk (and for some cheeses made
with a combination of goat's milk and cow's
milk). Imported chèvres are delicious, but there
are many wonderful chèvres made in this country, too. Chèvres can be mild, creamy, aged, dry,
and crumbly. For a salad dressing, a less expensive domestic chèvre works just as well as an
imported one.

Grilled Vegetable Ratatouille

Because we grill the vegetables instead of cooking them in a skillet, this ratatouille has a fresher flavor and texture than traditional ratatouille. Try it warm or at room temperature in summer, when the garden is overflowing with lots of fresh vegetables. Leftovers can be used to fill omelets, to layer in lasagne, or to top rice, pasta, risotto, or polenta. If you use dried oregano instead of fresh, perk up the dish with a handful of chopped flat-leaf parsley.

SERVES 8 TO 10

Safflower oil or canola oil, for
   oiling the grill

1 eggplant, cut into ½-inch-thick
   rounds

1 zucchini, quartered lengthwise

1 yellow squash, quartered
   lengthwise

1 red bell pepper, halved, seeded,
   and stem removed

1 red onion, cut into ½-inch-thick
   rounds

⅓ cup olive oil

⅓ cup balsamic or red wine
   vinegar

Salt and freshly ground black
   pepper to taste

2 tomatoes, cored and diced

2 tablespoons drained capers

6 fresh basil leaves, cut into very
   thin strips (chiffonade)

2 tablespoons chopped fresh
   oregano or marjoram or 2
   teaspoons dried oregano or
   marjoram

Juice of 1 lemon

1 • Brush the grill grates lightly with the safflower oil. Prepare a hot fire in a gas or charcoal grill.

2 • Toss the eggplant, zucchini, yellow squash, red bell pepper, and onion with the olive oil and vinegar in a large bowl. Season with salt and pepper.

3 • Place the vegetables on the hot grill and cook, turning once, until tender and slightly charred. (The eggplant and onion will take 5 to 6 minutes per side, the squash and bell pepper 3 to 4 minutes per side.)

4 • Place the grilled vegetables in a single layer in a baking dish and cool to room temperature.

5 • Dice the grilled vegetables and place them in a large bowl with the tomatoes, capers, basil, oregano, and lemon juice. Season with additional salt and pepper, if desired, and toss gently to mix. Serve immediately or refrigerate until ready to serve.

Old-Fashioned Chicken Salad

This classic salad is one of our most popular offerings—everyone loves it! If you're short on time, buy the chicken already cooked. This dish can be made a day in advance (add the eggs the day you are serving it). It's great for a cool, summer supper, on sandwiches, or for picnics.

SERVES 6 TO 8

4 cups shredded cooked chicken (page 58)

6 small sweet pickles, chopped, or about 1/3 cup drained pickle relish

3 ribs celery, chopped

3 tablespoons chopped fresh parsley

1 1/2 cups Old-Fashioned Salad Dressing (recipe follows)

2 hard-boiled eggs, peeled and chopped

Salt and freshly ground black pepper to taste

Combine the chicken, pickles, celery, parsley, dressing, and eggs together in a bowl. Season with salt and pepper and stir to mix. Serve immediately or refrigerate in an airtight container until ready to serve.

Old-Fashioned Salad Dressing

MAKES ABOUT 2 CUPS DRESSING

1 1/2 cups good-quality mayonnaise

1/2 cup sour cream

2 tablespoons Dijon mustard

2 tablespoons cider vinegar

1 tablespoon honey

Salt and freshly ground pepper to taste

Combine the mayonnaise, sour cream, mustard, vinegar, and honey in a bowl and whisk to mix until smooth and creamy. Season with salt and pepper and serve or refrigerate in an airtight container until ready to use.

Orzo with Grilled Zucchini and Sun-Dried Tomatoes

Try this easy pasta dish alongside Grilled Butterflied Leg of Lamb with Fresh Mint-Pepper Jelly (page 177) or Sautéed Chicken Breasts with Artichokes, Lemons, and Capers (page 165). It's also great for a quick vegetarian lunch or for picnics.

SERVES 6 TO 8

1 teaspoon salt

1 pound orzo

1/2 cup olive oil

Safflower oil or canola oil, for oiling the grill

1/4 cup balsamic vinegar

2 zucchini, sliced lengthwise into 1/4-inch slices

2 portobello mushrooms, stems discarded and caps wiped clean, cut into 1/4-inch slices

1/2 cup julienned sun-dried tomatoes

Juice of 1 lemon

1 yellow bell pepper, cored, seeded, and diced

1 bunch of arugula or watercress, washed, drained, and stems removed

8 large fresh basil leaves, cut into very thin strips (chiffonade)

8 ounces fresh mozzarella cheese, cut into 1-inch cubes

Salt and freshly ground black pepper to taste

Additional basil leaves, to garnish, optional

1 • Bring to a boil 3 quarts of water in a large pot. Add 1 teaspoon salt and the orzo and cook 3 to 5 minutes, stirring once or twice, until the pasta is just tender. Drain the orzo, rinse, and set aside to drain again. Add 1 tablespoon of the olive oil to the colander, toss with the orzo, and set aside to continue to drain.

2 • Heat a grill pan to the smoking point over medium-high heat. (Or lightly oil the grill grates with the safflower oil and heat a gas or charcoal grill to medium-high.)

3 • Whisk together 2 tablespoons of the olive oil and 2 tablespoons of the vinegar in a small bowl. Lightly brush the zucchini and mushrooms with the olive oil mixture. Place the slices, a few at a time, in the grill pan or on the grill grates and cook 3 to 4 minutes per side, until crisp-tender. Place on a plate to cool while the others are cooking.

4 • Mix together the sun-dried tomatoes, the remaining olive oil, remaining vinegar, and lemon juice in a bowl and set aside until ready to use.

5 • Coarsely chop the zucchini and mushrooms and place in a separate bowl with the orzo, yellow bell pepper, arugula, basil, and mozzarella. Add the sun-dried to-mato mixture, season with salt and pepper, and toss lightly to mix. Garnish with basil leaves if desired. Serve immediately or refrigerate until ready to serve.

variation: Instead of zucchini, portobello mush-rooms, and yellow pepper, toss the cooked orzo with about 3 cups of Grilled Vegetable Ratatouille (page 124).

Pesto Chicken Salad

This is one of our most popular salads; we offer it daily for both lunch and supper. Try it alongside cold pasta salad, or piled on a toasted baguette for an open-faced sandwich.

SERVES 6 TO 8

6 cups shredded cooked chicken (page 58)

1 cup Pesto Vinaigrette (recipe follows)

One 2-ounce jar (1/4 cup) pine nuts, toasted (page 141)

2/3 cup grated Parmesan cheese

1 bunch of arugula or watercress, washed, drained, and stems removed

6 fresh basil leaves, cut into very thin slices (chiffonade)

Salt and freshly ground black pepper to taste

Fresh basil, to garnish, optional

Toasted pine nuts, to garnish, optional

Grated Parmesan cheese, to garnish, optional

1 • Place the chicken in a bowl and add vinaigrette, pine nuts, and Parmesan and toss to mix.

2 • Add the arugula and basil, season with salt and pepper, and toss gently to mix. Garnish with additional fresh basil, toasted pine nuts, and grated Parmesan if desired.

Pesto Vinaigrette

This flavorful dressing can be made 2 to 3 days in advance. It's also delicious on grilled chicken, fish, or vegetables, sandwiches, or just about any salad.

MAKES ABOUT 1 1/2 CUPS VINAIGRETTE

1 cup Foster's Pesto (page 90)

3 tablespoons Champagne vinegar or white wine vinegar

Juice of 1 lemon

1/4 cup extra-virgin olive oil

Salt and freshly ground black pepper to taste

1 • Whisk together the pesto, vinegar, and lemon juice in a medium bowl.

2 • Add the olive oil slowly in a steady stream, whisking constantly, until all the oil has been incorporated. Season with salt and pepper. Refrigerate in an airtight container until ready to use or up to 3 days.

Roasted Chicken for Salads

At Foster's, we often roast bone-in breasts (with skin) for our salads. The bones and skin are removed after cooking (use the bones for soup or stock), but they impart flavor to the meat as it roasts. The skin acts as a natural "marinade"; the natural fats in the skin "baste" the chicken as it cooks. The result is always tender, juicy chicken.

Grilled Chicken Salad with Provençal Vinaigrette

This salad is particularly good in summer, when tomatoes are at their finest. The robust vinaigrette is best made ahead of time so that its flavors develop. Try it on other salads, especially those made with romaine, spinach, or other hearty greens. It's also tasty spooned on top of sliced fresh mozzarella or as a sauce for grilled fish or pasta.

SERVES 6 TO 8

Safflower oil or canola oil, for oiling the grill

6 boneless, skinless chicken breast halves (or 6 cups shredded cooked chicken, page 58)

1 red onion, cut into ½-inch rounds

5 tablespoons olive oil

3 tablespoons balsamic vinegar

½ cup julienned sun-dried tomatoes

1 cup drained, quartered artichoke hearts

3 plum tomatoes, cored and quartered

2 tablespoons drained capers

6 large fresh basil leaves, cut into very thin strips (chiffonade)

1 cup Provençal Vinaigrette (recipe follows)

Salt and freshly ground black pepper to taste

Basil leaves, to garnish

1 • Brush the grill grates lightly with the safflower oil. Prepare a hot fire in a gas or charcoal grill.

2 • Toss the uncooked chicken and the onion with the olive oil and vinegar in a large bowl. (If using cooked chicken, just toss the onion in the oil and vinegar in a bowl.)

3 • Grill the chicken about 7 to 8 minutes per side, turning once, until the breast feels firm to the touch and the juices run clear when the chicken is pierced in the thickest part with a knife. Set aside to cool 20 to 30 minutes. (Omit this step if using cooked chicken.)

4 • Meanwhile, grill the onion about 4 minutes per side or until slightly cooked but still crisp-tender. Chop the onion into small pieces and place in a large bowl. (Note: If you're using leftover cooked chicken and you don't want to fire up the grill just for the onion, you can broil or sauté it.)

5 • Slice the cooked chicken breasts on the diagonal into ½-inch-thick slices, 8 to 10 slices per breast half.

6 • Add the chicken, sun-dried tomatoes, artichoke hearts, plum tomatoes, capers, basil, vinaigrette, and salt and pepper to the bowl with the onion and toss gently to mix. Garnish with additional basil leaves if desired.

Provençal Vinaigrette

¼ cup balsamic vinegar

½ teaspoon red pepper flakes

1 plum tomato, cored and diced

2 tablespoons minced red onion

1 garlic clove, minced

1 tablespoon drained capers

3 fresh basil leaves, cut into very
thin strips (chiffonade)

¼ cup olive oil

½ cup canola or safflower oil

Salt and freshly ground black
pepper to taste

1 • Combine the vinegar, red pepper flakes, tomato, onion, garlic, capers, and basil in a medium bowl.

2 • Slowly add the olive oil and canola oil and whisk until all the oil is incorporated. Season with salt and pepper. Refrigerate in an airtight container until ready to use or up to 6 days.

Vinaigrette Dressing

There are probably as many variations on the vinaigrette as there are cooks. From light and tangy vinaigrettes—made with rice wine vinegar and flavorless canola oil—to rich and heady vinaigrettes—made with anchovy paste, mustard, and garlic—the combinations are almost endless. By simply changing the oil, the vinegar, and the herbs and spices, or by adding citrus juices, the vinaigrette changes dramatically, and so, therefore, does the resulting dish. Experiment with the many oils and vinegars available and see what you like best; it's easy!

Roasted Chicken, Sweet Potato, and Arugula Salad

Using sweet potatoes instead of white potatoes makes this an intriguing dish, indeed. It's delicious anytime, but especially in fall and winter, when sweet potatoes are in season.

SERVES 6 TO 8

6 bone-in chicken breast halves with skin (about 4 pounds)

3 sweet potatoes, peeled and cut into eighths

6 shallots, quartered

¼ cup olive oil

¼ cup balsamic vinegar

2 teaspoons fresh thyme or heaping ½ teaspoon dried thyme

6 leaves fresh basil, cut into very thin strips (chiffonade)

1 cup Herbed Balsamic Vinaigrette (recipe follows)

Salt and freshly ground black pepper to taste

1 bunch of arugula, washed, drained, and stems removed

1 • Preheat the oven to 450 degrees.

2 • Place the chicken in a roasting pan and roast until golden brown, the internal temperature is 165 degrees, and the juices run clear when pierced with the tip of a sharp knife in the thickest part, about 45 minutes. Cool, then remove and discard the skin and bones. Tear the chicken into large pieces and place in a large bowl.

3 • While the chicken cooks, toss the sweet potatoes and shallots with the olive oil, vinegar, and thyme in a large bowl to coat evenly. Spread evenly on a baking pan and roast about 30 minutes, until the potatoes are lightly browned and soft. (Note: The vinegar will evaporate and create a light glaze on the potatoes.) Remove from the oven and set aside to cool slightly.

4 • Add the sweet potatoes and shallots to the chicken and toss to mix. Add the basil and the vinaigrette and toss to coat. (This can be prepared a day in advance up to this point.) Season with salt and pepper. Add the arugula and toss lightly just before serving. Serve immediately.

Herbed Balsamic Vinaigrette

MAKES ABOUT 1 CUP VINAIGRETTE

⅓ cup balsamic vinegar

Juice of 1 lemon

2 tablespoons mixed chopped fresh basil, parsley, and thyme

1 teaspoon freshly ground black pepper

¼ cup olive oil

⅓ cup canola or safflower oil

1 • Combine the vinegar, lemon juice, herbs, and pepper in a small bowl and stir to mix.

2 • Slowly add the olive oil and the canola oil and whisk until all the oil is incorporated. Refrigerate in an airtight container until ready to use or up to 1 week.

Grilled Asparagus with Roasted Shallots and Cranberry Vinaigrette

If you don't want to fire up the grill, you can blanch or roast the asparagus instead. You might want to make a little extra vinaigrette to have on hand; it's delicious on mixed baby greens, grilled turkey and chicken, and most any sandwich. Like all vinaigrettes, this one can be made several days in advance and refrigerated until ready to use.

SERVES 4 TO 6

Safflower oil or canola oil, for oiling the grill

1/2 cup extra-virgin olive oil

Juice of 1 lemon

3 tablespoons red wine vinegar

Salt and freshly ground black pepper to taste

2 pounds asparagus, tough ends trimmed

10 shallots, cut in half, or 1 red onion, quartered

1/2 cup Cranberry Vinaigrette (recipe follows)

3 tablespoons chopped fresh chives or chopped fresh parsley or trimmed, minced scallions

1 • Brush the grill grates lightly with the safflower oil. Prepare a hot fire in a gas or charcoal grill and pre-heat the oven to 400 degrees.

2 • Whisk together the olive oil, lemon juice, vinegar, salt, and pepper in a small bowl.

3 • Toss the asparagus with half the olive oil mixture in a large bowl.

4 • Toss the shallots with the remaining olive oil mixture in a bowl, then spread the shallots out in 1 even layer in a baking dish. Roast the shallots, uncovered, 20 to 25 minutes or until tender and slightly crisp around the edges.

5 • While the shallots roast, place the asparagus on the grill grates (or use a grill basket or grill pan) and cook 5 to 7 minutes, turning often, until bright green and crisp-tender.

6 • Arrange the asparagus on a platter or individual plates and top with the shallots. Drizzle with vinai-grette, making certain that each serving has some of the dried cranberries. Sprinkle with the chives and season with additional salt and pepper if desired.

Cranberry Vinaigrette

¼ cup cranberry juice

3 tablespoons balsamic vinegar

1 shallot, minced

½ cup extra-virgin olive oil

1 tablespoon chopped fresh chives
or fresh parsley

½ cup dried cranberries or dried
cherries

Salt and freshly ground black
pepper to taste

Combine the cranberry juice, vinegar, and shallot in a bowl. Slowly add the olive oil and whisk until all the oil is incorporated. Mix in the chives and cranberries; season with salt and pepper. Refrigerate in an airtight container until ready to use.

Trimming Asparagus

No matter what color (white or green) or what size (thick or pencil-thin) the asparagus, the spears should be trimmed at the stem end. Very thin, very fresh asparagus will require minimal trimming; thicker asparagus will need to be trimmed about 1½ inches. (Save the trimmings for soup or for composting.) Thicker asparagus may also need to be peeled (use a paring knife or vegetable peeler), to remove the tough, fibrous skin.

Roasted New Potato Salad with Dijon Vinaigrette

Potato salads are one of Foster's most popular items, so we make several different kinds every day, all year round. Roasting—instead of boiling—the potatoes makes the skin slightly crispy, which adds a pleasant, earthy texture to the finished dish.

SERVES 8 TO 10

3 pounds red-skinned potatoes, washed and cut in half

$\frac{1}{4}$ cup olive oil

1 teaspoon salt

1 teaspoon freshly ground black pepper

2 tablespoons chopped fresh rosemary or 2 teaspoons dried rosemary

1 green bell pepper, cored, seeded, and diced

1 red bell pepper, cored, seeded, and diced

1 kosher dill pickle, chopped

2 ribs celery, cut on a diagonal into $\frac{1}{4}$-inch slices

2 tablespoons chopped fresh chives

1 tablespoon chopped fresh dill

1 cup Dijon Vinaigrette (recipe follows)

Salt and freshly ground black pepper to taste

1 • Preheat the oven to 400 degrees.

2 • Toss the potatoes with the olive oil, salt, pepper, and rosemary in a large, shallow baking dish. Spread in a single layer in the baking dish and roast uncovered 30 to 35 minutes, until the potatoes are slightly crisp and golden brown. Set aside to cool to room temperature.

3 • In a large bowl, toss the cooled potatoes with the green bell pepper, red bell pepper, pickle, celery, chives, dill, and vinaigrette. Season with salt and pepper and serve immediately. This salad is also great served warm.

Types of Potatoes for Salads

When shopping for potatoes for salads, look for potatoes that are about 2 inches in diameter. At Foster's, we usually use red-skinned potatoes or Yukon gold potatoes, which have less starch than russet potatoes. Other choices include Yellow Finn, fingerlings, Maine, or California long white potatoes. Figure about $\frac{1}{4}$ pound to $\frac{1}{3}$ pound of potatoes per person for a side dish serving.

Dijon Vinaigrette

3 tablespoons Dijon mustard

1 large egg or $1/4$ cup pasteurized
  eggs or $1/2$ cup good-quality
  mayonnaise

Juice of 1 lemon

1 tablespoon Champagne vinegar
  or white wine vinegar

$1/2$ cup olive oil

$3/4$ cup canola or safflower oil
  (omit if using mayonnaise)

Salt and freshly ground black
  pepper to taste

1 • Whisk together the mustard, egg or mayonnaise, lemon juice, and vinegar in a bowl until well blended.

2 • Add the olive oil and canola oil in a slow, steady stream, while whisking constantly, until all the oil is incorporated (omit the oils if using mayonnaise). Season with salt and pepper. The vinaigrette will be creamy, but not as thick as mayonnaise. Refrigerate in an airtight container until ready to use.

Southwestern Fried Chicken Salad

Just add a wedge of warm corn bread and thick slices of cold watermelon or blueberry pie for a summer feast. The chicken can be marinated overnight in the refrigerator, and then cooked the next day. The greens can be washed and drained the day before, then refrigerated to become nice and crisp.

SERVES 8 TO 10

1 cup buttermilk

1/2 teaspoon freshly ground black pepper

6 boneless, skinless chicken breast halves, cut into 1-inch strips

1 cup safflower or canola oil

1 cup all-purpose flour

1/2 cup yellow cornmeal

1 tablespoon paprika

1 teaspoon salt

1 red bell pepper, cored, seeded, and julienned

4 plum tomatoes, cored and diced

Juice of 3 limes

1/3 cup olive oil

1/4 cup chopped fresh cilantro

1 teaspoon ground cumin

1/2 teaspoon chili powder

1 ripe avocado

8 ounces mesclun salad greens, washed and drained

Salt and freshly ground black pepper to taste

1 • Mix the buttermilk and pepper in a large bowl. Add the chicken and let stand a minimum of 15 minutes at room temperature or overnight in the refrigerator.

2 • Heat the safflower oil in a large skillet over medium-high heat until hot but not smoking, 365 to 375 degrees.

3 • Combine the flour, cornmeal, paprika, and salt in a large bowl. Dip the chicken in the flour mixture, shake off the excess flour, and place in the hot oil. Do not crowd the pan or the chicken will "steam" instead of fry.

4 • Fry the chicken, uncovered, in batches, for 12 to 15 minutes, until golden brown and crispy. (Note: You may need to increase the heat when the chicken is added, which may reduce the temperature of the oil. If the chicken is browning too fast, lower the heat.) Drain the chicken on paper towels and cool slightly.

5 • Mix the red bell pepper, tomatoes, lime juice, olive oil, cilantro, cumin, and chili powder in a large bowl and set aside.

6 • Just before serving, peel and pit the avocado and cut into 1/2-inch slices.

7 • Place the greens on a platter and top with the fried chicken, tomato mixture, and avocado. Season with salt and pepper. Serve warm or at room temperature.

Tarragon Chicken Salad with Granny Smith Apples and Red Grapes

I've been making variations on this salad for at least twenty years, since I first made it at the SoHo Charcuterie in New York. At Foster's, we have served this salad since the day we opened in 1990, and it continues to be one of the most popular items on our menu. It keeps well for several days, so you can make it ahead of time, adding the apples and grapes the day you serve it.

SERVES 8 TO 10

6 cups shredded cooked chicken (page 58)

3 ribs celery, sliced on the diagonal into $\frac{1}{4}$-inch pieces

1 cup red seedless grapes, washed, drained, and cut in half

1 Granny Smith or other tart apple, cored and thinly sliced

$1\frac{1}{2}$ cups Tarragon Mayonnaise (recipe follows)

3 tablespoons chopped fresh parsley

Salt and freshly ground black pepper to taste

Parsley and celery leaves, to garnish, optional

1 • Combine the chicken, celery, grapes, apple, mayonnaise, and parsley in a large bowl and stir to mix thoroughly. Season with salt and pepper.

2 • Arrange on a platter or plates and garnish with parsley and celery leaves if desired. Serve immediately or refrigerate until ready to serve.

Tarragon Mayonnaise

This is also delicious on sandwiches or sliced tomatoes.

2 large eggs or ½ cup pasteurized
    eggs or 1 cup good-quality
    mayonnaise
3 tablespoons tarragon vinegar
Juice of 1 lemon
½ cup tarragon packed in vinegar,
    drained and stems removed, or
    ¼ cup dried tarragon soaked in
    3 tablespoons tarragon vinegar
1 cup canola or safflower oil (omit
    if using mayonnaise)
1 shallot, minced, or
    2 tablespoons minced red
    onion or scallion
Salt and freshly ground black
    pepper to taste

1 • Place the eggs or mayonnaise, vinegar, lemon juice, and tarragon leaves in the bowl of a food processor fitted with the metal blade. Process until well blended.

2 • Add the oil in a slow, steady stream down the feed tube, with the motor running, and process until all the oil is incorporated (omit the oil if using mayonnaise). The dressing will be thick and creamy.

3 • Add the shallot and blend until smooth. Season with salt and pepper. Refrigerate in an airtight container until ready to use or up to 1 week.

Grilled Chicken Salad with Tomatoes, Spinach, and Dijon Vinaigrette

Hearty enough to serve as a main course salad for lunch or supper, this salad is also delicious piled on a toasted baguette and served as an open-faced sandwich. You can prepare the salad a day in advance by combining everything except the spinach, tomatoes, and basil. Refrigerate, then toss with the remaining ingredients just before serving. This can also be made with roasted or poached chicken, if you are using leftover or purchased cooked chicken. Another make-ahead tip is a method we use at the Market: layer the spinach and tomatoes rather than tossing them; the salad will hold up better and look fresher longer.

SERVES 6 TO 8

Safflower oil or canola oil, for oiling the grill

6 boneless, skinless chicken breast halves (about 3 pounds)

$1/4$ cup olive oil

2 tablespoons chopped fresh parsley

2 tablespoons minced scallions

2 tablespoons Dijon mustard

$1^{1}/_{2}$ cups Dijon Vinaigrette (page 135)

6 plum tomatoes, cored and quartered

2 ribs celery, cut on a diagonal into $1/4$-inch slices

Salt and freshly ground black pepper to taste

4 cups firmly packed spinach, washed, drained, and stems removed

8 fresh basil leaves, cut into very thin strips (chiffonade)

1 • Brush the grill grates lightly with the safflower oil. Prepare a hot fire in a gas or charcoal grill.

2 • Toss the chicken with the olive oil, parsley, scallions, and mustard in a shallow bowl and let marinate 30 to 40 minutes at room temperature or overnight in the refrigerator.

3 • Grill the chicken, turning once, 7 to 8 minutes per side, until the breasts feel firm to the touch and the juices run clear when pierced in the thickest part with a knife. Set aside to cool, 20 to 30 minutes.

4 • Slice the chicken breasts on the diagonal into $1/4$-inch-thick slices, 8 to 10 slices per breast.

5 • Combine the chicken, vinaigrette, tomatoes, and celery in a medium bowl and toss to mix. Season with salt and pepper. Just before serving, toss with the spinach and basil.

variations: Try frisée or mesclun instead of spinach; use cherry tomatoes or tiny pear tomatoes if plum tomatoes are unavailable. In autumn, substitute grilled shiitake or portobello mushrooms for the tomatoes. Herbed Balsamic Vinaigrette (page 131) can be used instead of the Dijon Vinaigrette for a slightly different flavor.

Turkey Waldorf Salad with Dried Apricots and Chèvre Dressing

At Foster's, we use roasted turkey breast for this salad, but dark meat is fine, too. Try this salad on a bed of mixed greens or as the topping for an open-faced sandwich on toasted whole-grain bread.

SERVES 8 TO 10

3 pounds cooked boneless turkey breast

1/2 cup chopped dried apricots

1/2 cup dried cherries

2 ribs celery, chopped

1 Granny Smith or other tart apple, cored and thinly sliced

1/2 cup coarsely chopped toasted walnuts

2 cups Chèvre Dressing (recipe follows)

1/4 cup chopped fresh parsley

1/4 cup chopped fresh chives or chopped fresh parsley

Salt and freshly ground black pepper to taste

1 • Slice the cooked turkey breast into large pieces (about 1/2 inch thick and 1 1/2 inches long) and place in a large bowl.

2 • Add the apricots, cherries, celery, apple, walnuts, and dressing and mix until combined. Add the parsley and chives, toss to mix, and season with salt and pepper. Serve immediately or refrigerate in an airtight container until ready to serve or up to 1 day in advance.

variations: Smoked turkey or chicken can be used in place of regular roast turkey; golden raisins, currants, dried cranberries, or grapes can be substituted for the dried apricots. Try firm, tart pears instead of apples.

Chèvre Dressing

Also good on sandwiches or grilled chicken or fish, this creamy dressing keeps in the refrigerator up to 3 days.

MAKES ABOUT 2½ CUPS DRESSING

2 large eggs or ½ cup pasteurized
    eggs or 2 cups good-quality
    mayonnaise
3 tablespoons white wine vinegar
2 cups canola or safflower oil
    (omit if using mayonnaise)
½ cup peeled and chopped
    Granny Smith or other tart
    apple
½ cup crumbled, mild chèvre
2 tablespoons chopped fresh
    chives or chopped fresh parsley
Salt and freshly ground black
    pepper to taste

1 • Place the eggs or mayonnaise and vinegar in the bowl of a food processor fitted with the metal blade and pulse several times.

2 • Add the oil in a slow, steady stream down the feed tube, with the motor running, until the mixture has thickened. (Omit the oil if using mayonnaise.)

3 • Add the apple, chèvre, and chives and pulse until blended. Season with salt and pepper. (Note: If using mayonnaise instead of eggs, do not overprocess the mixture or it may break up.) Tightly covered, this dressing will keep in the refrigerator up to 3 days.

Toasting Nuts

To toast nuts, spread them on a baking pan in one layer and cook 10 to 12 minutes in a preheated 350-degree oven, stirring frequently and watching carefully to make sure the nuts do not burn. Or place the nuts in 1 layer in a dry skillet over medium heat. Cook and stir until pale golden brown. The nuts will continue to cook after they're removed from the oven or the skillet, so be careful not to overcook them.

Bow-Tie Pasta with Eggplant, Caramelized Onions, and Pine Nuts

If you like eggplant, you'll love this Mediterranean-style dish. The onions become sweet as they cook, and are a delicious foil to the earthy eggplant and tangy chèvre.

SERVES 10 TO 12

1 pound bow-tie pasta (farfalle), rotini or cavatelli

1/2 cup olive oil

2 Vidalia, Maui, Walla Walla, or other sweet onions, cut in half lengthwise and thinly sliced

1/4 cup balsamic vinegar

2 eggplants, peeled, diced, and cut into 1/2-inch cubes

4 garlic cloves, minced

3 roasted red bell peppers, peeled, cored, seeded, and julienned (page 40)

One 4-ounce jar (1/2 cup) pine nuts, toasted (page 141)

1/2 cup chopped fresh parsley

8 to 10 fresh basil leaves, cut into very thin strips (chiffonade)

1/2 cup Italian Vinaigrette (page 151)

Salt and freshly ground black pepper to taste

1 cup (4 ounces) crumbled creamy chèvre

1 • Preheat the oven to 400 degrees.

2 • Cook the pasta in a large pot of boiling, salted water, stirring occasionally, 8 to 10 minutes or until al dente. Drain and toss with 1 tablespoon of the olive oil and set aside.

3 • Heat 3 tablespoons of the olive oil in a medium skillet over medium-low heat. Add the onions and cook and stir about 10 minutes, until the onions are soft and translucent. Add 2 tablespoons of the balsamic vinegar, reduce heat to low, and cook and stir 20 to 25 minutes longer, until the onions are soft, brown, and caramelized. Set aside.

4 • Meanwhile, toss the remaining olive oil and remaining balsamic vinegar with the eggplant and garlic and mix to coat evenly. Spread in a single layer in a baking pan and place in the oven to roast for 25 to 30 minutes. Stir several times during the cooking process, until the eggplant is lightly brown and tender. Remove from the oven and set aside to cool.

5 • Combine the pasta, onions, eggplant-garlic mixture, roasted red bell peppers, pine nuts, parsley, basil, and vinaigrette and toss lightly to mix. Season with salt and pepper and add the chèvre. Toss gently to mix again. Serve immediately or refrigerate until ready to serve.

Shrimp Salad with Lemon-Dill Vinaigrette

You can cook the shrimp and toss it with the vinaigrette a day in advance, then mix with the vegetables just before serving. The Lemon-Dill Vinaigrette is also delicious drizzled over grilled fish or shrimp or on Cucumber, Avocado, and Tomato Salad (page 145).

SERVES 6 TO 8

3 bay leaves

2 tablespoons white distilled vinegar or white wine vinegar

2 pounds fresh jumbo shrimp, shells on

$\frac{1}{2}$ pound snow peas or sugar snap peas

1 red bell pepper, cored, seeded, and julienned

3 scallions, trimmed and julienned

3 carrots, peeled and julienned

2 tablespoons chopped fresh dill

2 tablespoons peeled, julienned fresh ginger

1 cup Lemon-Dill Vinaigrette (recipe follows)

1 bunch of watercress, washed, drained, and stems removed

Salt and freshly ground black pepper to taste

1 • Combine about 2½ quarts water, the bay leaves, and vinegar in a large pot and bring to a boil.

2 • Add the shrimp and cook 2 to 3 minutes, stirring occasionally, or until firm and pinkish in color. Do not overcook or the shrimp will be tough. Remove from the heat, drain, and rinse the shrimp with cold water until cooled. Peel the shrimp, leaving the tail section intact; set aside to drain.

3 • Meanwhile, bring a large saucepan of water to a boil. Add the snow peas and cook about 1 minute, until bright green and crisp-tender.

4 • Drain immediately and immerse the peas in a bowl of cold water to stop the cooking process. Set aside to drain thoroughly.

5 • Combine the red bell pepper, scallions, carrots, snow peas, dill, ginger, vinaigrette, and watercress in a large bowl with the shrimp. Season with salt and pepper and toss lightly to mix. Serve immediately or refrigerate until ready to serve.

Lemon-Dill Vinaigrette

¹⁄₄ cup white wine vinegar

Grated zest and juice of 2 lemons

2 tablespoons peeled, grated
    fresh ginger

2 tablespoons chopped fresh dill

¹⁄₂ cup canola or safflower oil

¹⁄₄ cup olive oil

Salt and freshly ground black
    pepper to taste

Combine the vinegar, lemon zest, lemon juice, ginger, and dill in a bowl. Slowly add the canola oil and olive oil and whisk until all the oil is incorporated. Season with salt and pepper and refrigerate in an airtight container until ready to use or up to 6 days.

Cucumber, Avocado, and Tomato Salad

This cool, easy salad is a variation on one that my mother makes all summer long. (She makes hers without avocado, which is also good.) Try this alongside Sautéed Soft-Shell Crabs with Cucumber-Lime Salsa (page 197) or Slow-Roasted Pork Roast with Sweet and Spicy Horseradish Sauce (page 183).

SERVES 8 TO 10

3 cucumbers

4 tomatoes, cored, cut into eighths

1 red onion, diced

2 scallions, trimmed and diced

2 tablespoons chopped fresh oregano

2 tablespoons chopped fresh dill

½ cup Oregano Vinaigrette (recipe follows)

Salt and freshly ground black pepper to taste

2 ripe avocados

1 • Use a vegetable peeler to remove alternating strips of cucumber peel so that you'll have white and green stripes. Cut the cucumbers crosswise into ¼-inch-thick rounds.

2 • Combine the cucumbers, tomatoes, onion, scallions, oregano, dill, and vinaigrette in a large bowl and toss gently, just to mix.

3 • Season with salt and pepper and refrigerate until ready to serve. This can be done 6 hours or up to a day in advance and refrigerated up to this point. Just before serving, peel and pit the avocados and cut into 2-inch slices. Place sliced avocados on top of the salad and serve immediately.

variation: Add 1 cup cubed (1-inch cubes) feta cheese and mixed greens or spinach for a more substantial, Greek-style salad.

Oregano Vinaigrette

This is also delicious on salads, green beans, potatoes, grilled fish, or grilled vegetables.

$1/3$ cup red wine vinegar

Juice of 1 lime

1 tablespoon sugar

2 tablespoons fresh oregano or
    marjoram or 2 teaspoons dried
    oregano or marjoram

1 teaspoon salt

1 teaspoon freshly ground black
    pepper

$1/2$ cup olive oil

Combine the vinegar, lime juice, sugar, oregano, salt, and pepper in a bowl. Slowly add the olive oil and whisk until all the oil is incorporated. Refrigerate in an airtight container until ready to use or up to 4 days.

Asian-Style Roasted Vegetables with Bok Choy and Hoisin Sauce

This unusual, Asian-inspired vegetable side dish includes bok choy—also known as Chinese white cabbage—a mildly flavored vegetable with tender outer leaves and a crunchy inner stalk. Serve cold or at room temperature with Grilled Tuna with Scallions and Wasabi Mustard (page 188), Herb-Grilled Salmon with Fresh Tomato-Orange Chutney (page 190), or Balsamic-Roasted Chicken (page 154).

SERVES 8 TO 10

½ cup hoisin sauce

Juice of 1 lemon

Juice of 1 orange

3 garlic cloves, minced

⅓ cup canola or safflower oil

¼ cup soy sauce (preferably light soy sauce)

1 pound green beans, stem end removed

1 bunch of baby carrots, peeled and trimmed, or 3 medium carrots, peeled and cut on the diagonal into 1-inch pieces

1 red onion, cut into eighths

1 red bell pepper, cored, seeded, and cut into quarters

8 ounces button mushrooms, wiped clean and stems removed

8 stalks bok choy (one 1-pound head), trimmed and cut on a diagonal into 4-inch pieces

½ cup chopped fresh parsley

2 tablespoons chopped fresh chives

Salt and freshly ground black pepper to taste

Additional herbs for garnish, optional

1 • Preheat the oven to 400 degrees.

2 • Combine the hoisin sauce, lemon juice, orange juice, garlic, oil, and soy sauce in a large bowl and whisk to blend.

3 • Add the beans, carrots, onion, red bell pepper, and mushrooms and toss until the vegetables are well coated.

4 • Spread the vegetables evenly in 1 layer in a roasting pan and top with any remaining marinade. Roast the vegetables, uncovered, 35 to 40 minutes, or until vegetables are tender and golden brown (see Note).

5 • Toss the hot, roasted vegetables with the bok choy, parsley, and chives in a large bowl. (The hot vegetables will slightly wilt the bok choy.) Season with salt and pepper; garnish with additional herbs if desired. Serve immediately or at room temperature.

note: You can add the bok choy to the other vegetables during the final 10 minutes of cooking if you prefer it slightly cooked.

variations: Napa cabbage, spinach, Swiss chard, or choy sum—a similar cabbage that looks like miniature bok choy—could be used in place of bok choy.

Lemon-Roasted Asparagus with Teriyaki Orange Salsa

Our salad chef, Laura Cyr, created this dish in late spring, when fresh asparagus was at its peak. Serve it warm or lightly chilled as a first course, or alongside Roast Pork Tenderloin with Dried Cherries and Rosemary (page 186).

SERVES 6

¼ cup olive oil

Juice of 1 lemon

2 pounds asparagus, tough ends trimmed

½ head Napa cabbage, cored and cut into 4-inch strips

¼ cup soy sauce

2 tablespoons firmly packed light brown sugar

2 tablespoons balsamic vinegar

Juice of 1 orange

2 tablespoons dry sherry or port or vermouth

1 tablespoon peeled, minced fresh ginger

2 oranges, peeled and sectioned

Salt and freshly ground black pepper to taste

2 tablespoons chopped chives or scallions

1 • Preheat the oven to 400 degrees.

2 • Combine the olive oil and lemon juice in a bowl. Add the asparagus and cabbage and toss to coat.

3 • Spread the asparagus and cabbage evenly in a baking pan and roast 10 to 12 minutes, turning once, until they are crisp-tender. Remove from the oven and set aside to cool.

4 • Mix the soy sauce, brown sugar, vinegar, orange juice, sherry, and ginger in a bowl and stir to blend. Add the oranges and toss to mix. Season with salt and pepper.

5 • Arrange the asparagus and cabbage on a platter and pour the orange mixture over the center. Season with additional salt and pepper if desired and sprinkle with chives. Serve immediately or at room temperature.

Crisp-Tender

Many of Foster's recipes use the term "crisp-tender." The Italian term "al dente" means the same thing: to cook until the food is just slightly resistant when you bite into it; it should not be soft or overcooked. Vegetables that are crisp-tender have a satisfying, mildly crunchy texture and usually have a higher vitamin content than long-cooked vegetables.

Succotash Salad with Garden Tomatoes

Instead of a warm side dish, we've taken the basic ingredients of succotash—corn, lima beans, and bell peppers—and added tomatoes, fresh herbs, and spicy jalapeño. This summer salad is particularly delicious with Southwestern Fried Chicken Salad (page 136) or Laura's Spicy Turkey Barbecue (page 166).

SERVES 8 TO 10

1 pound fresh or frozen shelled
   lima beans
¼ cup olive oil
Kernels from 2 ears fresh corn
   (1 cup fresh or frozen corn)
1 red bell pepper, cored, seeded,
   and diced, or banana peppers,
   poblano peppers, or sweet
   Italian peppers instead of the
   bell peppers
1 red onion, diced
1 jalapeño, seeded, and diced
2 tomatoes, cored and diced
1 tablespoon chopped fresh
   marjoram or oregano or basil
1 tablespoon red wine vinegar
Salt and freshly ground black
   pepper to taste

1 • Place the shelled beans in a large pot of boiling water. Reduce heat and simmer 10 to 15 minutes, uncovered, or until the beans are crisp-tender. Drain and rinse. Set aside to cool to room temperature.

2 • Heat the olive oil in a medium skillet. Add the corn, red bell pepper, and onion. Cook and stir over medium heat about 3 minutes, until the vegetables are just tender. Add the beans and jalapeño and cook 2 minutes longer, stirring occasionally.

3 • Remove the skillet from the heat and add the tomatoes, marjoram, and vinegar. Season with salt and pepper and serve immediately or refrigerate in an airtight container until ready to serve.

Tuscan White Bean Salad with Spinach, Olives, and Sun-Dried Tomatoes

Foster's variation on a simple Tuscan classic might be considered heresy to purists, but our customers are crazy about the addition of olives, sun-dried tomatoes, and spinach. It's a great dish for summer buffets, and is particularly delicious with Grilled Butterflied Leg of Lamb with Fresh Mint-Pepper Jelly (page 177) or Chicken Breasts Stuffed with Prosciutto and Sun-Dried Tomatoes (page 162). The salad can be made a day in advance; serve it lightly chilled or at room temperature.

SERVES 8 TO 10

1½ cups dried navy beans, rinsed and picked over

¼ cup olive oil

1 yellow onion, finely chopped

4 cups firmly packed spinach, washed, drained, and stems removed

½ cup chopped sun-dried tomatoes

½ pound fresh mozzarella cheese, cut into ½-inch cubes

½ cup pitted black olives, such as kalamata or niçoise

1 cup Italian Vinaigrette (recipe follows)

Salt and freshly ground black pepper to taste

1 • To quick-soak the beans: Place the beans in a large pot with water to cover by 3 inches and bring to a boil. Reduce heat and simmer, uncovered, 45 minutes. Remove from the heat, drain, and rinse.

2 • To cook the beans: Place the beans in a large pot and add enough water to cover by 3 to 4 inches. Bring to a boil, lower heat, and simmer, uncovered, 45 minutes to 1 hour, or until beans are tender but still firm. Drain and rinse the beans thoroughly. Set aside to cool.

3 • Heat the olive oil in a skillet over medium heat. Add the onion and cook and stir until slightly brown, about 5 minutes

4 • Toss the beans, onion, spinach, sun-dried tomatoes, mozzarella, and olives in a large bowl with the vinaigrette until just combined. Season with salt and pepper and serve immediately or refrigerate in an airtight container until ready to use or up to 1 day. If refrigerating, add the spinach just before serving.

Italian Vinaigrette

This vinaigrette is great on any type of mixed green, pasta, or marinated vegetable salads.

¼ cup red wine vinegar

3 garlic cloves, minced

1 teaspoon Dijon mustard

2 tablespoons chopped fresh
    oregano or 2 teaspoons dried
    oregano

¾ cup extra-virgin olive oil

Salt and freshly ground black
    pepper to taste

Combine the vinegar, garlic, mustard, and oregano in a small bowl. Add the olive oil in a slow, steady stream while whisking constantly until all the oil is incorporated. Season with salt and pepper and refrigerate in an airtight container until ready to use or up to 1 week.

entrées

Balsamic-Roasted Chicken • Braised Chicken Thighs with Chèvre Stuffing • Chicken-Arugula Meatballs • Chicken Marsala with Oven-Roasted Mushrooms and Onions • Chicken Breasts Stuffed with Prosciutto and Sun-Dried Tomatoes • Sautéed Chicken Breasts with Artichokes, Lemons, and Capers • Laura's Spicy Turkey Barbecue • Wine-Braised Boneless Turkey Breast with Sage and Thyme • Braised Fillet of Beef with Roasted Tomatoes and Mushrooms • Braised Short Ribs with Roasted Root Vegetable Puree • Cajun-Cut Rib Eye Steak • Spicy Grilled Standing Rib Roast • Grilled Butterflied Leg of Lamb with Fresh Mint-Pepper Jelly • Roast Leg of Lamb Stuffed with Italian White Beans and Spinach • Rack of Lamb with Jalapeño–Honey Mustard Glaze and Balsamic Vinegar Reduction • Slow-Roasted Pork Roast with Sweet and Spicy Horseradish Sauce • Roast Pork Tenderloin with Dried Cherries and Rosemary • Grilled Tuna with Scallions and Wasabi Mustard • Herb-Grilled Salmon with Fresh Tomato-Orange Chutney • Salmon Cakes with Crunchy Corn Relish • Pan-Seared Sea Scallops with Tom Thumb Tomatoes and Foster's Pesto • Mediterranean-Style Mussels with Toasted Focaccia • Sautéed Soft-Shell Crabs with Cucumber-Lime Salsa • Provençal Fish Stew with Rouille

Balsamic-Roasted Chicken

There's something incredibly satisfying about a really good roast chicken. It's familiar and homey, but never boring. At Foster's, we roast our chickens breast side down to begin, then turn them over to cook breast side up for the remainder of the cooking time. This method keeps the breast meat from becoming dry and overcooked and cooks the legs and thighs faster.

SERVES 2 TO 4

1 chicken (3½ to 4 pounds)

6 sprigs fresh marjoram or sage

1 lemon, cut in half

1 yellow onion, cut in half

¼ cup balsamic vinegar

½ cup dry white wine or apple
    juice

2 tablespoons olive oil

2 tablespoons chopped fresh
    rosemary or 2 teaspoons dried
    rosemary

Sea salt or kosher salt and freshly
    ground black pepper to taste

1 • Preheat the oven to 400 degrees.

2 • Remove the giblets and loose fat from the cavity of the chicken. Wash the chicken and pat dry. With your fingers, carefully loosen the skin from the chicken breast and place several sprigs of marjoram between the skin and the breast. Do the same where the breast meets the thigh.

3 • Place the chicken breast side up in a large roasting pan and squeeze the lemon juice over the chicken. Place the lemon halves along with the onion halves and any remaining marjoram into the cavity of the chicken.

4 • Pour the vinegar and wine over the chicken. Rub the breast of the chicken with the olive oil, rosemary, salt, and pepper and turn the chicken over, breast side down.

5 • Roast 30 minutes, basting occasionally with the pan juices. Turn the chicken breast side up and roast, basting often with the pan juices, 50 to 55 minutes longer, until the skin is golden brown, a meat thermometer registers 180 degrees in the thickest part of the thigh, and the juices run clear when the thigh is pierced with the tip of a sharp knife. (Note: Exact timing will depend on the size of the chicken. You should figure on 15 to 20 minutes per pound.)

6 • Transfer the chicken to a grooved carving board, cover loosely to keep it warm, and let rest 10 to 15 minutes before carving.

Braised Chicken Thighs with Chèvre Stuffing

Chicken thighs are rich in flavor and don't dry out as quickly as chicken breasts. This fast, easy dish is also delicious without the chèvre stuffing.

SERVES 4 TO 6

6 ounces creamy chèvre

2 tablespoons chopped fresh thyme or 2 teaspoons dried thyme

1 teaspoon salt

1 teaspoon freshly ground black pepper

6 chicken thighs, boned (about 1¼ pounds) (page 156)

3 tablespoons olive oil

1 yellow onion, minced

2 garlic cloves, minced

½ cup dry white wine

½ cup chicken broth (page 57)

8 cups firmly packed spinach, washed, drained, and stems removed

1 tablespoon chopped fresh parsley

1 tablespoon chopped fresh marjoram or 1 teaspoon dried marjoram

1 • Combine the chèvre, thyme, salt, and pepper in a small bowl and stir until well blended.

2 • Rinse the chicken thighs and pat dry. Working with 1 thigh at a time, open the thigh, place it skin side down on a work surface, and spread about 1 tablespoon of chèvre mixture in the center of the thigh. Roll the chicken flesh over the stuffing to close, then secure with a toothpick or tie with kitchen string. Continue with the remaining thighs and stuffing, until all the thighs are stuffed.

3 • Heat the olive oil in a large skillet over medium heat. Add the onion and cook 3 to 4 minutes, stirring constantly, until soft and translucent. Move the onions to 1 side of the skillet.

4 • Add the chicken thighs and cook about 5 minutes on 1 side. Add the garlic and stir. Turn the chicken thighs and continue to cook 5 minutes more, until nicely brown.

5 • Add the wine and chicken broth. Season with additional salt and pepper to taste, reduce heat, cover, and simmer 15 to 20 minutes, until the chicken is thoroughly cooked and the juices run clear when the thigh is pierced with the tip of a sharp knife in the thickest part. Transfer the chicken to a platter.

6 • Add the spinach, parsley, and marjoram to the skillet and cook and stir about 2 minutes, until the spinach has wilted. Remove from the heat. Place a serving of spinach on each plate. Remove the string or toothpicks from the chicken and place 1 or 2 thighs on top of the spinach. Spoon the pan juices over the chicken and serve immediately.

variations: Try Herbed Cream Cheese (page 96) instead of the chèvre for a slightly different flavor and texture. For a leaner dish, discard the chicken skin and omit the chèvre stuffing; stuff with wilted spinach.

A Simple Way to Remove a Chicken Thigh Bone

Find the side of the thigh that is naturally split. Reach into the opening with your fingers and pull out the bone and its cartilage. Using a sharp boning knife, move the knife blade along the bone to detach the bone from the skin. It's really simple.

Chicken-Arugula Meatballs

A lighter version of classic meatballs, these are flavored with pine nuts, raisins, and arugula. Try this over angel hair pasta sprinkled with chopped fresh arugula, or pass the meatballs as a hot hors d'oeuvre. Leftover meatballs are delicious as a filling for a hoagie-style sandwich: spread crusty Italian bread with warm Zesty Tomato Sauce (page 222), tomato chutney, or Foster's Pesto (page 90), add the meatballs, then top with fresh arugula if desired.

SERVES 6 TO 8

2 pounds ground chicken (use all white meat or a mixture of white and dark meat, which will result in a slightly moister, more richly flavored meatball)

2 cups fresh, unseasoned bread crumbs (page 158)

³/₄ cup grated Parmesan cheese

1 yellow onion, grated

1 rib celery, grated (discard fibrous parts)

3 garlic cloves, minced

¹/₃ cup golden raisins, chopped

One 2-ounce jar (¹/₄ cup) pine nuts, chopped

¹/₃ cup Foster's Arugula Pesto (page 236) or ¹/₃ cup Foster's Pesto (page 90)

¹/₂ teaspoon salt

¹/₂ teaspoon freshly ground black pepper

2 large eggs

1 bunch of arugula, washed, drained, stems removed, and chopped

4 tablespoons olive oil

¹/₂ cup dry white wine

¹/₂ pound capellini, cooked al dente

1 • Combine the chicken, ¹/₂ cup of the bread crumbs, ¹/₂ cup of the Parmesan, onion, celery, garlic, raisins, pine nuts, 2 tablespoons of the pesto, salt, pepper, and eggs in a large bowl and stir to mix. Add about 1 cup of the chopped arugula to the chicken mixture and stir to mix until all ingredients are well blended.

2 • Shape the mixture into eighteen to twenty 2-inch round meatballs. Lightly roll each meatball in the remaining bread crumbs and chill 1 hour until ready to cook. (Note: Chilling keeps the meatballs from breaking apart when cooked.)

3 • Heat the olive oil in a large skillet over medium-high heat and cook the meatballs in 2 small batches for about 2 minutes before rotating and turning to brown all over, 6 to 8 minutes total browning time. (It is important not to turn the meatballs too early, or they may fall apart. Let them form a golden brown, crusty exterior before turning.) Reduce heat and cook 4 to 6 minutes longer. Add 1 tablespoon additional oil if necessary. Remove the meatballs from the skillet and keep warm.

4 • Add the wine to the skillet and deglaze, scraping all the brown bits from the bottom. Add the pasta, the remaining pesto, and the meatballs to the skillet and toss in the remaining arugula. Cook about 1 minute, just until the arugula wilts. Remove from the heat and sprinkle with the remaining Parmesan cheese. Serve immediately.

variations: Instead of cooking the meatballs on top of the stove, you can bake them in a cast-iron skillet in the oven as follows: Heat half of the olive oil in a large cast-iron skillet in a preheated 400-degree oven for 5 minutes. Add the meatballs in 1 layer, then cook, uncovered, 15 to 18 minutes, turning once, until golden brown on all sides and cooked through. Repeat with the remaining olive oil and meatballs. Ground turkey can be substituted for the chicken if you prefer; spinach can be used instead of arugula for a slightly milder flavor.

Making Fresh Bread Crumbs

Purchased bread crumbs are fine in a pinch, but homemade bread crumbs taste better and are worth the effort. Bread crumbs are not just a "filler." In Italian cooking, especially, bread crumbs are an essential ingredient, used to add flavor and texture. To make fresh bread crumbs (also called soft bread crumbs), put good-quality, firm bread such as sourdough or Italian white bread (not soft, white sliced sandwich bread) in a food processor or blender and process into fine crumbs. You can store bread crumbs in the refrigerator, or freeze them until ready to use. You can also season the bread crumbs with fresh or dried herbs, salt, pepper, or finely grated Parmesan or Romano cheese.

Chicken Marsala with Oven-Roasted Mushrooms and Onions

This variation on veal Marsala is easy to make, yet special enough for an important dinner party. The boneless chicken breasts are flattened to about ⅓ inch thick, so they cook very quickly, like veal cutlets. The creamy sauce is made right in the pan. We like to serve this dish on a bed of Classic Mashed Potatoes (page 214) or lightly wilted spinach (page 213).

SERVES 4

4 boneless, skinless chicken
    breast halves

3 tablespoons Dijon mustard

8 fresh sage leaves

2 ounces pancetta, very thinly
    sliced

6 tablespoons olive oil

2 tablespoons balsamic vinegar

8 ounces button mushrooms,
    cleaned

10 cipollini onions or shallots,
    cut in half (or quartered if large)

½ cup all-purpose flour

1 cup sweet Marsala

¾ cup heavy cream

Salt and freshly ground black
    pepper to taste

1 • Preheat the oven to 400 degrees.

2 • Rinse the chicken and pat dry. Flatten each chicken breast half by placing it between 2 sheets of wax paper or plastic wrap and pounding it with the flat bottom of a heavy pan until it is about ⅓ inch thick in all places.

3 • Working with 1 flattened breast half at a time, spread 2 teaspoons of the mustard onto one side of each breast and press 2 sage leaves into the mustard side of the breast. Set aside. Repeat with remaining breast halves.

4 • Heat a large skillet over medium-high heat and cook the pancetta 4 to 5 minutes, turning occasionally, until it is crisp and lightly brown. Remove the pancetta and set aside on a paper towel to drain. Set the skillet aside.

5 • Meanwhile, while the pancetta is cooking, place 2 tablespoons of the olive oil, the vinegar, mushrooms, and onions into a baking dish and toss to mix. Roast in the oven about 30 minutes, stirring several times during the cooking process.

6 • Add the remaining olive oil to the skillet after the pancetta has been removed and lower the heat to medium. Dredge each breast in the flour to coat both sides lightly, shaking off any excess flour, and place in the skillet.

7 • Cook the chicken breasts, turning once, 3 to 4 minutes per side (exact timing will depend on the size of the breasts), until the breasts are golden brown and slightly crispy. Remove the breasts from the skillet and set aside.

8 • Raise heat to medium-high. Add the Marsala to the skillet, scraping the bottom of the pan to loosen any browned bits. Stir and reduce the Marsala by half. Add the cream, stir, and bring to a boil. Reduce heat to a low boil and continue to cook 2 to 3 minutes, until the sauce is slightly thick and creamy and coats the back of a spoon.

9 • Return the chicken and pancetta to the skillet with the sauce to reheat. Season with salt, pepper, and the remaining mustard and sage. To serve, top the chicken with the pancetta, roasted mushrooms, and cipollini. Spoon the sauce over the chicken and serve immediately.

variations: If pancetta is not available, substitute bacon. For a lower-calorie dish, eliminate the pancetta and cream.

Prosciutto and Pancetta

These flavorful cured meats from Italy are primarily used as seasoning. Both are available in most specialty food stores and in many supermarkets nationwide.

Prosciutto is dry-cured, unsmoked ham that is slightly sweet, mildly spicy, and much less salty than dry-cured American country hams. It does not have to be cooked before eating. Prosciutto is good to have on hand to flavor salads, pasta, scrambled eggs, and baked potatoes or to layer on sandwiches. Prosciutto is available in vacuum-packed packages, which can be refrigerated for several weeks or frozen up to 6 months.

Pancetta—also known as Italian bacon—is salted, flavored with black pepper and garlic, then rolled up and pressed into a log shape. It is then cured, but not smoked, and should be cooked before eating. Most often, it is thinly sliced and sautéed until the edges are crispy and golden brown. Pancetta keeps well refrigerated; or cut it into small pieces and cover with plastic wrap. Pancetta will freeze up to 6 months. When ready to use, partially defrost the pancetta, then slice it; it's easier to slice thinly when it's partially frozen.

Chicken Breasts Stuffed with Prosciutto and Sun-Dried Tomatoes

The naturally sweet, concentrated flavor of sun-dried tomatoes and the mildly salty prosciutto complement simple grilled chicken deliciously. The stuffing goes under the skin, which flavors the breast meat and produces crispy skin. This recipe calls for bone-in chicken breasts with the skin and the wing. If you don't want to trim the breasts yourself, have the butcher do it for you.

SERVES 4

4 bone-in chicken breast quarters, with skin

½ cup julienned sun-dried tomatoes

½ cup olive oil

2 tablespoons balsamic vinegar

2 tablespoons sherry vinegar

2 tablespoons chopped fresh rosemary or 2 teaspoons dried rosemary

1 lemon, cut in half

4 very thin slices (about 2 ounces) prosciutto

8 basil leaves

Salt and freshly ground black pepper to taste

1 tablespoon unsalted butter

½ cup dry sherry

1 tablespoon chopped fresh parsley

2 bunches of arugula, washed, drained, and stems removed

1 • Cut the chicken breast meat away from the rib cage and discard the bone. Cut off the first 2 joints of the tip of the wing, leaving the tiny "leg." Loosen the skin from the meat of the breast but do not remove it completely; leave 1 side attached. Rinse the chicken, pat dry, and set aside.

2 • Soak the tomatoes in ½ cup hot water, covered, for about 5 minutes. Drain and place in a bowl. (Note: If using oil-packed sun-dried tomatoes, do not soak them; proceed directly to step 3.)

3 • Toss the reconstituted tomatoes with ¼ cup of the olive oil, balsamic vinegar, sherry vinegar, and 1 tablespoon of the rosemary. Add the lemon juice to the tomato mixture and reserve the squeezed lemon halves. Set aside.

4 • Place 1 half-slice of prosciutto between the skin and meat of each breast. Divide the tomatoes in half; set 1 half aside for later use. Place 7 to 8 strips of sun-dried tomatoes on top of each piece of prosciutto and top with a basil leaf. Pull the chicken skin over the prosciutto, tomatoes, and basil and sprinkle with the remaining rosemary. Season with salt and pepper and set aside.

5 • Heat the remaining olive oil and the butter in a large cast-iron skillet over medium-high heat. Add the chicken, skin side down, and the reserved lemon halves. Cook 7 to 8 minutes, until the skin is crispy and golden brown and the edges of the chicken breast start to turn opaque. Turn the chicken over and add the sherry and parsley. Reduce heat to me-

dium and cook 8 to 10 minutes longer, until the chicken is opaque throughout. (Note: The exact timing will depend on the size of the chicken breasts.)

6 • Toss the arugula in a bowl with the reserved tomatoes and marinade and the additional prosciutto. Season with additional salt and pepper and divide among 4 plates. Top each bed of arugula with a chicken breast. Spoon any remaining pan liquid over the breast and serve immediately.

variations: You can grill the chicken instead of cooking it in a skillet. The prosciutto can be omitted, and watercress, spinach, or mixed salad greens can be substituted for the arugula.

How to Prepare Chicken *Suprêmes*

At Foster's, we often use what the French call *suprêmes,* which are boneless breasts of chicken (the term also applies to pheasant, duck, and other poultry) with the wing joint still attached. To prepare a *suprême,* use a sharp boning knife to cut the breast meat away from the rib cage, as you would if preparing a completely boneless breast. Cut off the wing tips, leaving the section closest to the breast attached. You can "French" the bone if desired: loosen the skin of the wing from the bone and use the back (dull side) of a knife to scrape the meat toward the breast. Don't forget to save the breastbones and wing tips for making stock or soup.

Sautéed Chicken Breasts with Artichokes, Lemons, and Capers

This quick, easy dish is delicious any time of year, but especially in summer, since the lemons, artichokes, and capers add vibrant—but light—flavors. Try this on a bed of lightly wilted spinach (page 213) or Classic Mashed Potatoes (page 214) or with Risotto Cakes with Roasted Tomatoes and Foster's Arugula Pesto (page 234).

SERVES 4

4 boneless, skinless chicken breast halves (about 6 ounces each)

Salt and freshly ground black pepper to taste

2 tablespoons fresh thyme or 2 teaspoons dried thyme

1/3 cup all-purpose flour

3 tablespoons unsalted butter

1 tablespoon olive oil

One 14-ounce can artichoke hearts (packed in water), drained and cut in half

1/4 cup drained capers

1 lemon, sliced into paper-thin rounds

6 bay leaves

1 cup dry white wine

1 • Rinse the chicken and pat dry. Flatten each chicken breast half by placing it between 2 sheets of wax paper or plastic wrap and pounding it with the flat bottom of a heavy pan until the chicken is about 1/3 inch thick in all places. Season with salt, pepper, and thyme, pressing them into the breast meat.

2 • Dust the breasts lightly with the flour, shaking off any excess flour.

3 • Heat the butter and olive oil in a large skillet over medium-high heat. Add the chicken breasts; top with artichokes, capers, and lemon slices. Cook the breasts 4 to 5 minutes per side, turning once, until light brown and crispy. (Note: Reduce the heat if the breasts are browning too quickly.)

4 • Add the bay leaves and wine and reduce heat to a simmer, as you scrape the bottom of the pan to loosen any brown bits. Simmer about 5 minutes longer, stirring occasionally, until the sauce is slightly reduced and thickened. Discard the bay leaves.

5 • Season with additional salt and pepper if desired and serve immediately, topped with the artichokes, capers, lemon slices, and the sauce.

variations: Instead of pounding the breasts, you can slice through the breasts to make 2 thin "cutlets."

Laura's Spicy Turkey Barbecue

Created by one of the cooks at the Market, Laura Cyr, this dish is an easy variation on classic southern pulled pork barbecue. Like traditional pork barbecue, this lighter version also cooks slow and long, until it is fork-tender. However, unlike pork barbecue, you don't need a smoker or a barbecue pit—a standard oven is fine. At Foster's, we serve this as a sandwich on soft buns with Asian Cole Slaw with Corn and Frisée (page 111), but you could also serve it in soft flour tortillas as a main course, accompanied by cole slaw, Black Bean and Yellow Rice Salad (page 115), or Cucumber, Avocado, and Tomato Salad (page 145), corn on the cob, and sliced tomatoes. For a southern-style hors d'oeuvre, pile the barbecue onto bite-sized Old-Fashioned Buttermilk Biscuits (page 16) and serve warm.

SERVES 8 TO 10 FOR SANDWICHES OR A MAIN COURSE

One 5-pound boneless turkey breast

2 cups cider vinegar

1 cup apple juice

$\frac{1}{2}$ cup Worcestershire sauce

$\frac{1}{2}$ cup firmly packed light brown sugar

1 tablespoon red pepper flakes

1 tablespoon freshly ground black pepper

2 cups Foster's Sweet and Tangy Barbecue Sauce (recipe follows)

1 • Preheat the oven to 300 degrees.

2 • Place the turkey breast in a large, deep roasting pan.

3 • Mix the vinegar, apple juice, Worcestershire sauce, brown sugar, red pepper flakes, and black pepper in a bowl or large measuring cup. Stir to mix, and pour over the turkey.

4 • Cover the turkey and roast 3 to 3½ hours, basting and turning frequently until the meat comes apart easily when pulled with a fork.

5 • Remove the turkey from the oven and cool slightly. Pull the breast meat apart in large chunks with a fork and place on a serving platter; keep warm. Heat the barbecue sauce in a small saucepan if necessary, pour half the sauce on top of the turkey, and serve the remaining sauce on the side.

Foster's Sweet and Tangy Barbecue Sauce

The addition of fresh ginger and fresh orange juice gives this barbecue sauce a very fresh, slightly spicy flavor. The addition of coffee helps cut the acidity of the tomatoes. The sauce is great on chicken, pork, and beef; it's easy to make and keeps almost indefinitely in the refrigerator.

MAKES ABOUT 1 QUART SAUCE

3 cups canned crushed tomatoes

1 cup firmly packed light brown sugar

1 cup cider vinegar

¾ cup Worcestershire sauce

¼ cup brewed strong coffee

¼ cup fresh orange juice

2 tablespoons peeled, julienned fresh ginger

Juice of 2 lemons

2 garlic cloves, minced

1 tablespoon dry mustard

1 tablespoon freshly ground black pepper

1 tablespoon red pepper flakes

1 • Combine the tomatoes, brown sugar, vinegar, Worcestershire sauce, coffee, orange juice, ginger, lemon juice, garlic, mustard, black pepper, and red pepper flakes in a large saucepan over medium-high heat.

2 • Bring to a low boil, reduce heat to low, and simmer 30 to 45 minutes, until the mixture has thickened and reduced by about one-quarter. Use immediately or refrigerate in an airtight container until ready to use.

Wine-Braised Boneless Turkey Breast with Sage and Thyme

Braising—instead of roasting—ensures that the turkey breast stays tender and moist. In this recipe, the tender breast meat is removed from the carcass, resulting in two breast halves, which will cook faster than a whole, bone-in turkey breast. Serve this easy dish warm or at room temperature as a main course; leftovers are delicious in sandwiches, soups, and salads.

SERVES 6 TO 8

One 5-pound boneless turkey breast, separated into halves

10 to 12 fresh sage leaves

$\frac{1}{4}$ cup fresh thyme or 1 heaping tablespoon dried thyme

$\frac{1}{4}$ cup all-purpose flour

3 tablespoons unsalted butter

2 tablespoons olive oil

1 red onion, thinly sliced

1 small bunch of baby carrots, trimmed and scrubbed, or 3 large carrots, peeled and cut on the diagonal

1 cup apple juice, preferably unfiltered

$1\frac{1}{2}$ cups dry white wine

Juice of 1 orange

Juice of 1 lemon

Salt and freshly ground black pepper to taste

Additional fresh sage leaves, to garnish, optional

1 • Preheat the oven to 375 degrees.

2 • Rinse the turkey and pat dry. Place the sage and thyme under the skin of each breast half and press them onto the breast meat. Dredge the breast halves in the flour, shaking off any excess flour.

3 • Heat the butter and olive oil in a large, ovenproof skillet or Dutch oven over medium-high heat and add the turkey, skin side down, and the onion and carrots. Cook the turkey about 5 minutes per side, until lightly brown. Stir the onion and carrots occasionally while the turkey is cooking.

4 • Add the apple juice, wine, orange juice, lemon juice, and salt and pepper. Remove the skillet from the heat and place in the oven uncovered, basting frequently, 40 to 45 minutes, or until the internal temperature is 155 to 160 degrees. Remove the turkey from the oven and let rest on a carving board, loosely covered, about 10 minutes, before slicing.

5 • Carve each breast half crosswise on the diagonal into $\frac{1}{4}$- to $\frac{1}{2}$-inch-thick slices. Spoon the pan juices, carrots, and onions on top, garnish with additional sage leaves, and serve immediately.

variations: Try other herbs—such as oregano and fresh parsley—instead of the sage and thyme. Button mushrooms, chopped celery, or cabbage can be added to the carrots and onions for a slightly different flavor. This is also great served on a bed of steamy basmati rice or savory stuffing.

Braised Fillet of Beef with Roasted Tomatoes and Mushrooms

This special-occasion dish is ready in almost no time at all, a real plus for impromptu entertaining. You can use roasted tomatoes any time a recipe calls for canned tomatoes or when fresh tomatoes are not at their peak.

SERVES 4

Four 2-inch-thick beef tenderloin fillets (about 2 pounds total)

4 tablespoons olive oil

1 teaspoon cracked black peppercorns

2 tablespoons fresh rosemary or 2 teaspoons dried rosemary

6 plum tomatoes, cored and cut in half lengthwise

8 ounces button or cremini mushrooms, wiped cleaned

$1/4$ cup balsamic vinegar

$1/2$ cup dry red wine

Salt to taste

Classic Mashed Potatoes (page 214)

1 • Preheat the oven to 400 degrees.

2 • Rub each fillet evenly with 2 teaspoons of the olive oil and coat with the cracked black pepper and rosemary. Press the pepper and rosemary into the fillet with the back of a fork to adhere.

3 • Toss the remaining olive oil with the tomatoes and mushrooms in a bowl and set aside.

4 • Heat a cast-iron skillet over medium-high heat to the smoking point, 10 to 12 minutes. Add the beef, tomatoes, and mushrooms. Cook the beef about 3 minutes on each side. Stir the tomatoes and mushrooms several times while the beef is cooking.

5 • Add the vinegar and wine. Place the skillet and its contents in the oven and cook 15 to 18 minutes for rare steaks (internal temperature will be 115 to 120 degrees when a meat thermometer is inserted in the center of the steak). Stir several times to coat the vegetables and meat with the pan juices during the cooking process.

6 • Transfer the fillets to a plate (reserving vegetables and pan juices), cover loosely , and let rest about 5 minutes. Return the skillet to the burner and boil the liquid with the vegetables over high heat until it becomes slightly thick, 3 to 4 minutes. Season with salt.

7 • Serve as follows: Spoon a serving of mashed potatoes on each serving plate. Top the potatoes with 1 fillet. Spoon the pan juices and vegetables over the fillet and potatoes. Serve immediately.

Using a Cast-Iron Skillet

Cast-iron skillets—the same kind our grand-mothers used—are indispensable in the kitchen. They heat evenly, and they hold heat well. Plus, they can go from stovetop right into the oven for dishes that require combination cooking (searing or browning followed by longer, slower cooking). Because cast-iron skillets can withstand such high temperatures, they brown food beautifully. They can be used in place of a grill when you don't want to fire up the outdoor grill or if you only have a small amount of food to cook, such as a small steak, a fish fillet, or a few boneless, skinless chicken breasts. They are also great to use on top of a grill for something you might want to sear or cook at a high heat without smoking up the kitchen.

Braising

This moist-heat cooking method is most often used for meat and sometimes poultry. The braising technique involves the browning of the meat or poultry in fat (usually a combination of oil and butter) to sear the exterior and seal in the flavor and juices. Next, a liquid—usually broth or wine or a combination of the two—is added and the dish is cooked until tender.

Braised Short Ribs with Roasted Root Vegetable Puree

Browned in a skillet, then braised slowly in the oven, these beef short ribs are great served with a bit of horseradish or Beet-Horseradish Mustard (page 92) on the side. They're also delicious on a bed of creamy polenta or Classic Mashed Potatoes (page 214). The vegetable puree goes well with grilled chicken or fish.

SERVES 4 TO 6

12 beef short ribs, bone-in (about 3½ to 4 pounds)

2 tablespoons chopped fresh rosemary or 2 teaspoons dried rosemary

Salt and freshly ground pepper to taste

⅓ cup all-purpose flour

¼ cup olive oil

4 shallots, quartered

2 carrots, peeled and chopped

2 parsnips, peeled and chopped

3 cups port

3 cups beef or chicken broth (page 57)

1 tablespoon tomato paste

Roasted Root Vegetable Puree (recipe follows)

1 • Preheat the oven to 350 degrees.

2 • Season the ribs with rosemary, salt, and pepper by rubbing them into the meat of the ribs to adhere. Lightly coat each side of the ribs with flour, shaking off any excess flour.

3 • Heat the olive oil in a large, deep, ovenproof skillet or Dutch oven over medium-high heat. Add the ribs and cook about 2 minutes on all sides, until brown, about 8 minutes total. Transfer the ribs to a plate and set aside. Add the shallots, carrots, and parsnips to the same skillet and cook and stir about 5 minutes, until tender and lightly brown.

4 • With the vegetables still in it, deglaze the skillet by adding the port and cooking over medium-high heat 10 to 12 minutes, until the liquid has reduced by half. Add the broth and tomato paste and stir to mix thoroughly. Remove the skillet from the heat.

5 • Return the ribs to the skillet, cover, and cook in the oven about 2½ hours, until the meat is fork-tender and almost falling off the bone. Turn the ribs several times during the cooking process. (Note: You can roast the vegetables for the vegetable puree while you roast the ribs.)

6 • Transfer the cooked ribs and the shallots, carrots, and parsnips to a plate (reserve the pan juices); cover and keep warm. Place the skillet with its juices over medium-high heat and boil to reduce the liquid by about two-thirds. The liquid will become thick, almost like a glaze. Spoon the glaze over the ribs and the shallots, carrots, and parsnips (you can add the

ribs and vegetables back to the pan for a few minutes if they need to be warmed).

7 • Reheat the vegetable puree in the oven or microwave oven if necessary. Spoon the vegetable puree onto individual plates, top each serving with 2 or 3 short ribs and some of the whole roasted vegetables, and drizzle with the glaze from the ribs. Serve immediately.

Roasted Root Vegetable Puree

MAKES ABOUT 4 CUPS PUREE

2 carrots, peeled and quartered

2 parsnips, peeled and quartered

2 small turnips, peeled and quartered

2 small Yukon gold potatoes, peeled and quartered

1/2 fennel bulb, cored and quartered

1/2 cup peeled and coarsely chopped celeriac

1/4 cup olive oil

Salt and freshly ground black pepper to taste

2 tablespoons unsalted butter

1/4 cup pan juices from the ribs

1/2 cup milk, half-and-half, or heavy cream

1 • Place the carrots, parsnips, turnips, potatoes, fennel, and celeriac in a baking dish and toss with the olive oil, salt, and pepper. Spread out evenly in the dish.

2 • Place in the oven along with the ribs and roast, uncovered, 1 to 1¼ hours, until the vegetables are soft to the touch and cooked through. Stir several times during the cooking process to coat with oil and to make sure the vegetables are cooking evenly.

3 • Cool the vegetables for 10 to 15 minutes, until they are still warm but not hot. Place the roasted vegetables in the bowl of a food processor fitted with the metal blade. Add the butter, pan juices from the ribs, and milk, and puree until smooth. Season with additional salt and pepper.

variation: To make the Root Vegetable Puree as a separate recipe to serve alongside chicken or fish, prepare the vegetables as directed but roast in a preheated 400-degree oven for 40 to 45 minutes or until the vegetables are soft to the touch and cooked through. Stir several times during the cooking process to coat with oil and to make sure the vegetables are cooking evenly. You can add rosemary, thyme, or chives to the vegetables as they roast for added flavor. Add ¼ cup additional milk in place of the pan juices. You can use just about any combination of root vegetables that you like, about 2 pounds total.

Cajun-Cut Rib Eye Steak

This tender, thick-cut rib eye steak is seasoned with hot spices, seared on top of the stove, then finished in the oven.

SERVES 2 TO 3

One 1½-pound rib eye steak

½ cup port or dry red wine

2 tablespoons Dijon mustard

2 tablespoons soy sauce

2 tablespoons Worcestershire sauce

2 teaspoons freshly cracked black peppercorns

¼ teaspoon ground red pepper (cayenne)

1 tablespoon chopped fresh rosemary or 1 teaspoon dried rosemary

1 roasted red bell pepper, peeled, cored, seeded, and diced page 40)

1 roasted jalapeño, peeled, seeded, and diced (page 40)

1 • Place the steak in a deep glass or earthenware baking dish and set aside.

2 • Combine the port, mustard, soy sauce, and Worcestershire sauce in a small bowl and stir to blend thoroughly. Pour this mixture over the steak. Press half the black pepper, ground red pepper, and rosemary onto each side of the steak, turning it to coat both sides in the port mixture. Marinate, refrigerated, overnight, or up to 2 hours before cooking at cool room temperature.

3 • Preheat the oven to 425 degrees.

4 • Heat a large, heavy, cast-iron skillet over medium-high heat to the smoking point, 10 to 12 minutes.

5 • Place the steak in the hot skillet and cook on each side for about 3 minutes. Pour any remaining marinade on top of the steak. Toss the red bell pepper and jalapeño in the skillet and place the skillet in the oven.

6 • Cook about 15 minutes for rare steak (internal temperature 115 to 120 degrees), about 20 minutes for medium-rare steak (internal temperature 125 to 130 degrees). Transfer the steak to a carving board, cover loosely, and let rest 5 minutes before slicing. Carve into ½-inch slices and serve immediately, topped with pan juices and peppers.

variations: Substitute a T-bone steak for the rib eye steak. Omit the jalapeño for a milder-tasting dish.

Cooking Steaks: Some Basics

Steaks are a tender cut of meat that have enough marbling to keep the meat from drying. This is important, since steaks are usually cooked by one of the dry-heat methods: grilling, broiling, or pan-searing. To avoid overcooking or undercooking, always have the steaks at room temperature before cooking. Use an instant-read thermometer to check the internal temperature. Once the steaks are done, let them rest at room temperature for at least 5 minutes before slicing. (Note: All cuts of meat will continue to cook as they rest at room temperature, but because steaks are a small cut, they cook even more than the larger cuts as they rest.)

To make sure a steak doesn't end up medium-well when what you wanted was medium-rare, undercook the steak, and use an instant-read thermometer to test for doneness. If it is too rare, return it to the grill, skillet, or broiling pan and continue to cook to the desired degree of doneness. Remember, depending on the size or thickness of the cut, the steak will continue to cook as it rests for 5 minutes.

- Rare: 115 to 120 degrees.
- Medium-rare: 125 to 130 degrees.
- Medium: 135 to 145 degrees.
- Medium-well: 150 to 160 degrees.
- Well: 160 to 165 degrees. At this temperature, the meat is usually overcooked unless it is a slow-roasted, fatty, juicy cut.

Spicy Grilled Standing Rib Roast

Standing rib roasts are usually cooked in the oven, but they're delicious grilled, too. We grill this roast on a charcoal or gas grill over indirect heat (that is, not directly over live flames), so it can withstand a long cooking time without burning. Try this roast with Beet-Horseradish Mustard (page 92) and Roasted New Potato Salad with Dijon Vinaigrette (page 134.)

SERVES 8 TO 10

Safflower oil or canola oil, for oiling the grill

1 cup dry red wine

$1/2$ cup Dijon mustard

$1/4$ cup olive oil

1 jalapeño, seeded and minced

2 tablespoons chopped fresh rosemary or 2 teaspoons dried rosemary

2 teaspoons kosher salt

1 tablespoon coarsely ground black pepper

$1/2$ teaspoon ground red pepper (cayenne)

One 4-rib standing rib roast (prime rib, 9 to 10 pounds, chine bone removed)

1 • Brush the grill grates lightly with the safflower oil. Prepare a hot fire to 1 side in a gas or charcoal grill. (Note: Having the charcoal or gas heat to 1 side allows for indirect-heat cooking on the other side of the grill. You must have a grill with a lid.) Let the coals burn until they turn gray.

2 • Whisk the wine, mustard, olive oil, jalapeño, rosemary, salt, black pepper, and ground red pepper in a small bowl until well blended.

3 • Place the roast, bone side down, meaty side up, in a large roasting pan and spoon about one-fourth of the wine mixture over the top and sides of the roast. Remove the roast from the pan and place on the side of the grill that is not over the coals. Cover with the grill lid and cook 2 to $2^{1}/2$ hours, basting frequently with the marinade and rotating the roast 2 to 3 times during the cooking for even cooking and browning. Add more charcoal to the fire if necessary. You want a medium fire, not extremely hot, so if you add charcoal, add a small amount at a time. The roast is done (medium-rare) when the internal temperature is between 125 and 130 degrees when tested with a meat thermometer inserted in the center of the roast (or 115 to 120 degrees for rare, 135 to 145 degrees for medium; the meat will continue to cook 5 to 10 degrees as it rests). (Note: It is important to use a meat thermometer for this recipe because all grills are different and heat can vary considerably.)

4 • Remove the roast from the grill, place on a grooved carving board, cover loosely, and let rest for 20 to 30 minutes.

5 • Run a sharp knife between the bones and the meat, separating the meat from the bones. Carve into ½-inch slices. Pour the juices that have collected in the carving board over the meat and serve immediately. (Note: The rib bones are great separated and put back on the grill for a few minutes, with a little of the basting liquid or barbecue sauce.)

variations: Baste the roast with Foster's Sweet and Tangy Barbecue Sauce (page 167) or other barbecue sauce during the final 30 minutes of cooking, then serve with the barbecue sauce.

Grilling Basics

When using a charcoal fire, light the coals 30 to 35 minutes before you start cooking, for a hot fire. For a medium fire, light the coals 40 to 45 minutes before, and for a low fire, 45 to 50 minutes. (Gas grills take less time to heat.) I like to use hardwood lump charcoal, such as Kingsford, since it starts easily and burns evenly. Wood and wood chips—such as hickory and mesquite—can be added to the charcoal fire for flavor.

Grilled Butterflied Leg of Lamb with Fresh Mint-Pepper Jelly

Butterflied lamb cooks faster and more evenly, and is easier to trim of fat and silverskin, than a whole leg of lamb. A butterflied leg has more surface area than a whole leg, so there's more flavor from the marinade and the grill. The lamb can be marinated up to 2 days in advance.

SERVES 6 TO 8

One 4$\frac{1}{2}$- to 5-pound butterflied leg of lamb, trimmed of excess fat and silverskin

8 garlic cloves, cut in half, smashed lightly with the flat side of a knife blade

$\frac{1}{4}$ cup fresh rosemary or 1 heaping tablespoon dried rosemary or a mixture of rosemary, marjoram, and oregano

3 tablespoons olive oil

$\frac{1}{2}$ cup Marsala or dry red wine

3 tablespoons chopped fresh mint

1 teaspoon kosher salt

1 tablespoon freshly ground black pepper

Safflower oil or canola oil, for oiling the grill

1 recipe Foster's Seven Pepper Jelly with Fresh Mint (recipe follows)

1 • Make about 8 small incisions on the fatty side of the lamb and insert a smashed garlic half and some rosemary into each slit. Rub the lamb on both sides with the olive oil, Marsala, remaining garlic and rosemary, mint, salt, and pepper. Cover and refrigerate overnight or let stand 1 hour at cool room temperature.

2 • Brush the grill grates lightly with the safflower oil. Prepare a hot fire in a gas or charcoal grill.

3 • If the lamb has been in the refrigerator, bring it to room temperature. Remove the meat from the marinade and drain slightly, allowing some of the marinade to remain on the lamb for added flavor.

4 • When the fire is medium-hot (if using charcoal, the coals will be gray and slightly glowing), place the lamb on the grill and cook 15 to 20 minutes per side (depending on how hot the fire is), basting frequently with the remaining marinade. Move the lamb to the side on the grill away from the direct heat and continue to cook 10 to 15 minutes longer, turning once, or until the internal temperature registers 130 to 135 degrees for medium-rare or 140 to 145 degrees for medium.

5 • Remove the lamb from the grill and let rest, lightly covered, on a carving board 10 minutes before slicing. Carve into thin, $\frac{1}{4}$-inch slices and serve immediately with Foster's Seven Pepper Jelly with Fresh Mint.

Foster's Seven Pepper Jelly with Fresh Mint

1 cup Foster's Seven Pepper Jelly
   or your favorite pepper jelly
1/4 cup chopped fresh mint
3 tablespoons red wine vinegar
1 teaspoon freshly ground black
   pepper

Combine the jelly with the mint, vinegar, and pepper in a bowl and whisk until all ingredients are blended. Refrigerate in an airtight container until ready to use or up to 1 week.

Roast Leg of Lamb Stuffed with Italian White Beans and Spinach

When the lamb is sliced, the "stuffing" of white beans and green spinach is a pretty contrast to the pink lamb. Not only does this dish make a beautiful presentation, it's also easy to make, and a good dish for serving a hungry crowd. This is delicious served with Lentil, Spinach, and Feta Salad with Sour Cherry Vinaigrette (page 120) or grilled or pan-cooked escarole.

SERVES 6 TO 8

1 cup dried cannellini beans or navy beans, rinsed and picked over, or 2 cups canned cannellini or navy beans, rinsed and drained

6 tablespoons olive oil

6 garlic cloves, smashed with flat side of a knife

8 cups firmly packed spinach, washed, drained, and stems removed

One 4½- to 5-pound boneless leg of lamb, trimmed of excess fat and silverskin

½ cup dry red wine

1 tablespoon freshly ground black pepper

1 teaspoon kosher salt

1 tablespoon chopped fresh rosemary or 1 teaspoon dried rosemary

1 • Preheat the oven to 425 degrees.

2 • Place the beans in about 6 cups of water and bring to a boil. Cook until tender, about 1 hour. Drain, rinse, and set aside to cool. (Note: If using canned beans, omit this step, and proceed directly to step 3.)

3 • Heat 2 tablespoons of the olive oil in a large skillet over medium heat. Add 3 cloves of the garlic and cook and stir for 1 to 2 minutes. Add the spinach and cook 1 to 2 minutes, until just wilted, stirring constantly. Remove from the heat and set aside to cool.

4 • Lay the lamb fat side down on a cutting board or other work surface. Spread about ½ cup of the beans and ½ cup of the spinach-garlic mixture evenly over the center part of the surface. Reserve the remaining beans and spinach.

5 • Roll the leg up lengthwise into a log and tie with kitchen twine. Place in a baking dish.

6 • Make several slits in the fat of the lamb and stuff the remaining garlic into the slits. Coat the outside of the lamb with the wine, 2 tablespoons of the olive oil, the pepper, salt, and rosemary.

7 • Heat the remaining olive oil in a large ovenproof skillet or Dutch oven and brown the rolled lamb evenly on all sides, about 10 minutes total. Add the wine marinade to the pan and roast 55 minutes to 1 hour for medium-rare (about 12 minutes per pound) or until a meat thermometer registers 130 to 135 degrees (140 to 145 degrees for medium, 1 hour 10 minutes to 1 hour 15 minutes) when inserted into

the thickest part of the leg. Baste the lamb with pan juices several times during the cooking process. Remove from the oven, cover loosely, and let the lamb rest about 10 minutes before carving.

8 • Remove the twine, place the lamb on a carving board, and slice the lamb into ¼- to ½-inch slices. Reheat the reserved cooked beans and spinach in the same skillet and serve alongside the lamb.

Rack of Lamb with Jalapeño–Honey Mustard Glaze and Balsamic Vinegar Reduction

Spicy peppers, sweet mustard, and a tangy vinegar reduction are a tasty accent to this elegant cut of lamb. The Balsamic Vinegar Reduction has no added fat, and the lamb marinade has very little, so this dish is healthful, too. Serve this warm with Balsamic-Roasted Vegetables (page 113) or Grilled Vegetable Ratatouille (page 124).

SERVES 4

Two 1¹/₂-pound racks of lamb
   (8 or 9 chops per rack)
¹/₄ cup olive oil
6 tablespoons Honey Mustard
   (page 91)
1 jalapeño, seeded and minced
1 teaspoon kosher salt
2 tablespoons freshly ground
   black pepper
¹/₄ cup chopped fresh rosemary or
   1 heaping tablespoon dried
   rosemary
8 garlic cloves, minced
¹/₂ cup Balsamic Vinegar
   Reduction (recipe follows)

1 • Preheat the oven to 450 degrees.

2 • Trim any excess fat off the bones and ribs of the lamb (see page 182 on how to French a chop).

3 • Combine the olive oil, mustard, jalapeño, salt, pepper, rosemary, and garlic in a small bowl and mix well.

4 • Stand the ribs up together in a roasting pan with the rib bones intertwined, fat side facing out. Brush or spoon the olive oil mixture onto the fat side of the 2 racks of lamb.

5 • Roast for 25 to 30 minutes for medium-rare; the internal temperature in the center of the rack will register 130 to 135 degrees. Remove the lamb from the oven, cover loosely, and let rest 5 to 10 minutes before slicing into individual chops. Serve immediately with Balsamic Vinegar Reduction.

Balsamic Vinegar Reduction

1 shallot, minced, or
    2 tablespoons minced
    onion
$1/3$ cup balsamic vinegar
Juice of 2 oranges
$1/4$ cup brewed coffee
$1/2$ cup dry red wine
1 teaspoon freshly ground black
    pepper
1 teaspoon chopped fresh
    rosemary or $1/4$ heaping
    teaspoon dried rosemary

1 • Place the shallot in a small saucepan over medium heat until it begins to sizzle.

2 • Immediately add the vinegar, orange juice, coffee, and wine. Increase heat to high. Boil until reduced by half, about 5 minutes.

3 • Remove from the heat and stir in the pepper and rosemary. Spoon onto the lamb chops and serve immediately.

How to French a Chop

When referring to ribs or chops, "to French" means to cleanly scrape away the meat 1 or 2 inches from the end of the rib bones, which creates a neat, elegant look. A butcher can do it for you, but it's quite easy to do yourself. Simply use the dull side of a knife and pare and scrape the fat and meat away.

Slow-Roasted Pork Roast
with Sweet and Spicy Horseradish Sauce

We use fresh ham for this flavorful roast, which is particularly delicious in spring or summer with Roasted New Potato Salad with Dijon Vinaigrette (page 134) or Black Bean and Yellow Rice Salad (page 115, shown on page 185). The word "ham" usually brings to mind cured pork, but the word actually refers to the hog's hind leg, generally from the hipbone to the middle of the shank bone. Fresh ham, then, is unprocessed; it is not cured, dried, or salted, so it tastes like other tender cuts of fresh pork, such as the loin and pork chops. At Foster's, we don't slice this roast; instead, we serve it in large, tender pulled chunks for a more casual presentation.

SERVES 8 TO 10

One 7- to 8-pound fresh ham or fresh pork shoulder, skin on, bone-in

$\frac{1}{2}$ cup cider vinegar

$\frac{1}{2}$ cup balsamic vinegar

1 cup Foster's Seven Pepper Jelly or your favorite pepper jelly

1 tablespoon red pepper flakes

1 tablespoon freshly ground black pepper

1 tablespoon salt

2 cups Sweet and Spicy Horseradish Sauce (recipe follows)

1 • Preheat the oven to 350 degrees.

2 • Place the pork in a large roasting pan. Pierce the skin and fat of the pork—without going through to the meat—all over with a fork and set aside.

3 • Mix together the cider vinegar, balsamic vinegar, pepper jelly, red pepper flakes, black pepper, and salt in a bowl and stir until well blended. Brush the pork generously with the basting liquid and add about 2 cups water to the bottom of the pan.

4 • Cover and place in the oven to roast for 5½ to 6 hours, basting frequently, until a meat thermometer inserted in the thickest part registers 220 to 225 degrees, the skin is browned and crisp, and the meat is falling-off-the-bone tender. Let rest for 20 to 30 minutes before serving. To serve, remove the skin, pull the pork into large pieces, and serve with the horseradish sauce.

Sweet and Spicy Horseradish Sauce

This sauce can be made 4 to 5 days in advance. It's delicious on sandwiches and most pork and lamb dishes.

One 5-ounce jar prepared
    horseradish, drained
1 cup Foster's Seven Pepper Jelly
    or your favorite pepper jelly
¼ cup balsamic vinegar
1 teaspoon freshly ground black
    pepper

Combine the horseradish, pepper jelly, vinegar, and pepper in a bowl and whisk until well blended. Spoon the sauce on top of the pulled pork or refrigerate in an airtight container until ready to use.

Temperatures for Cooking Pork

When cooking fresh pork (the term "fresh" is used to differentiate it from cured pork, or ham), take care not to overcook it. Chops and loins are quite lean, and will be dry and lacking in flavor if cooked too long. Trichinae are destroyed at 138 degrees, but to be on the safe side, most professional chefs serve pork between 145 and 150 degrees. The USDA recommends that pork prepared at home be cooked to an internal temperature of 160 to 165 degrees. Remember, however, that even after cooked pork is removed from the oven, it will continue to cook about 10 degrees as it rests. To avoid overcooking, we suggest that you remove the pork from the oven when a meat thermometer reaches 145 degrees in the thickest part. Then cover the pork loosely for 5 to 10 minutes. As it rests at room temperature, it will cook another 10 degrees, to 155 degrees. (For pork, 155 to 160 degrees is considered medium; 170 to 180 degrees is considered well-done.)

Roast Pork Tenderloin with Dried Cherries and Rosemary

Pork tenderloin—as its name suggests—is a very tender section of the loin. The loin is usually sold in separate portions: the blade end, the sirloin end, and the center loin. The tenderloin is a small, cylindrical muscle that is the tenderest part of the sirloin end. Pork tenderloin is much less expensive than beef tenderloin, and since it cooks quickly and is an elegant cut of meat, it makes a great dish for entertaining. The cherry-rosemary marinade results in a very aromatic dish that's delicious served warm or at room temperature.

SERVES 6

Two 1-pound pork tenderloins

$1/2$ cup dried cherries

$1/3$ cup dry red wine

$1/4$ cup balsamic vinegar

$3/4$ cup good-quality, all-natural cranberry juice or unfiltered apple juice

4 garlic cloves, minced

6 shallots, cut in half lengthwise

3 tablespoons fresh rosemary or 3 teaspoons dried rosemary

2 tablespoons olive oil

Salt and freshly ground black pepper to taste

1 • Preheat the oven to 375 degrees.

2 • Rinse the pork loin, pat dry, and place in a shallow glass or ceramic baking dish. Set aside.

3 • Whisk together the cherries, wine, vinegar, cranberry juice, garlic, shallots, and rosemary in a bowl. Pour this mixture over the pork, cover, and refrigerate 2 to 3 hours or overnight, turning the pork several times.

4 • Heat the olive oil in a large, ovenproof skillet over medium heat. Remove the pork from the marinade (reserve the marinade) and place the pork in the heated skillet. Cook the pork on all sides, 5 to 6 minutes total time, until light brown.

5 • Pour the reserved marinade over the pork and place the skillet in the oven. Roast, basting several times, 20 to 25 minutes or until a meat thermometer registers 150 to 155 degrees for medium (160 degrees— about 5 minutes longer—for medium-well). The meat will be a very light pink color. (Note: The pork will continue to cook after it is removed from the oven.)

6 • Remove the pork from the baking dish and place on a grooved carving board. Cover the pork loosely and let it rest 5 to 10 minutes before carving.

7 • Season with salt and pepper. Slice into $1/4$-inch pieces and spoon the pan juices over the pork. Serve immediately.

variations: Dried cranberries or raisins can be substituted for the dried cherries.

roast pork

Grilled Tuna with Scallions and Wasabi Mustard

A marinade of fresh ginger, soy sauce, orange juice, and honey gives this dish an Asian flavor. Although fresh wasabi is almost impossible to find in this country, wasabi powder is widely available. Mixed with Dijon mustard, orange juice, and honey, the wasabi-mustard mixture is also good on sandwiches and salads.

SERVES 4

Four 1¼-inch-thick tuna steaks (about 8 ounces each)

8 scallions, trimmed

¼ cup olive oil

¼ cup light soy sauce

Juice of 2 oranges

2 tablespoons peeled, grated fresh ginger

1 tablespoon honey

Salt and freshly ground black pepper to taste

Safflower oil or canola oil, for oiling the grill

1 russet potato, halved, for rubbing on the grill

⅓ cup fresh cilantro, to garnish, optional

½ cup Wasabi Mustard (recipe follows)

1 • Place the tuna steaks and scallions in a large baking dish. Combine the olive oil, soy sauce, orange juice, ginger, honey, salt, and pepper in a bowl and stir to mix well. Spoon the soy sauce mixture over the tuna steaks and scallions, cover, and refrigerate several hours to marinate.

2 • Brush the grill grates lightly with the safflower oil. Prepare a hot fire in a gas or charcoal grill. Rub the grates with the cut side of the russet potato (the starch from the potato keeps the fish from sticking).

3 • Remove the tuna steaks and scallions from the marinade and drain slightly. Place the tuna on the hot fire and grill about 3 minutes per side for medium steaks. Spoon the marinade over the top while the fish cooks. (Note: Do not overcook; the inside should be pink, not gray.) Remove the tuna from the grill and transfer to a plate.

4 • While the tuna is cooking, grill the scallions 3 to 4 minutes, turning several times. Spoon the remaining marinade over the top while the scallions cook.

5 • Place the tuna on a platter or individual plates, garnish with grilled scallions and cilantro, and serve immediately with Wasabi Mustard.

Wasabi Mustard

½ cup Dijon mustard

1 teaspoon wasabi powder

1 tablespoon honey

Grated zest and juice of 1 orange

½ teaspoon salt

1 teaspoon freshly ground black
  pepper

Combine the mustard, wasabi powder, honey, orange zest, orange juice, salt, and pepper in a small bowl and stir until well combined. Serve immediately or refrigerate in an airtight container until ready to use.

Cooking Tuna

At Foster's, we serve tuna slightly pink, so that it's not dry or overcooked. Always buy tuna from a reputable fishmonger and ask for sashimi-grade tuna, which is the best choice.

Herb-Grilled Salmon with Fresh Tomato-Orange Chutney

Delicious served warm or at room temperature, this is an elegant party dish that cooks quickly. The tart tomato-orange chutney can be made several hours in advance or the day before.

SERVES 6

Safflower oil or canola oil, for oiling the grill

1 russet potato, halved, for rubbing on the grill

One 3-pound boneless salmon fillet, skin on, scales removed (Note: One side of an average-sized salmon is about 3 pounds)

Juice of 1 orange

2 tablespoons olive oil

6 fresh basil leaves

3 or 4 sprigs fresh dill

Salt and freshly ground black pepper to taste

2 cups Fresh Tomato-Orange Chutney (recipe follows)

Fresh herb leaves, for garnish

1 • Brush the grill grates lightly with the safflower oil. Prepare a very hot fire in a gas or charcoal grill. The fire should be bright red and flaming hot. Rub the grates with the cut side of the russet potato (the starch from the potato keeps the fish from sticking). (Note: You can use a stovetop grill pan instead of an outdoor grill, if desired, although the flavor will not be quite the same.)

2 • Place the salmon on a piece of heavy-duty aluminum foil, skin side down. Drizzle the orange juice over the flesh side of the salmon. Coat evenly with the olive oil, basil, dill, salt, and pepper. Lightly press the herb leaves into the flesh so they adhere.

3 • Place the salmon flesh side down (skin side up) on the grill (reserve the foil) and cook 6 to 8 minutes.

4 • Turn the salmon over and place it skin side down on the foil. Pour the remaining orange juice over the salmon. Put the salmon in the foil on the grates over the fire and cook uncovered 8 to 10 minutes longer, until the fish starts to flake but is still a little fleshy in the center. (Note: The fish will continue to cook as it rests.) Remove from the grill and let rest, loosely covered, for 3 to 4 minutes.

5 • Remove the skin and discard. Transfer the fish to a platter or serve portions on individual plates. Serve immediately, topped with chutney and fresh herb leaves.

Fresh Tomato-Orange Chutney

½ pint yellow pear tomatoes or
   cherry tomatoes, cut in half
½ pint red grape tomatoes or
   cherry tomatoes, cut in half
¼ cup olive oil
2 tablespoons balsamic vinegar
2 large navel oranges
4 scallions, trimmed and minced
2 tablespoons peeled, grated
   fresh ginger
Grated zest and juice of 1 lemon
1 jalapeño, seeded and minced
½ teaspoon mustard seeds
½ teaspoon fennel seeds
1 teaspoon cracked mixed
   peppercorns
5 or 6 fresh basil leaves, cut into
   very thin strips (chiffonade)
Salt and freshly ground black
   pepper to taste

1 • Preheat the oven to 400 degrees.

2 • Toss the yellow pear tomatoes and red grape toma-toes with 2 tablespoons of the olive oil and the vin-egar to coat evenly. Spread in a single layer on a baking pan and place in the oven to roast about 30 minutes. Remove from the oven and set aside.

3 • Grate the zest from the oranges and place the zest in a bowl. Trim the peel and the white pith from the oranges and discard. Cut the oranges into sections and add them to the bowl with the zest.

4 • Add the tomatoes, scallions, ginger, and the remain-ing olive oil, the lemon zest, lemon juice, jalapeño, mustard seeds, fennel seeds, peppercorns, basil, salt, and pepper in a bowl and stir to mix thoroughly. Re-frigerate in an airtight container until ready to use or up to 3 days.

Salmon Cakes with Crunchy Corn Relish

We serve this dish for brunch, lunch, and supper or as a first course. It's easy, fast, and a terrific way to use leftover salmon from last night's dinner. The Crunchy Corn Relish (page 193) can be made 3 or 4 days in advance and is delicious as an alternate sauce for Sautéed Soft-Shell Crabs (page 197) or Herb-Grilled Salmon (page 190). This recipe is also great made with crab instead of salmon.

MAKES ABOUT TWELVE 2½-INCH CAKES; SERVES 6

2 pounds cooked salmon (poached or grilled), cooled to room temperature

1 cup fresh bread crumbs (page 158)

½ cup Basil Mayonnaise (page 92), or good-quality mayonnaise mixed with ¼ cup finely chopped fresh basil

1 tablespoon Dijon mustard

2 large eggs

½ red onion, minced

3 scallions, trimmed and minced

1 jalapeño, seeded and minced

1 tablespoon chopped fresh basil

1 teaspoon chopped fresh dill

1 teaspoon hot sauce (such as Tabasco or Texas Pete)

1 teaspoon salt

½ teaspoon freshly ground black pepper

¼ cup canola or safflower oil

1 recipe Crunchy Corn Relish (recipe follows)

1 • Preheat the oven to 250 degrees.

2 • Carefully break up the salmon with a fork into large chunks in a large bowl. Add ½ cup of the bread crumbs, the mayonnaise, mustard, eggs, onion, scallions, jalapeño, basil, dill, hot sauce, salt, and pepper and stir just until mixed. Do not overmix; the salmon pieces should be bite-sized chunks, not fine flakes.

3 • Form the mixture into twelve 2½-inch cakes about 1½ inches thick. Coat both sides of the cakes lightly with the remaining bread crumbs, shaking off any excess crumbs.

4 • Heat the oil over medium-high heat in a large, non-stick skillet. Cook 6 to 8 salmon cakes at a time, about 3 minutes per side, turning only once, until light golden brown. Remove from the oil and place on a paper towel to drain. Transfer the cooked, drained cakes to a baking dish and place in the oven to keep warm while the remaining cakes cook. Serve immediately with Crunchy Corn Relish.

Crunchy Corn Relish

Kernels from 4 ears fresh corn
(2 cups fresh or frozen corn)

$1/2$ red onion, diced

$1/4$ cup dry white wine

3 tablespoons white wine vinegar

1 tablespoon peeled, julienned
fresh ginger

3 tablespoons fresh thyme or
1 tablespoon dried thyme

3 garlic cloves, minced

1 tablespoon pink peppercorns

2 teaspoons whole coriander
seeds

1 tablespoon sugar

2 bay leaves

1 green bell pepper, cored,
seeded, and diced

1 red bell pepper, cored, seeded,
and diced

7 scallions, trimmed and cut into
thinly sliced rounds

6 fresh basil leaves, cut into very
thin strips (chiffonade)

Salt and freshly ground black
pepper to taste

1 • Place the corn, onion, wine, vinegar, ginger, thyme, garlic, peppercorns, coriander, sugar, and bay leaves in a medium saucepan over low heat. Stir and cook about 10 minutes, until the seasonings are incorporated. Remove from the heat and set aside to cool.

2 • Meanwhile, in a separate bowl, combine the green bell pepper, red bell pepper, scallions, and basil in a large bowl and stir to mix.

3 • Add the corn mixture to the pepper mixture and stir to mix. Season with salt and pepper. Refrigerate in an airtight container until ready to use. Discard the bay leaves before serving.

Pan-Seared Sea Scallops with Tom Thumb Tomatoes and Foster's Pesto

We like Tom Thumb tomatoes in this recipe because of their crunchy texture and sugary-sweet taste, but you can use cherry tomatoes or grape tomatoes or a variety of small red and yellow tomatoes. If tomatoes and basil are not in season, try Cucumber-Lime Salsa (page 198) or Crunchy Corn Relish (page 193) with this dish instead. When cooking sea scallops, a nonstick skillet is better than a grill if you want a crispy, golden crust. When choosing scallops, look for those that are firm and translucent, slightly pinkish in color, with a mild aroma of the sea. These make a great first course or hors d'oeuvre topped with a small dollop of Foster's Pesto (page 90).

SERVES 4 TO 6

1½ pounds sea scallops (24 to 30 scallops)

3 tablespoons olive oil

1 tablespoon balsamic vinegar

6 fresh basil leaves, cut into very thin strips (chiffonade)

Freshly ground black pepper to taste

1 pint Tom Thumb tomatoes or cherry tomatoes or other small tomatoes, cut in half

Grated zest and juice of 2 limes

Salt to taste

½ cup Foster's Pesto (page 90)

8 to 10 fresh basil leaves, to garnish, optional

1 • Remove the small muscle on the sides of the scallops if necessary. Rinse the scallops and set aside to drain; pat dry. Place the scallops in a large bowl with the olive oil, vinegar, basil, and pepper. Toss to coat the scallops evenly.

2 • Heat a large, nonstick skillet over high heat until hot but not smoking. Add the scallops in 2 batches and sear about 1½ minutes per side, until golden brown and slightly crispy. (Note: The scallops will continue to cook after you remove them from the skillet, so be careful not to overcook.) Transfer the scallops to a plate, cover lightly, and keep warm while the remaining scallops are cooking.

3 • Add the tomatoes to the pan and sear slightly. Reduce heat to medium-high and cook for 2 to 3 minutes, until the tomatoes are lightly cooked and just beginning to turn brown. Add the lime zest and lime juice, and season with salt.

4 • Divide the tomato mixture onto 6 plates and top with 5 to 6 scallops and a dollop of pesto. Garnish with fresh basil leaves if desired. Serve immediately.

Mediterranean-Style Mussels with Toasted Focaccia

This robust dish can be served as a first course or as a main dish for a light, casual lunch or supper. The mussels can be scrubbed and cleaned a day in advance; the tomato-broth mixture can also be made a day ahead and reheated just before cooking the mussels. If you can't find focaccia, substitute good-quality, day-old country-style Italian bread.

SERVES 4 TO 6

2 leeks, trimmed and cut in half lengthwise

¼ cup plus 2 tablespoons olive oil

2 carrots, peeled and chopped

1 small fennel bulb, cored and thinly sliced

6 plum tomatoes, cored and chopped

8 garlic cloves, lightly smashed with the flat side of a knife

2½ cups dry white wine

2 cups fish broth (page 57) or bottled clam juice

4 bay leaves

1 teaspoon salt (omit if using clam juice)

1 teaspoon freshly ground black pepper

1 teaspoon red pepper flakes

3 to 4 pieces day-old focaccia, cut in half

3 pounds mussels, debearded and scrubbed

10 fresh basil leaves, cut into very thin strips (chiffonade)

⅓ cup chopped fresh parsley

1 • Preheat the oven to 400 degrees.

2 • Soak the leeks in a large bowl filled with cold water for about 10 minutes. Rinse, drain, and slice into ¼-inch half-rounds.

3 • Heat ¼ cup of the olive oil in a large, deep skillet or Dutch oven over medium-low heat. Add the leeks, carrots, fennel, and tomatoes and cook and stir about 15 minutes. (Note: Reduce the heat if the vegetables are browning too quickly.) Add the garlic and cook and stir 2 to 3 minutes longer.

4 • Add the wine, broth, bay leaves, salt, black pepper, and red pepper flakes; reduce heat and simmer about 15 minutes.

5 • Meanwhile, brush the focaccia with the remaining olive oil, place on a baking sheet, and toast in the oven 10 to 12 minutes, until golden brown and crusty. Remove from the oven and set aside.

6 • Increase heat to high for the skillet and add the mussels, basil, and parsley. Cover and cook until all the mussels are open, 3 to 4 minutes, stirring occasionally. (Note: So that the mussels don't overcook, remove them as soon as they open; place in a bowl and cover to keep warm as the remaining mussels cook and open.) Remove the skillet from the heat and discard any unopened mussels. Add the mussels you removed back to the pot to warm. Discard the bay leaves.

7 • Place 1 piece of toasted focaccia in the bottom of each bowl and ladle the mussels and liquid with vegetables over the focaccia. Serve immediately.

Sautéed Soft-Shell Crabs with Cucumber-Lime Salsa

Serve this dish when live soft-shell crabs (blue crabs that have shed their shells) are available, from April to mid-September.

SERVES 4

8 live soft-shell crabs

16 fresh basil leaves

$2/3$ cup all-purpose flour

$1/3$ cup yellow cornmeal

$1/2$ teaspoon ground red pepper (cayenne)

$1/2$ teaspoon salt

$1/2$ teaspoon freshly ground black pepper

$1/2$ cup canola or safflower oil

2 cups Cucumber-Lime Salsa (recipe follows)

2 lemons, cut into quarters

1 • Preheat the oven to 200 degrees.

2 • Clean the crabs by clipping the face right behind the eyes and tail flap. Pull up both sides of the top shell and remove the gills. Rinse well and pat dry. Place a basil leaf under each area where you removed the gills.

3 • Mix the flour and cornmeal in a bowl with the red pepper, salt, and black pepper. Dip each crab in the flour mixture and shake off any excess flour. Set aside.

4 • Heat half the oil in a large skillet over medium-high heat until very hot and a pinch of flour sizzles when dropped in the oil. Add the crabs 4 at a time and cook, uncovered, 2 to 3 minutes per side until golden brown. (Note: The oil has to be quite hot so the crabs will brown. However, be careful when turning the crabs, as the hot oil sometimes "pops.") Transfer the crabs to drain on a paper-towel-lined baking sheet, then place in the oven to keep warm while the others are cooking, adding the remaining olive oil as needed. Season with additional salt and pepper if desired.

5 • Spoon $1/2$ cup of the salsa onto each plate. Squeeze fresh lemon juice over each crab. Place 2 crabs on top of each of the pools of salsa, and serve immediately.

Cucumber-Lime Salsa

2 cups fresh cilantro (about 2
    bunches), washed and stems
    removed
7 scallions, trimmed and chopped
Juice of 2 limes
$1/4$ cup honey
1 tablespoon distilled white
    vinegar
1 teaspoon salt
$1/2$ teaspoon freshly ground black
    pepper
$1/3$ cup olive oil
2 cucumbers, peeled, seeded, and
    diced

1 • Place the cilantro, scallions, lime juice, honey, vinegar, salt, and pepper in the bowl of a food processor fitted with the metal blade and process on high speed until pureed.

2 • Slowly add the olive oil, with the motor running, until all the oil is incorporated. Remove from the bowl of the processor, place in a bowl with the cucumbers, and stir to blend. Refrigerate in an airtight container until ready to use or up to 1 day.

Provençal Fish Stew with Rouille

This soup is great served right from the pot when you have a large crowd. Offer a platter of Crostini (page 104) topped with rouille on the side, and let guests serve themselves. The soup base can be made several days in advance; add the fresh fish just before serving.

MAKES ABOUT 3 QUARTS STEW; SERVES 6 TO 8

¼ cup olive oil

1 red onion, chopped

2 leeks, trimmed and split lengthwise

½ fennel bulb, with 1 inch of fronds attached, halved lengthwise, cored, and thinly sliced

2 ribs celery, chopped

2 carrots, peeled and chopped

6 garlic cloves, peeled and smashed

One 28-ounce can whole tomatoes

8 cups fish broth (page 57)

1 cup dry white wine

2 teaspoons salt

1 teaspoon freshly ground black pepper

1 teaspoon dried marjoram

1 teaspoon red pepper flakes

Grated zest and juice of 2 oranges

One 2-pound red snapper or grouper, filleted (bones and head reserved)

1 pound mussels, scrubbed and debearded

12 small littleneck clams, cleaned

1 pound large shrimp, shells on

2 teaspoons saffron threads

2 tablespoons very thinly sliced basil leaves (chiffonade)

6 to 8 pieces Crostini (page 104)

1 cup Rouille (Spicy Red Pepper Sauce) (recipe follows)

1 • Heat 3 tablespoons of the olive oil in a Dutch oven or a large, heavy saucepan over medium heat. Add the onion; cook and stir about 10 minutes or until softened.

2 • Meanwhile, soak the leeks in a large bowl filled with cold water for about 10 minutes; rinse, drain, and slice into ¼-inch half-rounds. Add the leeks to the onion and cook and stir 5 minutes longer, until the leeks have softened.

3 • Add the fennel, celery, and carrots and cook and stir 10 minutes more. Add the garlic and cook 2 minutes longer, stirring occasionally.

4 • Add the tomatoes, broth, wine, salt, pepper, marjoram, and red pepper flakes. Reduce heat to low and simmer, uncovered, 50 minutes to 1 hour.

5 • Increase heat to medium-high and add the orange zest and juice, snapper, mussels, clams, shrimp, and saffron and stir to mix. Cook, stirring occasionally, 6 to 7 minutes, until all the clams and mussels have opened and the snapper begins to flake. Remove from the heat and sprinkle with the basil. Discard any clams or mussels that fail to open.

6 • Spoon a portion of the soup with some of each fish into individual serving bowls. Top each crostino with a dollop of rouille and place on top of each serving of soup. Serve immediately.

Rouille (Spicy Red Pepper Sauce)

2 thick slices light bread, such as
    sourdough, a French baguette,
    or crusty Italian bread

½ cup water

1 teaspoon red pepper flakes

1 roasted red bell pepper, peeled,
    cored, seeded, and chopped
    (page 40)

12 roasted garlic cloves (page 63)

1 tablespoon olive oil

2 teaspoons kosher salt

½ teaspoon freshly ground black
    pepper

1 • Place the bread and water in a bowl to soak for about 5 minutes. Squeeze the water from the bread; discard the water and place the bread in the bowl of a food processor fitted with the metal blade.

2 • Add the red pepper flakes, roasted red bell pepper, garlic, olive oil, salt, and pepper and puree until the mixture is a smooth paste.

3 • Refrigerate in an airtight container until ready to use or up to 1 week. Bring to room temperature before serving.

foster's old-fashioned favorites

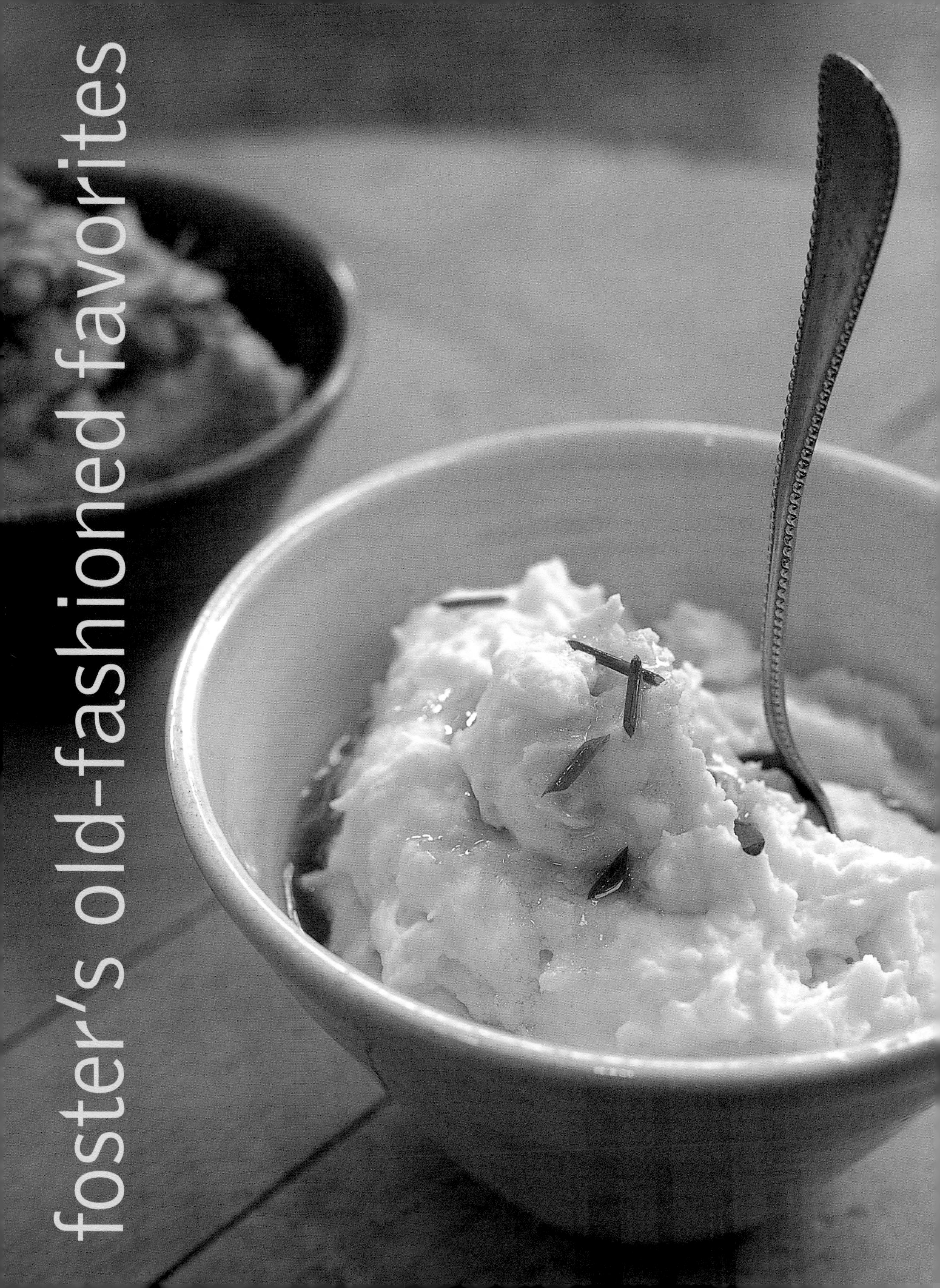

Chicken Potpie with Foster's Herb Biscuits • Chicken Chilaquiles with Spicy Tomatillo Salsa • Savory Black-Eyed Pea Cakes • Crispy Mashed Potato Cakes with Easy Applesauce • Grilled Portobello Mushrooms Stuffed with Parmesan Mashed Potatoes • Classic Mashed Potatoes • Creamy Corn Pudding with Roasted Red Pepper Sauce • Baked Capellini with Chicken and Four Cheeses • Grilled Eggplant Parmesan with Fresh Mozzarella and Zesty Tomato Sauce • Ratatouille Meat Loaf • Southwestern Shepherd's Pie with Chicken and Chili Mashed Potatoes • Potato Gratin with Tomatoes, Chèvre, and Thyme • Deep-Dish Roasted Tomato, Mushroom, and Caramelized Shallot Pie • Baked Potato Casserole Topped with Crispy Onion Rings • Foster's Seasonal Vegetable Plate • Risotto Cakes with Roasted Tomatoes and Foster's Arugula Pesto • Upscale Mac and Cheese • Squash Pudding with Roasted Tomato Vinaigrette

Chicken Potpie with Foster's Herb Biscuits

This dish can be made in advance and reheated. However, the topping—whether you use biscuits, phyllo, or puff pastry—is best if added the day you're serving it, since it tends to absorb the juices from the chicken mixture.

SERVES 8 TO 10

One 4- to 4¹/₂-pound chicken

1 recipe (uncooked) Old-Fashioned Buttermilk Biscuits with herb variation (page 17)

6 tablespoons (³/₄ stick) unsalted butter

4 carrots, peeled and chopped

4 ribs celery, chopped

8 ounces fresh button mushrooms, wiped clean and thinly sliced

¹/₄ cup all-purpose flour

5 cups chicken broth (use the reserved liquid from poaching the chicken)

One 10-ounce box frozen green peas or 2 cups cooked fresh green peas

1 tablespoon chopped fresh sage or 1 teaspoon dried sage

Salt and freshly ground black pepper to taste

Egg wash: 1 egg beaten with 2 tablespoons milk

1 • Preheat the oven to 375 degrees.

2 • Place the chicken in a large pot and add just enough water to cover by about 1 inch. Bring the water to a boil and reduce heat to low. Simmer about 45 minutes, or until the juices run clear when the thigh is pierced in the thickest part.

3 • Prepare the biscuits as the recipe directs, but do not bake them. Set aside.

4 • Remove the chicken from the pot and set aside until cool enough to handle. Reserve 5 cups of the cooking liquid and set aside.

5 • Melt the butter in a large skillet over medium-high heat and add the carrots, celery, and mushrooms. Cook, stirring frequently, about 10 minutes, until light brown.

6 • Add the flour and cook, stirring frequently, 3 to 4 minutes longer, until light brown. Slowly whisk in the broth and bring to a low boil, whisking constantly.

7 • Add the peas and sage. Season with salt and pepper and stir to mix. Reduce heat and simmer, stirring occasionally, 10 to 15 minutes or until thick and creamy.

8 • Remove the skin from the chicken and discard. Pull the meat off the bones in large chunks and stir the chicken into the vegetable mixture. Remove from the heat and transfer the mixture into a 9 by 13-inch baking dish.

9 • Top with the uncooked biscuits. Brush the biscuits with the egg wash and bake 25 to 30 minutes, until the biscuits are golden brown and the chicken mixture is bubbling around the edges. Serve immediately.

Chicken Chilaquiles with Spicy Tomatillo Salsa

Chilaquiles were originally created in Mexico to use up leftovers, but we came up with a dish that's really worth making whether you have leftover chicken or not. You can fry the tortillas in advance and make the salsa ahead, too.

SERVES 8 TO 10

Twelve 5$\frac{1}{2}$-inch corn tortillas, cut into pie-shaped quarters

$\frac{1}{4}$ cup canola or safflower oil

One 8-ounce can chopped green chilies (about 1 cup), drained

2 cups Spicy Tomatillo Salsa (recipe follows)

$\frac{1}{4}$ cup chopped fresh cilantro

7 scallions, trimmed and chopped

One 8-ounce package cream cheese, cut into $\frac{1}{2}$-inch cubes

$\frac{1}{4}$ cup drained, crumbled feta cheese

$\frac{1}{2}$ cup sour cream

$\frac{1}{2}$ cup heavy cream

1 teaspoon salt

1 teaspoon freshly ground black pepper

4 cups shredded cooked chicken (page 58)

1$\frac{1}{2}$ cups (6 ounces) grated Monterey Jack cheese

1$\frac{1}{2}$ cups (6 ounces) grated Cheddar cheese

1 • Preheat the oven to 350 degrees.

2 • Arrange the tortillas in a single layer on 2 large baking sheets. Brush the tortillas lightly with the oil and bake 8 to 10 minutes, until crisp and very light brown.

3 • Stir together the chilies, salsa, cilantro, scallions, cream cheese, feta, sour cream, heavy cream, salt, and pepper in a large bowl until well combined. Fold in the chicken and mix well.

4 • Combine the Monterey Jack and Cheddar together in a separate bowl.

5 • Arrange half the tortillas in the bottom of a 9 by 13-inch baking dish. Spread half the chicken mixture over the tortillas. Sprinkle half the cheese over the chicken mixture.

6 • Arrange the remaining tortillas over the cheese mixture, spread with the remaining chicken mixture, and top with the remaining cheese mixture.

7 • Bake, uncovered, 30 to 35 minutes, until the mixture is bubbling around the sides and the cheese is golden brown. Serve immediately.

Spicy Tomatillo Salsa

1 pound fresh tomatillos, husked
    and rinsed
4 fresh serrano chilies, stemmed
$1/4$ cup olive oil
$1/2$ cup vegetable broth (page 56) or
    water, if needed

1 • Preheat the oven to 500 degrees.

2 • Toss the tomatillos and chilies with the olive oil and place on a baking sheet. Bake 15 to 20 minutes, until the tomatillos have softened and have begun to split open.

3 • Place the tomatillos in the bowl of a food processor fitted with the metal blade and pulse to a coarse puree. Add the chilies and pulse several times more. The puree should be the consistency of a thin salsa. If necessary, thin with a small amount of broth.

variations: The chilaquiles are great with the addition of almost any bean—try black beans, navy beans, kidney, or pinto. You can substitute shredded cooked beef, pork, or turkey for the chicken. Foster's Salsa (page 90) can be used instead of the Spicy Tomatillo Salsa. If you don't want to cook your own tortillas, use purchased tortilla chips instead. Try this dish with different kinds of peppers—it's particularly good with poblanos—and if you want something less spicy, replace the serranos with bell peppers.

Tomatillos

This fruit looks like a small green tomato with a thin, papery husk. Its tart flavor is a welcome addition to southwestern fare, especially in salsas. Sauces and salsas made with tomatillos are a nice accompaniment to simply prepared fish, complementing the fish as a squeeze of fresh lemon would.

Savory Black-Eyed Pea Cakes

We serve these as a vegetarian entrée, as an hors d'oeuvre topped with Foster's Salsa (page 90) or Granny Foster's Chili Sauce (page 43), or as a side dish to Wine-Braised Boneless Turkey Breast with Sage and Thyme (page 168) or Roast Pork Tenderloin with Dried Cherries and Rosemary (page 186). At Foster's, we use frozen black-eyed peas since they're available all year round and they taste terrific. Since black-eyed peas are traditionally served on New Year's Day for good luck, this makes a festive party dish to celebrate January 1.

MAKES NINE 3-INCH CAKES

4 cups fresh or frozen black-eyed
  peas
1 red onion, diced
1/2 red bell pepper, cored, seeded,
  and diced
1 jalapeño, seeded and diced
1 cup (4 ounces) grated Parmesan
  cheese
2 large eggs
2 tablespoons all-purpose flour
2 garlic cloves, minced
1 tablespoon chopped fresh
  oregano or 1 teaspoon dried
  oregano
1 teaspoon salt
1 teaspoon freshly ground black
  pepper
1/4 cup chopped fresh parsley
2 1/2 cups fresh bread crumbs
  (page 158)
1/3 cup canola or safflower oil

1 • Place the peas in a saucepan and cover with water by 2 inches. Bring to a boil and reduce heat to medium-low. Cook, uncovered, 30 to 40 minutes, until the peas are tender but still holding their shape.

2 • Preheat the oven to 300 degrees.

3 • Drain the peas and divide in half. Mix half the peas in a large bowl with the onion, red bell pepper, jalapeño, Parmesan, eggs, flour, garlic, oregano, salt, pepper, parsley, and 1 cup of the bread crumbs. Mash with a potato masher until well blended.

4 • Fold in the reserved peas and mix thoroughly. Scoop out about 1/2 cup of the mixture and form into 3-inch cakes 1/2 inch thick. Repeat, to make 9 or 10 cakes.

5 • Dip each cake into the remaining bread crumbs to coat both sides. Shake off any excess bread crumbs.

6 • Heat half the oil in a large, nonstick skillet over medium-high heat and cook 6 to 8 of the cakes at a time (do not crowd the skillet), uncovered, 4 to 5 minutes per side or until light golden brown and crispy on the outside. (Note: Turn the cakes only once; if you turn them too often, they will fall apart. If the cakes are browning too quickly, reduce heat slightly.)

7 • Drain on paper towels. Place on a baking sheet and keep warm in the oven while the remaining cakes are cooking. Add the remaining oil to the skillet and

cook the remaining cakes. Serve immediately topped with Foster's Salsa (page 90), Granny Foster's Chili Sauce (page 43), or Foster's Seven Pepper Jelly.

variations: For creamier cakes, use a mild, creamy chèvre—such as Montrachet—instead of Parmesan cheese. If you like spicy food, choose hot peppers such as jalapeño or serrano instead of milder bell peppers or banana peppers.

Peppers: Hot, Medium, and Mild

bell peppers Although green peppers will eventually turn red if left on the vine, some varieties of bell peppers are grown for their colors, such as the yellow, orange, and purple ones. Red, yellow, and orange peppers are milder than the green and purple varieties, which are slightly more assertive.

italian sweet peppers These long, mild green peppers are often grilled or sautéed.

banana peppers Pale yellow in color, these mild, sweet peppers are about 5 inches long and are enjoyed raw, grilled, roasted, or sautéed.

jalapeños These hot green or red peppers can be used whole, or remove the seeds and veins, which eliminates some of the heat.

poblano peppers Available fresh, canned, and dried (dried poblanos are known as ancho chilies), these peppers range in color from green to red—red poblanos are sweeter than the green. Poblanos can be mild or somewhat hot.

habanero peppers An extremely hot pepper, habaneros are available fresh and dried and range in color from light green to bright orange.

serrano peppers A very hot pepper that can be found in specialty stores fresh, dried, canned, pickled, or packed in oil.

Crispy Mashed Potato Cakes with Easy Applesauce

Crunchy on the outside and soft on the inside, these savory cakes are a terrific way to use up leftover mashed potatoes. They can be made several hours before serving (just reheat in a 400-degree oven for 5 to 7 minutes) and everyone loves them—especially kids. At the Market, we recommend them as a side dish to Chicken Marsala with Oven-Roasted Mushrooms and Onions (page 159) or Balsamic-Roasted Chicken (page 154). The spicy homemade applesauce is really easy, too, and is also great with Roast Pork Tenderloin with Dried Cherries and Rosemary (page 186).

MAKES SIX 4-INCH CAKES

3 pounds russet potatoes, peeled and halved

6 tablespoons (¾ stick) unsalted butter

⅓ cup milk

⅓ cup grated Parmesan cheese

1 teaspoon salt

½ teaspoon freshly ground black pepper

¾ cup fresh bread crumbs (page 158)

1 large egg

2 scallions, trimmed and minced

2 tablespoons chopped fresh parsley

3 tablespoons all-purpose flour

⅓ cup canola or safflower oil

1 cup Easy Applesauce (recipe follows)

1 • Place the potatoes in a large saucepan and add cold water to cover by 2 inches. Bring to a low boil and cook, uncovered, 25 to 30 minutes or until tender when pierced with the tip of a sharp knife.

2 • Drain the potatoes, return them to the saucepan, and add the butter, milk, and Parmesan. Season with salt and pepper and mash with a potato masher until smooth. Set aside to cool slightly. (Note: The cakes stay together better if the potatoes aren't hot, so you can cook the potatoes ahead of time—even the day before.)

3 • Add half the bread crumbs, egg, scallions, and parsley to the potato mixture and stir to mix.

4 • Form about ½ cup of the potato mixture (you can use a large ice cream scoop) into 4-inch cakes about ½ inch thick.

5 • Mix the remaining bread crumbs and flour in a bowl. Coat both sides of each cake with the bread crumb mixture.

6 • Heat the oil in a large, nonstick skillet over medium-high heat until the oil is hot enough to sizzle when you drop in a small amount of the flour–bread crumb mixture. Cook the potato cakes in the oil 4 to 5 minutes per side, until light brown and crispy. (Note: During the cooking process, you may need to lower the heat or add more oil; you want just enough oil to cover the bottom of the pan.) Serve hot with Easy Applesauce.

variations: Top the cakes with a small dollop of applesauce or caviar, then top with chèvre or crème fraîche. Or omit the applesauce and drizzle with Chive Oil (page 215). To serve as an appetizer, form the cakes into 2-inch rounds. Try Yukon gold potatoes for a slightly different flavor and color. Use different herbs or add spinach or peas.

Easy Applesauce

This spicy applesauce keeps in the refrigerator for up to 1 month.

MAKES ABOUT 5 CUPS APPLESAUCE

4 pounds Granny Smith or other tart apples, peeled, cored, and chopped

1½ cups sugar

½ cup apple juice or water

Juice of 1 lemon

1 tablespoon ground cinnamon

½ teaspoon ground cloves

1 • Place the apples in a heavy saucepan with the sugar, apple juice, and lemon juice.

2 • Cook over medium-high heat about 10 minutes, uncovered, stirring frequently, until the sugar begins to dissolve and the apples begin to break up.

3 • Add the cinnamon and cloves. Stir and cook about 5 minutes more. Refrigerate in an airtight container until ready to use or up to 1 month.

Grilled Portobello Mushrooms Stuffed with Parmesan Mashed Potatoes

This easy, make-ahead dish can be served as a vegetarian main course with a side dish of Balsamic-Roasted Vegetables (page 113). Or serve as a side dish for Chicken Breasts Stuffed with Prosciutto and Sun-Dried Tomatoes (page 162) or Braised Chicken Thighs with Chèvre Stuffing (page 155). When choosing portobello mushrooms, look for those that have a pleasant, earthy scent and are firm to the touch. Be sure to check the gills, which should not be wet.

SERVES 8

Safflower oil or canola oil, for oiling the grill

1 recipe Classic Mashed Potatoes (page 214)

¼ cup olive oil

2 tablespoons balsamic vinegar

8 portobello mushroom caps, cleaned and stems removed (reserve stems for another use)

1 teaspoon salt

½ teaspoon freshly ground black pepper

1 cup sour cream

¼ cup grated Parmesan cheese

2 scallions, trimmed and chopped

1 • Brush the grill grates lightly with the safflower oil. Prepare a hot fire in a gas or charcoal grill.

2 • Preheat the oven to 400 degrees.

3 • Prepare the potatoes as the recipe directs.

4 • Mix the olive oil and vinegar together in a small bowl. Brush the mushrooms with the olive oil mixture, then sprinkle with the salt and pepper.

5 • Place the mushrooms on the hot grill and cook 2 to 3 minutes on each side or until lightly grilled but still firm. Transfer the mushrooms to a baking dish gill side up.

6 • Add the sour cream and Parmesan to the potatoes and stir to mix.

7 • Fill each mushroom cap with ½ to ¾ cup of the potato mixture. Top with the scallions and place in the oven to bake for 10 to 15 minutes or until the potato mixture is heated through and puffy.

variations: Chopped, lightly wilted spinach (page 213) can be folded into the potato filling before cooking. For a more rustic dish, use red-skinned potatoes and leave the skin on before mashing. To cook the mushrooms indoors, place them gill side up on a lightly oiled baking pan and roast, uncovered, in a preheated 400-degree oven for 12 to 15 minutes or until the caps are slightly crispy around the edges.

Wilted Spinach

This fast, easy dish can be used as a bed or side dish for grilled chicken, meat, or fish. Or chop wilted spinach and toss with cooked pasta, olive oil, and chopped garlic. To wilt spinach, heat olive oil in a large skillet over high heat. Add fresh, cleaned, stemmed spinach and toss in the oil 1 to 2 minutes or just until wilted. Remove the spinach from the skillet immediately or it will overcook. For extra flavor, you can add freshly squeezed lemon juice to taste or a sprinkle of grated Parmesan cheese.

Classic Mashed Potatoes

There's nothing more comforting than honest-to-goodness, homemade mashed potatoes, enriched with butter and whole milk. This recipe is a favorite at Foster's and at my own table, as well. Try them alongside Salmon Cakes with Crunchy Corn Relish (page 192) or Braised Short Ribs with Roasted Root Vegetable Puree (page 171) or as a "bed" for Braised Fillet of Beef with Roasted Tomatoes and Mushrooms (page 169) or Sautéed Soft-Shell Crabs (page 197). These creamy mashed potatoes can also be scooped into individual soup bowls, and then topped with hot Chicken, Leek, and Fennel Soup (page 61) or Fiery Three-Bean Chili (page 75).

SERVES 8 TO 10

4 pounds russet potatoes, peeled and cut in half (about 6 potatoes)

8 tablespoons (1 stick) unsalted butter, cut into chunks

¾ cup whole milk

Salt and freshly ground black pepper to taste

Chive Oil (recipe follows)

1 • Place the potatoes in a large saucepan and add enough cold water to cover by 2 inches. Bring to a low boil and cook, uncovered, 25 to 30 minutes, until the potatoes are tender when pierced with the tip of a sharp knife.

2 • Drain the potatoes and return them to the saucepan while still warm. Add the butter and milk and mash with a potato masher until all the butter and milk are incorporated and the potatoes are creamy. (Note: If you like smooth mashed potatoes, use an electric hand mixer instead of a masher and beat until smooth.) Season with salt and pepper; drizzle with Chive Oil, and serve immediately.

variations: For low-fat mashed potatoes, omit the butter and add just enough skim milk, plain yogurt, or buttermilk, plus a few teaspoons of olive oil, to reach the desired consistency. Either way—classic or low-fat—the potatoes can be flavored with blue cheese; pureed roasted garlic; Parmesan cheese; chopped caramelized onions; cooked, crumbled bacon; or chopped fresh herbs. Different types of potatoes can also be used: try Yukon gold, new potatoes (with or without the peel), or peeled sweet potatoes.

Chive Oil

1 cup chopped fresh chives
½ cup chopped fresh parsley
1 cup olive oil
1 teaspoon salt

1 • Place the chives, parsley, oil, and salt in the container of a blender and blend at high speed for about 3 to 4 minutes, until completely pureed.

2 • Strain the mixture through a sieve, pressing with the back of a wooden spoon to remove all the fibrous threads of the chives.

3 • Refrigerate in an airtight container until ready to use. Remove from the refrigerator 1 hour before serving and shake to blend thoroughly.

Creamy Corn Pudding with Roasted Red Pepper Sauce

This light, gentle side dish is delicious with Slow-Roasted Pork Roast with Sweet and Spicy Horseradish Sauce (page 183).

SERVES 6 TO 8

1 tablespoon unsalted butter, softened

Kernels from 3 ears fresh corn (1½ cups fresh or frozen corn)

2 scallions, trimmed and minced

½ red bell pepper, cored, seeded, and diced

1 jalapeño, seeded and minced

1 tablespoon yellow cornmeal

2 tablespoons sugar

2 teaspoons chopped fresh marjoram or basil or ½ heaping teaspoon dried marjoram or basil

2 teaspoons salt

1 teaspoon freshly ground black pepper

1 cup half-and-half

5 large eggs, beaten

1 cup (4 ounces) grated sharp Cheddar cheese

1 cup Roasted Red Pepper Sauce (recipe follows)

1 • Preheat the oven to 350 degrees.

2 • Rub the butter on the bottom and sides of a 3-quart soufflé dish or deep casserole dish.

3 • Combine the corn, scallions, red bell pepper, jalapeño, cornmeal, sugar, marjoram, salt, and pepper in a large bowl and stir to mix.

4 • Whisk the half-and-half and eggs together in a separate bowl; stir in the cheese. Mix the egg mixture with the corn mixture, and stir to combine. Pour the mixture into the prepared soufflé dish and bake 55 minutes to 1 hour, or until puffy and light golden brown. (Note: The pudding will be very moist and soft in the center.)

5 • Remove from the oven and let stand at room temperature 5 to 10 minutes before serving. Serve warm with Roasted Red Pepper Sauce.

variations: Use diced, sautéed summer squash in place of the corn. Use pepper Jack cheese instead of Cheddar for a spicier flavor. Or substitute chèvre or cream cheese for a milder taste.

Roasted Red Pepper Sauce

2 roasted red bell peppers,
    peeled, cored, and seeded
    (page 40)
3 garlic cloves, chopped
6 fresh basil leaves
¼ cup olive oil
1 tablespoon white wine vinegar
1 tablespoon lemon juice
Salt and freshly ground black
    pepper to taste

1 • Place the roasted red bell peppers, garlic, and basil in the bowl of a food processor fitted with the metal blade and puree until smooth, about 1 minute.

2 • Slowly add the olive oil down the feed tube, with the motor running, until all the oil is incorporated. Add the vinegar and lemon juice and process until combined. Season with salt and pepper and refrigerate in an airtight container until ready to use or up to 1 week.

FOSTER'S OLD-FASHIONED FAVORITES | 217

Baked Capellini with Chicken and Four Cheeses

Created by my sister, Judy Edwards, this creamy, comforting dish can be made ahead and reheated, so it's great for serving a crowd, especially a crowd with kids.

SERVES 8 TO 10

One 4$\frac{1}{2}$- to 5-pound chicken or 4 cups shredded cooked chicken (page 58)

8 ounces capellini or spaghetti

1 tablespoon olive oil

6 tablespoons ($\frac{3}{4}$ stick) unsalted butter

1 yellow onion, chopped

1 green or red bell pepper, cored, seeded, and diced

2 jalapeños, seeded and minced

4 ribs celery, chopped

8 ounces button mushrooms, wiped clean and stems removed

$\frac{1}{4}$ cup all-purpose flour

2 cups chicken broth (reserved from cooking the chicken, or use canned or homemade broth if substituting cooked chicken)

One 14-ounce can (about 2 cups) chopped tomatoes

1 cup (4 ounces) grated Italian Fontina cheese

$\frac{1}{2}$ cup grated mozzarella cheese

$\frac{1}{2}$ cup grated provolone cheese

1 tablespoon chopped fresh parsley

1 teaspoon red pepper flakes

1 tablespoon salt

1 teaspoon freshly ground black pepper

1 cup (4 ounces) grated Parmesan cheese

1 • Place the chicken in a large pot and cover with water. Bring to a boil, reduce heat, and simmer 45 minutes to 1 hour or until the juices run clear when a thigh is pierced in the thickest part. Remove the chicken from the liquid (reserve the liquid) and cool to room temperature.

2 • Remove 2 cups of the chicken broth from the pot and set aside. (Reserve the remaining broth for another use.)

3 • Preheat the oven to 350 degrees.

4 • Grease a 9 by 13-inch glass baking dish and set aside.

5 • Prepare the capellini according to package directions until al dente. Rinse, drain, and toss in a colander with the olive oil and set aside to drain.

6 • Remove the chicken meat from the bones and set aside. Discard the skin and reserve the bones for stock or soup, if desired. Shred the chicken into bite-sized pieces.

7 • Melt the butter over medium-high heat in a skillet and add the onion, bell pepper, jalapeños, celery, and mushrooms. Cook and stir 4 to 5 minutes, until the vegetables are soft. Add the flour and reduce heat to low; cook about 3 minutes longer, stirring constantly.

8 • Add the 2 cups of reserved chicken broth and stir constantly until the liquid comes to a boil and is thick enough to coat the back of a wooden spoon, about 1 minute.

9 • Add the tomatoes, Fontina, mozzarella, provolone, parsley, red pepper flakes, salt, and pepper and remove from the heat.

10 • Add the chicken and capellini to the sauce mixture

and toss just to blend; do not overmix or the capellini will break.

11 • Pour the mixture into the baking dish and bake, uncovered, 25 to 30 minutes, or until bubbling around the edges and golden brown on top. Sprinkle with the Parmesan and serve immediately.

variations: Although at Foster's we use a blend of Italian cheeses, like Fontina, mozzarella, provolone, and Parmesan, if you're making this for children (or for die-hard traditionalists), try it with 16 ounces of Velveeta in place of the Fontina, mozzarella, and provolone. This is also great with different types of pasta.

Grilled Eggplant Parmesan with Fresh Mozzarella and Zesty Tomato Sauce

I prefer this version of eggplant Parmesan to the traditional recipe because this variation is much lighter and the flavors are more defined than the classic fried eggplant Parmesan. Although this is a hearty vegetarian main course, it's also good as a side dish with Balsamic-Roasted Chicken (page 154) or Pesto Chicken Salad (page 127). This dish is best served soon after you make it, at room temperature. However, the eggplant and sauce can be prepared 1 day in advance and you can assemble the dish and reheat it just before serving.

SERVES 6

Safflower oil or canola oil, for oiling the grill

4 tomatoes, cored and cut into 1/2-inch-thick rounds

2 eggplants, cut into 1/2-inch-thick rounds

1/2 cup olive oil

2 garlic cloves, minced

2 tablespoons balsamic vinegar

2 tablespoons basil leaves, cut into very thin strips (chiffonade)

3 cups Zesty Tomato Sauce (recipe follows)

1 cup (4 ounces) grated Parmesan cheese

1/2 pound fresh mozzarella cheese, sliced into 1/4-inch-thick rounds

1/2 cup julienned roasted red bell peppers (page 40)

Salt and freshly ground black pepper to taste

Fresh basil leaves, to garnish, optional

1 • Brush the grill grates lightly with the safflower oil. Prepare a hot fire in a gas or charcoal grill. The coals should be red and glowing.

2 • Place the sliced tomatoes and eggplants on a baking sheet.

3 • Combine the olive oil, garlic, vinegar, and 1 tablespoon of the basil in a bowl and stir until blended. Brush the eggplant and tomatoes on both sides with a generous amount of this mixture.

4 • Grill the tomatoes 1 to 2 minutes per side. (You just want to flavor them; don't overcook them or they'll begin to fall apart.) Remove the tomatoes from the grill and set aside.

5 • Grill the eggplant until tender and slightly brown, 4 to 5 minutes on each side. Remove from the grill and set aside. (Note: The exact cooking times will depend on the heat of the fire.)

6 • Spoon enough tomato sauce on the bottom of a baking dish or onto individual serving plates to cover the bottom of the dish or plate in a thin layer.

7 • Make "stacks" by beginning with the largest slices of ingredients and working up to the smaller slices. Place a layer of eggplant on the tomato sauce, and then add a slice of tomato. Sprinkle with some of the Parmesan, then top with a slice of mozzarella, another slice of tomato, a slice of eggplant, several slices of roasted red pepper, another slice of mozzarella, another slice of tomato, and about 1/4 cup of the tomato sauce. Top with 4 or 5 pieces of roasted

eggplant

red bell pepper, a sprinkle of Parmesan, and salt and pepper. Garnish with the remaining basil chiffonade and basil leaves if desired. Repeat until you have 6 stacks. Any additional tomato sauce can be served on the side. Any additional vegetables can be chopped and used to garnish the top. Serve at room temperature or slightly warm.

variation: Substitute mild chèvre for the mozzarella to give a slightly different flavor. Use other grilled vegetables—such as zucchini or yellow squash—instead of eggplant.

Zesty Tomato Sauce

MAKES ABOUT 4 CUPS SAUCE

2 tablespoons olive oil

1 red onion, diced

2 garlic cloves, minced

$\frac{1}{4}$ cup balsamic vinegar

$\frac{1}{2}$ cup dry red wine

One 28-ounce can chopped
   tomatoes

2 tablespoons chopped fresh
   marjoram or oregano or
   2 teaspoons dried marjoram
   or oregano

Salt and freshly ground black
   pepper to taste

1 • Heat the oil in a saucepan over medium heat. Add the onion and cook, stirring occasionally, for 3 minutes or until softened.

2 • Add the garlic and cook 2 minutes more, stirring constantly.

3 • Add the vinegar and wine and simmer rapidly, uncovered, stirring occasionally, 3 to 4 minutes, until the liquid is reduced by half. Add the tomatoes with their juices, reduce heat to low, and continue to simmer, stirring occasionally, until thickened, about 20 minutes.

4 • Remove from the heat. Add the marjoram, salt, and pepper. Refrigerate in an airtight container until ready to serve.

Ratatouille Meat Loaf

Foster's Grilled Vegetable Ratatouille (page 124) is made with diced, grilled vegetables, so the vegetables are crisp-tender, not soft like traditional ratatouille. When grilled rata-touille is added to meat loaf, the result is a visually appealing "confetti" effect. The rata-touille can also be served alongside the meat loaf as a sauce and makes good use of leftover grilled eggplant, peppers, and tomatoes from last night's dinner. A layer of mozzarella in the meat loaf's center makes a delicious surprise.

SERVES 6 TO 8

2 pounds ground chuck or ground turkey

1½ cups Grilled Vegetable Ratatouille (page 124)

½ cup ketchup

2 large eggs

1 cup fresh bread crumbs (page 158)

1 teaspoon dried marjoram

1½ teaspoons salt

1 teaspoon freshly ground black pepper

4 ounces mozzarella cheese, cut into ¼-inch-thick rounds

1 roasted red bell pepper, peeled, cored, seeded, and julienned (page 40)

1 • Preheat the oven to 350 degrees.

2 • Combine the ground beef, ratatouille, ketchup, eggs, bread crumbs, marjoram, salt, and pepper in a large bowl and stir to mix until thoroughly combined.

3 • Pack half the mixture into a lightly greased 9 by 5 by 3-inch loaf pan. Place a layer of mozzarella on top of the mixture, keeping the cheese in the center of the loaf. Place the roasted pepper down the center of the cheese and top with another layer of cheese. Place the remaining ground beef mixture on top of the cheese and pack firmly. Tap the pan on the counter several times to settle the mixture.

4 • Bake 50 to 55 minutes, uncovered, until the juices run clear and the top of the meat loaf is brown.

5 • Remove from the oven and carefully pour off the drippings in the pan. Let the meat loaf rest 15 to 20 minutes before turning out of the pan and slicing. Slice into 1-inch slices and serve warm topped with additional Grilled Vegetable Ratatouille or Zesty To-mato Sauce (page 222).

variations: Use smoked mozzarella instead of fresh mozzarella. If you don't have time to make the ratatouille, use a mixture of lightly sautéed diced eggplant, peppers, and zucchini.

Southwestern Shepherd's Pie with Chicken and Chili Mashed Potatoes

This dish is homey and economical. The filling can be prepared a day in advance, then warmed before topping it with the potatoes. The chili mashed potatoes also make a delicious side dish for a grilled steak.

SERVES 8 TO 10

3 tablespoons olive oil

2 tablespoons unsalted butter

1 red onion, diced

2 ribs celery, diced

1 red bell pepper, cored, seeded, and diced

1 green bell pepper, cored, seeded, and diced

3 garlic cloves, minced

1 jalapeño, seeded and minced

$1/4$ cup all-purpose flour

8 cups shredded cooked, chicken (page 58)

$3/4$ cup dry white wine

3 cups chicken broth (page 57)

$1/4$ cup chopped fresh parsley

2 teaspoons chopped fresh thyme or $1/2$ heaping teaspoon dried thyme

1 teaspoon red pepper flakes

Kernels from 2 ears fresh corn (1 cup fresh or frozen corn)

Salt and freshly ground black pepper to taste

1 recipe Classic Mashed Potatoes (page 214)

2 teaspoons chili powder

Fresh parsley and fresh thyme, to garnish, optional

1 • Preheat the oven to 400 degrees.

2 • Heat the olive oil and butter in a large skillet over medium heat. Add the onion and cook, stirring frequently, until slightly brown, about 5 minutes. Add the celery, red bell pepper, and green bell pepper and cook 3 minutes more, stirring occasionally. Add the garlic and jalapeño and cook 3 minutes more, stirring occasionally.

3 • Add the flour and cook, stirring constantly, until the flour starts to brown slightly, about 5 minutes. Add the chicken and wine and stir until the wine begins to evaporate, about 1 minute. Slowly add the chicken broth, and continue to cook, stirring frequently, until the mixture begins to thicken and coats the back of a spoon. Reduce heat to low, bring the mixture to a low boil, and cook 5 to 10 minutes or until the mixture thickens and is creamy.

4 • Remove from the heat and add the parsley, thyme, red pepper flakes, and corn. Season with salt and pepper, and transfer the mixture to a 9 by 13-inch baking dish.

5 • To make the chili mashed potatoes, mix Classic Mashed Potatoes with 1 teaspoon of the chili powder in a bowl until well combined.

6 • Spoon the chili mashed potatoes on top of the chicken and bake 20 to 30 minutes or until the potato peaks are slightly brown and the chicken mixture is bubbling around the sides of the dish. Remove from the oven, sprinkle with the remaining chili powder and the parsley and thyme, if desired. Serve immediately.

variations: For a more traditional shepherd's pie, eliminate the southwestern spices and add diced, sautéed celery and chopped, cooked spinach to the filling mixture. The chili mashed potato topping can be made with any kind of potato; try Yukon gold potatoes or sweet potatoes for a particularly buttery taste and texture. You can also try cooked lamb or beef in place of the chicken.

Potato Gratin with Tomatoes, Chèvre, and Thyme

A lighter variation of the classic French potato gratin, this flavorful side dish (or first course) reheats beautifully. Try it with Balsamic-Roasted Chicken (page 154) or Cajun-Cut Rib Eye Steak (page 173).

SERVES 10 TO 12

8 tablespoons (1 stick) unsalted butter, melted

8 Yukon gold or russet potatoes, peeled

Salt and freshly ground black pepper to taste

3 tablespoons fresh thyme or 3 teaspoons dried thyme

2 cups (8 ounces) crumbled chèvre

1 cup (4 ounces) grated Parmesan cheese

1 tomato, cored and thinly sliced into 1/4-inch rounds

2 cups half-and-half or whole milk or heavy cream

1 cup fresh bread crumbs (page 158)

variation: Any type of potato and just about any type of cheese that melts well or semisoft cheese can be used for this dish. Try sweet potatoes, blue cheese, Monterey Jack, Swiss, Gruyère, or Cheddar. Eliminate the tomatoes, if desired. If you prefer a richer, more traditional gratin, substitute heavy cream for the half-and-half.

1 • Preheat the oven to 400 degrees.

2 • Brush the bottom and sides of a 9 by 13-inch baking dish with 2 tablespoons of the melted butter.

3 • Slice 2 of the potatoes as thinly as possible, about 1/8 inch thick. Arrange a layer of potatoes on the bottom of the baking dish. Top with a second layer of potatoes. (Note: It is best to slice the potatoes as needed per layer because the starch in the potatoes helps hold the layers together.) Brush lightly with a portion of the melted butter, sprinkle with salt and pepper, about 2 teaspoons of the thyme, 2 tablespoons of the chèvre, and 1/3 cup of the Parmesan.

4 • Slice and add 2 more layers of potatoes, brush with a portion of the melted butter, sprinkle with salt and pepper, about 2 teaspoons of the thyme, 2 tablespoons chèvre, and 1/3 cup of the Parmesan.

5 • Add a single layer of tomatoes and top with 2 tablespoons of the chèvre, 1/3 cup of the Parmesan, about 2 teaspoons of the thyme, and salt and pepper.

6 • Continue this process with 2 more layers of potatoes. Press the potatoes firmly with the palm of your hand to pack all the ingredients together. Brush with some of the melted butter, sprinkle with the remaining thyme, salt, pepper, and the remaining crumbled chèvre.

7 • Pour the half-and-half over the potatoes and top with the bread crumbs. Sprinkle with the remaining butter and bake, covered, 45 to 50 minutes. Uncover and bake 30 to 40 minutes longer, until the gratin is bubbling and golden on top and the potatoes are soft when pierced with the tip of a sharp knife. Let rest 10 to 15 minutes before serving. Serve warm.

Deep-Dish Roasted Tomato, Mushroom, and Caramelized Shallot Pie

This savory pie is one that our customers love to take home and serve for Sunday brunch or as part of a buffet, or to take to a potluck supper.

SERVES 8 TO 10

Crust

4 cups all-purpose flour

2 teaspoons salt

1/2 pound (2 sticks) cold, unsalted butter, cut into small pieces

3/4 cup ice cold water

1 • Place the flour and salt in the bowl of a food processor fitted with the metal blade. Add the butter and pulse 10 to 12 times, until the mixture resembles coarse cornmeal.

2 • Add the water slowly, about 1/4 cup at a time (you may not need all the water), as you pulse 3 to 4 more times, until the mixture just begins to cling together.

3 • Remove the dough from the bowl and place on a lightly floured work surface. Knead the dough several times just until it comes together. Do not overwork the dough. Divide the dough into 2 equal pieces and pat each piece into a flat rectangle. Wrap in plastic wrap and refrigerate several hours or overnight.

4 • Let the dough rest at room temperature 10 to 15 minutes. Roll each piece on a lightly floured surface into a 9 by 13-inch rectangle about 1/8 inch thick. Place 1 piece of the rolled-out dough in a 9 by 13-inch baking dish and press into the bottom and up the sides of the dish. Place the other piece on a baking sheet. Cover both with plastic wrap and refrigerate a minimum of 2 hours or overnight.

- -

Filling

8 plum tomatoes, cored and cut in half lengthwise

6 shallots, thinly sliced

1/4 cup olive oil

2 tablespoons balsamic vinegar

1 pound cremini or shiitake mushrooms, cleaned and thinly sliced

1 • Preheat the oven to 400 degrees.

2 • Toss the tomatoes and shallots with 2 tablespoons of the olive oil and the vinegar in a bowl. Transfer to a baking pan and spread the mixture out in a single, even layer. Cook 20 to 25 minutes, until the tomato skins start to shrivel. Remove from the oven and set aside.

3 • Heat the remaining olive oil in a skillet over medium-

1 cup ricotta cheese

1 cup (4 ounces) grated
mozzarella cheese

1½ cups (about 6 ounces)
crumbled creamy chèvre

3 large eggs

1 garlic clove, minced

Juice of 1 lemon

2 tablespoons chopped fresh
marjoram or 4 teaspoons dried
marjoram

2 tablespoons chopped fresh
parsley

2 teaspoons salt

2 teaspoons freshly ground black
pepper

Egg wash: 1 large egg beaten with
2 tablespoons milk

high heat and cook and stir the mushrooms 3 to 4 minutes until light golden brown. Remove from the heat and set aside.

4 • Stir the ricotta, mozzarella, chèvre, eggs, garlic, lemon juice, marjoram, parsley, salt, and pepper in a large bowl and set aside.

5 • Add the roasted tomato-shallot mixture to the mushrooms and stir to mix. Spoon half the mixture into the chilled, dough-lined baking dish.

6 • Spread half the cheese mixture on top of the tomato-mushroom mixture. Top with remaining mushroom mixture, then finish with the remaining cheese mixture.

7 • Cut 10 to 12 holes in the remaining sheet of dough with a ½-inch cookie cutter or knife. Place the sheet of dough on top of the cheese topping; trim and crimp the edges. Brush with egg wash and bake 40 to 45 minutes, until the pastry is golden brown and the mixture is bubbling. (Note: Cover if the top is browning too quickly.) Let stand 10 to 15 minutes before serving; serve warm.

variations: Add 2 cups wilted spinach (page 213) and/or 2 cups shredded cooked chicken (page 58) to the mushroom mixture for a slightly different flavor. Try rosemary or basil instead of marjoram. Frozen phyllo, frozen puff pastry, or purchased pie dough can be used instead of the homemade crust to save time.

Baked Potato Casserole Topped with Crispy Onion Rings

You can use leftover baked potatoes for this hearty side dish. If you don't have time to bake potatoes, boiled or steamed potatoes work just as well. This dish can be made a day in advance and reheated just before serving. It's delicious served with Braised Fillet of Beef with Roasted Tomatoes and Mushrooms (page 169) or Laura's Spicy Turkey Barbecue (page 166).

SERVES 8 TO 10

1 tablespoon unsalted butter, softened

4 russet potatoes, scrubbed

2 tablespoons olive oil

10 slices bacon

2 cups half-and-half

1 tablespoon chopped fresh oregano or 1 teaspoon dried oregano

2 teaspoons salt

1 teaspoon freshly ground black pepper

1½ cups (6 ounces) grated Cheddar cheese

2 cups Crispy Onion Rings (recipe follows)

1 • Preheat the oven to 400 degrees.

2 • Butter a 9 by 13-inch baking dish and set aside.

3 • Rub the potatoes with the olive oil to coat lightly and bake 55 minutes to 1 hour or until tender when pierced with a knife. Remove from the oven and set aside until cool enough to handle. Chop the potatoes into 1-inch cubes and set aside.

4 • Lower the oven temperature to 350 degrees.

5 • Lay the bacon in a single layer on a baking pan and bake in the oven until crisp. Remove from the oven and place on a paper towel to drain, then crumble coarsely.

6 • Layer the ingredients in the prepared dish as follows: Place half the potatoes in the bottom of the baking dish; top with half of the bacon. Pour 1 cup of the half-and-half, half the oregano, half the salt, half the pepper, and half the cheese over the potatoes. Repeat the process, ending with the cheese, and top with onion rings.

7 • Bake 25 to 30 minutes or until the potato mixture is hot and bubbling around the edges of the dish. Cover if the onion rings begin to brown too quickly.

Crispy Onion Rings

2 cups canola or safflower oil
1 yellow onion, cut into
    1/4-inch rounds
1 cup buttermilk
1 cup all-purpose flour
2 tablespoons cornstarch
Salt and freshly ground black
    pepper to taste

1 • Heat the oil in a large, deep skillet over medium-high heat to about 375 degrees or until a sprinkle of flour dropped in the oil sizzles.

2 • Separate the onion slices into rings and place in a bowl with the buttermilk to soak.

3 • Mix the flour and cornstarch together in a separate bowl and season with salt and pepper.

4 • Remove the onion rings one at a time from the buttermilk, dip into the flour, shaking off any excess flour, and place directly into the hot oil.

5 • Fry in small batches, 3 to 5 minutes per batch, until the onion rings are golden brown and crispy. Remove from the oil and place on a paper towel to drain. Season with additional salt and pepper if desired and set aside until ready to use.

Baking Bacon

Cooking bacon in the oven is easier than cooking it in a skillet since you don't have to turn the bacon while it cooks. It's neater, too: there's no spattered grease to clean up. To bake bacon, preheat oven to 400 degrees. Lay the bacon strips in 1 layer in a roasting pan. Bake 10 to 15 minutes, until crispy. Drain the bacon on paper towels and discard the bacon grease.

Foster's Seasonal Vegetable Plate

Our customers love the variety this lunch special offers (which changes daily and reflects the seasons) and the fact that it's so healthy. We think of it as a contemporary version of the "meat-and-threes" offerings at country diners and coffee shops throughout the South. But instead of meat loaf, mashed potatoes, and turnip greens, our customers choose from an array of steamed, sautéed, and raw vegetables, plus a seasonal selection of composed salads and side dishes. What could possibly be more healthful or more delicious? Use the suggestions below as a guide to create your own vegetable plate. At Foster's, we serve it with Granny Foster's Chili Sauce (page 43), which is a tangy complement to the veggies, and add a basket of warm Old-Fashioned Buttermilk Biscuits (page 16) or Jalapeño Corn Muffins (page 7).

The Vegetables

Steamed baby green beans; sautéed pattypan squash; pan-fried new potatoes; fried okra; baby radishes; sliced tomatoes sprinkled with coarse sea salt; alfalfa, pea, or radish sprouts; lima beans; black-eyed peas; roasted sweet potatoes; roasted winter squash; mashed potatoes; grilled zucchini; grilled summer squash; cole slaw; grilled, roasted, or stewed tomatoes; corn pudding; steamed carrots; steamed cabbage, and just about any recipe in the "Salads and Sides" chapter (pages 108–151).

Risotto Cakes with Roasted Tomatoes and Foster's Arugula Pesto

This make-ahead dish can be served as a vegetarian entrée, as a first course, or as a side dish to Sautéed Chicken Breasts with Artichokes, Lemons, and Capers (page 165), Balsamic-Roasted Vegetables (page 113), or Braised Chicken Thighs with Chèvre Stuffing (page 155). You can also make the risotto cakes small, and serve them as an hors d'oeuvre. The cakes can be formed the day before and cooked at the last minute. The tomatoes can be roasted and the pesto prepared up to 3 days ahead of time.

MAKES TWELVE TO FIFTEEN
2½-INCH CAKES; SERVES 6 TO 8

6 tablespoons olive oil

1 yellow onion, diced

2 garlic cloves, minced

2 cups Arborio rice

1 cup dry white wine

5 cups chicken broth (page 57)

4 cups firmly packed fresh
spinach, washed, drained,
and stems removed

1 cup (4 ounces) grated Parmesan
cheese

2 tablespoons fresh thyme or
2 teaspoons dried thyme

2 tablespoons fresh rosemary or
2 teaspoons dried rosemary

2 tablespoons unsalted butter

1 recipe Oven-Roasted Tomatoes
(recipe follows)

1 cup Foster's Arugula Pesto
(page 236)

1 • Heat 4 tablespoons of the olive oil in a large saucepan over medium-high heat. Add the onion and cook, stirring constantly, 3 to 4 minutes, until translucent. Add the garlic and cook 2 minutes longer, stirring frequently.

2 • Add the rice and cook 5 minutes, stirring constantly, or until most of the rice has turned light golden. Add the wine and boil until reduced by half, stirring constantly.

3 • Meanwhile, place the broth in a separate saucepan and bring to a boil. Reduce heat so the broth is at a low simmer. Slowly add 1 cup of the hot broth to the rice, stirring constantly, until the liquid is absorbed. Repeat this process—adding 1 cup of broth at a time—until all the broth is absorbed. This should take 20 to 25 minutes.

4 • Stir in the spinach until it has wilted, 2 to 3 minutes. Stir in the Parmesan, thyme, and rosemary and remove from the heat. Spread the mixture evenly in a greased 9 by 13-inch baking dish and chill in the refrigerator several hours or overnight.

5 • Cut twelve 2½-inch circles out of the chilled risotto with a biscuit cutter or cookie cutter. (You can form leftover risotto mixture into cakes, too, if desired.)

6 • Heat the butter and remaining olive oil over medium heat in a 12-inch nonstick skillet. Cook 6 to 8 risotto cakes at a time for about 3 minutes per side, turning only once, until the cakes are golden brown and

crispy. Remove from the pan, drain on a paper towel, and place in the oven to keep warm while you cook the remaining cakes.

7 • To serve, place 2 risotto cakes on each plate or arrange them all on a platter. Top each cake with 3 or 4 tomatoes, several of the onion slices or a small portion of the onion, and about a tablespoon of pesto. Serve immediately.

Oven-Roasted Tomatoes

Roasting makes the tomatoes more intense, because the natural sugars become concentrated as the water in the fruit evaporates.

MAKES ABOUT 2 CUPS TOMATOES

12 fresh plum tomatoes (about
   2 pounds), cored and cut in half
1 red onion, thinly sliced
¼ cup olive oil
2 tablespoons balsamic vinegar
4 garlic cloves, minced
2 tablespoons fresh rosemary or
   2 teaspoons dried rosemary
2 tablespoons fresh thyme or
   2 teaspoons dried thyme
Salt and freshly ground black
   pepper to taste

1 • Preheat the oven to 400 degrees.

2 • Combine the tomatoes, onion, olive oil, vinegar, garlic, rosemary, thyme, salt, and pepper in a baking pan and toss until the tomatoes are coated evenly with the mixture.

3 • Spread the tomato mixture evenly in the baking pan and bake 40 to 45 minutes, stirring occasionally, until the tomatoes are very soft, the vinegar has caramelized, and the tomatoes begin to shrivel.

Foster's Arugula Pesto

This robust pesto is delicious with pasta, and dresses up grilled chicken or fish. You can also mix it into your favorite vinaigrette or use it as a sandwich spread.

5 cups firmly packed arugula, washed, drained, and stems removed

½ cup firmly packed parsley

½ cup slivered almonds

Juice of 1 lemon

9 garlic cloves, crushed or minced

½ cup extra-virgin olive oil

½ cup grated Parmesan cheese

Salt and freshly ground black pepper to taste

1 • Combine the arugula, parsley, almonds, lemon juice, and garlic in the bowl of a food processor fitted with the metal blade. Pulse several times until a paste forms, stopping several times to scrape down the sides of the bowl.

2 • With the motor running, slowly add the olive oil and process until the mixture is smooth.

3 • Add the Parmesan, salt, and pepper and pulse several times until well mixed. Refrigerate in an airtight container until ready to use.

Arugula

"Arugula" is one of the names for a salad green whose popularity originated in Italy. It's also known as rocket, rugula, and rucola. Mature arugula has a peppery taste, somewhat like watercress. However, tiny young arugula leaves have a very delicate flavor. Like watercress, arugula is sold in bunches. It's also frequently added to mesclun and "field lettuce" mixes. Baby arugula is somewhat fragile once it is picked, but it's easy to grow and will reseed itself in areas where there is no hard winter freeze. We use it at the Market to make a unique arugula pesto that's delicious on pasta, grilled fish, chicken, vegetables, sandwiches, and grilled or toasted bread, as well as for a pizza base in place of marinara or pizza sauce.

Upscale Mac and Cheese

A dressed-up version of macaroni and cheese, this dish can be made ahead and reheated.

SERVES 6 TO 8

1 pound orecchiette pasta

1 cup sour cream

1 tablespoon olive oil

6 tablespoons (¾ stick) unsalted butter

1 yellow onion, diced

⅓ cup all-purpose flour

3 cups milk

2 roasted red bell peppers, peeled, cored, seeded, and pureed (page 40)

1½ cups (6 ounces) grated sharp Cheddar cheese

½ cup grated Parmesan cheese

3 ounces cream cheese, cut into 1-inch pieces

8 cups firmly packed spinach, washed, drained, and stems removed

½ cup sun-dried tomatoes

Juice of 1 lemon

2 teaspoons salt

1 teaspoon freshly ground black pepper

2 tablespoons fresh marjoram or 2 teaspoons dried marjoram

1 • Preheat the oven to 350 degrees.

2 • Lightly grease a 9 by 13-inch baking dish and set aside.

3 • Cook the pasta according to package directions until al dente. Rinse and drain well. Put the pasta in a large bowl and toss with the sour cream just until mixed. Set aside.

4 • Heat the olive oil and butter in a skillet over medium heat and add the onion. Cook and stir 3 to 4 minutes, until the onion is translucent.

5 • Stir the flour into the onion mixture and cook, stirring constantly, about 3 minutes, until the flour cooks and turns light brown.

6 • Slowly whisk in the milk and cook, stirring constantly, until the mixture comes to a boil and thickens, 3 to 4 minutes.

7 • Remove the sauce from the heat and stir in the pureed peppers, Cheddar, Parmesan, cream cheese, spinach, sun-dried tomatoes, and lemon juice. Stir until the cheese has melted and the spinach has wilted.

8 • Add the cheese mixture to the pasta–sour cream mixture. Add the salt, pepper, and marjoram and toss until well blended.

9 • Transfer to the prepared baking dish and bake, uncovered, 40 to 45 minutes or until bubbling around the edges and slightly brown on top. Remove from the oven and let rest for about 10 minutes before serving. Serve warm.

variations: Other small pasta shapes such as ziti or penne can be used in place of the orecchiette. Diced ham, diced cooked chicken, or sautéed chopped tomatoes, mushrooms, peppers, or summer squash can be added for an even more robust dish.

Squash Pudding with Roasted Tomato Vinaigrette

This easy summer casserole is delicious as a side dish, or as a light supper accompanied by grilled, seasonal vegetables. Since the squash is sautéed just until crisp-tender, the resulting dish has the appealing texture of garden-fresh squash. The cornmeal thickens the dish slightly and also adds a very mild, earthy flavor.

SERVES 6 TO 8

2½ cups milk

1 cup yellow cornmeal

¼ cup olive oil

3 yellow squash, diced

1 red bell pepper, cored, seeded, and diced

5 large eggs

1 tablespoon chopped fresh thyme or 1 teaspoon dried thyme

2 tablespoons chopped fresh chives or minced scallions

1 cup (4 ounces) crumbled creamy chèvre

Roasted Tomato Vinaigrette (recipe follows)

1 • Preheat the oven to 350 degrees.

2 • Lightly butter a 2-quart soufflé dish and set aside.

3 • Bring the milk to a low boil in a medium saucepan. Remove from the heat and slowly whisk in the cornmeal.

4 • Heat the olive oil in a skillet over medium heat. Add the squash and red bell pepper and cook, stirring frequently, 3 to 5 minutes until crisp-tender, and set aside.

5 • Mix together the eggs, thyme, chives, and chèvre in a bowl. Add the milk mixture and the squash mixture and stir until well blended.

6 • Pour the mixture into the prepared dish and bake 45 to 50 minutes, until the top is lightly brown and puffy, but it is still slightly soft in the center. Cool 10 to 15 minutes before serving so that the pudding sets. Serve with the vinaigrette spooned on top of each serving. Serve immediately.

variations: For a slightly different texture and flavor, substitute 1 cup fresh corn kernels for 1 cup of the squash. Make the pudding spicy by adding jalapeños or other hot peppers. Use Cheddar, Fontina, or pepper Jack in place of chèvre.

Roasted Tomato Vinaigrette

Oven-roasted tomatoes add a tart-sweet flavor to this vinaigrette, which is also delicious drizzled on salads or grilled fish, chicken, or vegetables.

MAKES ABOUT 1¹/₂ CUPS VINAIGRETTE

5 plum tomatoes, cored and
   chopped

2 shallots, chopped

¹/₃ cup olive oil

2 teaspoons salt

1 teaspoon freshly ground black
   pepper

2 teaspoons chopped fresh chives

¹/₃ cup champagne vinegar or
   white wine vinegar

1 • Preheat the oven to 400 degrees.

2 • Toss the tomatoes, shallots, and olive oil in a baking pan. Arrange the tomatoes in 1 layer and roast 30 to 40 minutes until the tomatoes are slightly brown and the skins begin to shrivel. Remove from the oven, reserving the oil in the pan, and cool slightly.

3 • Place the salt, pepper, chives, vinegar, tomatoes, shallots, and the oil from the roasting pan in a bowl and whisk until well blended and all the oil is incorporated.

variation: If you don't have time to roast tomatoes, use chopped fresh tomatoes instead and reduce the olive oil to 2 tablespoons.

market desserts

Chunky Peanut Butter Cookies • Classic Sugar Cookies • Chocolate Chip Cookies • Crispy Gingersnaps • Coconut Macaroons • Chocolate Whoppers • "Nutty Buddy" Shortbread • Classic Oatmeal Cookies • Blondies • Foster's Brownies • Lemon Bars with Blueberries • Chewy Apple-Pecan Bars • Super-Moist Carrot Cake with Cream Cheese Frosting • Chocolate Espresso Layer Cake with Mocha Latte Frosting • Devil's Food Cake with Chocolate Satin Frosting • Blackberry Jam Cake with Blackberry Cream Cheese Frosting • Buttermilk Cake with Fresh Strawberries and Cream • Coconut Cake with Lemon Curd Filling and Seven-Minute Frosting • German Chocolate Cake with Coconut-Pecan Caramel Frosting • Four-Layer Blueberry Gingerbread Cake with Mocha Cream • Chocolate Pound Cake • Lemon-Almond Pound Cake • Cream Cheese Pound Cake • Turtle Cheesecake • Basic Piecrust • Lemon Chess Pie with Sour Cherries • Coconut Custard Pie • French Silk Pie • Key Lime Pie with Walnut–Graham Cracker Crust • Chocolate Meringue Pie • Bourbon-Pecan Pie • Silky Pumpkin Pie • Fresh Peach Pie with Cream Cheese Crust • Fresh Strawberry Shortcake • Strawberry-Rhubarb Crisp • Say's Bread Pudding with Bourbon Icing • Fresh Peach Cobbler

Chunky Peanut Butter Cookies

We top these big, old-fashioned cookies with extra chopped peanuts for a super-nutty flavor. They're one of our bestsellers; try them and you'll see why. The dough can be made ahead and refrigerated in an airtight container up to 1 week.

8 tablespoons (1 stick) unsalted butter, softened

½ cup creamy peanut butter

½ cup firmly packed light brown sugar

½ cup granulated sugar

1 large egg

½ teaspoon pure vanilla extract

1½ cups all-purpose flour

1 teaspoon baking soda

¼ teaspoon salt

½ cup coarsely chopped roasted peanuts, optional

2 tablespoons granulated sugar, for sprinkling on top

1 • Preheat the oven to 375 degrees.

2 • Lightly grease 2 baking sheets and set aside.

3 • Cream together the butter, peanut butter, brown sugar, and granulated sugar in a bowl with an electric mixer until well combined.

4 • Add the egg and vanilla and mix until all ingredients are combined.

5 • Sift together the flour, baking soda, and salt in a separate bowl and stir to mix.

6 • Slowly add the flour mixture to the peanut butter mixture while beating or stirring until smooth and well blended. Do not overmix.

7 • Scoop the dough with a ¼-cup (2-ounce) ice cream scoop or a heaping tablespoon and drop onto the prepared baking sheets about 3 inches apart. Press flat with the back of a fork dipped in 2 tablespoons of the granulated sugar. Each cookie should be about ¼ inch to ½ inch thick.

8 • Sprinkle with the chopped peanuts and the remaining granulated sugar.

9 • Bake 12 to 15 minutes (or 10 to 12 minutes for soft, chewy cookies), until golden brown. Cool 5 to 10 minutes on the baking sheets before removing the cookies to a baking rack to cool completely.

variations: Add 1 cup semisweet chocolate chips or chopped, roasted peanuts to the batter for a chunkier cookie.

Classic Sugar Cookies

We use this traditional dough for Christmas cookies, Valentine's Day cookies, and more. The dough keeps beautifully, and can be cut out and decorated as you like.

8 tablespoons (1 stick) unsalted butter, softened

1 cup sugar

1 large egg

¼ cup milk

Grated zest and juice of 1 lemon

½ teaspoon pure vanilla extract

2½ cups all-purpose flour

½ teaspoon baking powder

½ teaspoon salt

1 recipe Royal Icing (recipe follows)

1 • Cream the butter and sugar together in a bowl with an electric mixer until light and fluffy.

2 • Add the egg to the butter mixture and beat until well combined. Add the milk, lemon zest, lemon juice, and vanilla and mix well.

3 • Sift together the flour, baking powder, and salt in a separate bowl and stir to mix.

4 • Add the flour mixture to the butter-sugar mixture and beat until well combined, but do not overmix.

5 • With floured hands, remove the dough from the bowl and form into a flat round. Wrap with plastic and refrigerate for at least 1 hour or up to 5 days.

6 • Preheat the oven to 350 degrees.

7 • Lightly grease 2 baking sheets and set aside.

8 • Remove the dough from the refrigerator. Let stand at room temperature 15 to 20 minutes if it is too hard to roll out.

9 • On a lightly floured surface, roll into a round about ¼ inch thick. Cut with cookie cutters; place the cookies on the prepared baking sheets about 3 inches apart.

10 • Bake 12 to 15 minutes, until the cookies are lightly golden around the edges only. Cool 5 to 10 minutes on the baking sheets before removing the cookies to a baking rack to cool completely.

11 • To decorate, brush with a layer of thin Royal Icing and sprinkle with colored sugar or use a pastry bag and pipe on thick Royal Icing for added designs.

Royal Icing

1 large egg white

1 tablespoon fresh lemon juice

2 to 3 cups confectioners' sugar
    (use 2 cups for thin Royal Icing
    to spread on the cookies; use
    3 cups for thick Royal Icing to
    pipe on decorations)

1 • Combine the egg white and lemon juice in a bowl
    and beat with an electric mixer until frothy.

2 • Slowly add the sugar, about ½ cup at a time, until
    well blended, light, and fluffy.

3 • Add several drops of food coloring, if color is de-
    sired, and beat until well blended. Use immediately
    or refrigerate in an airtight container up to 2 days.

Chocolate Chip Cookies

Our basic chocolate chip cookie is really big and packed with chocolate chips and nuts. We make hundreds of these cookies every day; it's clearly everyone's favorite. The dough can be made up to 6 days in advance and refrigerated until ready to bake.

$\frac{1}{2}$ pound (2 sticks) unsalted butter, softened

1 cup granulated sugar

$1\frac{1}{4}$ cups firmly packed light brown sugar

2 teaspoons pure vanilla extract

3 large eggs

3 cups all-purpose flour

1 teaspoon baking soda

$\frac{1}{4}$ teaspoon salt

3 cups (18 ounces) semisweet chocolate chips

$1\frac{1}{2}$ cups coarsely chopped walnuts

1 • Preheat the oven to 350 degrees.

2 • Lightly grease 2 baking sheets and set aside.

3 • Cream together the butter, granulated sugar, and brown sugar in a bowl with an electric mixer and beat until light and fluffy. Add the vanilla and mix.

4 • Add the eggs to the butter mixture one at a time, beating well after each addition.

5 • Sift together the flour, baking soda, and salt in a separate bowl and stir to mix.

6 • Add the flour mixture to the butter mixture and stir just until the dry ingredients are moist and blended. Do not overmix.

7 • Fold in the chocolate chips and nuts until all ingredients are thoroughly mixed. (Note: The dough can be refrigerated in an airtight container up to 6 days at this point.)

8 • Scoop the dough with a $\frac{1}{4}$-cup (2-ounce) ice cream scoop or by the heaping tablespoon, and drop onto the prepared baking sheets about 3 inches apart. Press the cookies with the back of a spatula to a thickness of $\frac{1}{4}$ inch.

9 • Bake 15 to 18 minutes, until the cookies are firm and light brown. Cool 5 to 10 minutes on the baking sheets before removing the cookies to a baking rack to cool completely.

variations: Pecans can be substituted for the walnuts, or omit the nuts entirely. Use white chocolate chips or chocolate chunks.

Crispy Gingersnaps

Flavored with cinnamon and cloves as well as ginger, these crispy cookies are great with vanilla ice cream or frozen yogurt. They also make a delicious piecrust in place of graham cracker crumbs.

1 cup vegetable shortening or
    8 tablespoons (1 stick)
    unsalted butter, softened

1¼ cups sugar

1 large egg

½ cup molasses

2 cups all-purpose flour

1 teaspoon baking soda

2 teaspoons ground ginger

1 teaspoon ground cinnamon

1 teaspoon ground cloves

½ teaspoon salt

Additional sugar, to garnish,
    optional

1 • Preheat the oven to 350 degrees.

2 • Lightly grease 2 baking sheets and set aside.

3 • Cream together the shortening and 1 cup of the sugar in a large bowl with an electric mixer until the mixture is light and fluffy.

4 • Add the egg to the sugar mixture and beat well. Slowly add the molasses and beat until well blended.

5 • Sift together the flour, baking soda, ginger, cinnamon, cloves, and salt in a separate bowl and stir to mix.

6 • Add the flour mixture to the sugar and egg mixture and beat until just combined; do not overmix.

7 • Scoop the dough with a ¼-cup (2-ounce) ice cream scoop or by the heaping tablespoon and drop onto the prepared baking sheets about 3 inches apart.

8 • Press the cookies flat with the back of a spatula to a thickness of about ¼ inch. Sprinkle the cookies with the remaining sugar.

9 • Bake 15 to 18 minutes, until the cookies are crispy and crackled on the top. Cool 5 to 10 minutes on the baking sheets before removing the cookies to a baking rack to cool completely.

Coconut Macaroons

These big, sticky macaroons keep really well. They're absolute heaven for coconut lovers!

7 egg whites

2$\frac{1}{2}$ cups sugar

2 tablespoons honey

2 teaspoons pure vanilla extract

6 cups (16 ounces) sweetened
    flaked coconut

1$\frac{1}{4}$ cups all-purpose flour

1 • Combine the egg whites, sugar, honey, and vanilla in a bowl (or in a double boiler) and place over a large saucepan of simmering water. Cook and stir constantly for 8 to 10 minutes, until the sugar dissolves. The mixture will look milky in color.

2 • Combine the coconut and flour in a separate bowl and toss to mix.

3 • Remove the egg white mixture from the heat and stir in the coconut mixture. Cover and refrigerate until firm, about 1 hour or overnight.

4 • Preheat the oven to 300 degrees.

5 • Lightly grease 2 large baking sheets and set aside.

6 • Remove the batter from the refrigerator and scoop with a $\frac{1}{4}$-cup (2-ounce) ice cream scoop or by the heaping tablespoon and drop onto the prepared baking sheets about 3 inches apart.

7 • Bake 15 to 20 minutes, until golden brown but still soft and creamy in the center. Cool 5 to 10 minutes before removing the macaroons to a baking rack to cool completely.

variation: Dip cooled cookies halfway into 6 to 8 ounces melted semisweet chocolate; let stand 15 to 20 minutes for the chocolate to set.

COCON...

LEMON
BARS

Chocolate Whoppers

We offer these big, chewy super-chocolaty cookies at the Market daily—everyone loves them! Inspired by a similar cookie made at the SoHo Charcuterie back in the early eighties, these cookies keep well, freeze beautifully, and, since they're soft, ship well, too.

MAKES ABOUT 1 DOZEN 2½- TO 3-INCH COOKIES

6 ounces semisweet chocolate (preferably high-quality baking chocolate, such as Valrhona or Callebaut), chopped into large chunks

2 ounces unsweetened chocolate, chopped into large chunks

6 tablespoons (¾ stick) unsalted butter

2 large eggs

1 tablespoon plus 2 teaspoons instant espresso powder

2 teaspoons pure vanilla extract

¾ cup sugar

⅓ cup all-purpose flour

1 teaspoon baking powder

½ teaspoon salt

2 cups coarsely chopped walnuts

1 cup (6 ounces) semisweet chocolate chips

1 • Preheat the oven to 325 degrees.

2 • Lightly grease 2 baking sheets and set aside.

3 • Melt together the semisweet chocolate, unsweetened chocolate chunks, and butter in a double boiler over low heat until just melted, stirring occasionally. (Note: Do not overheat; remove from the heat as soon as chocolate has melted.) Stir to blend the chocolate and butter, and set aside.

4 • Cream together the eggs, espresso powder, and vanilla in a large bowl with an electric mixer. Add the sugar and mix until thick and creamy.

5 • Sift together the flour, baking powder, and salt in a separate bowl and stir to mix. Set aside.

6 • Add the chocolate mixture to the egg mixture and blend until well combined. Add the flour mixture and stir just until the dry ingredients are moist.

7 • Fold in the walnuts and chocolate chips. (Note: The batter will be very moist—similar to the consistency of cake batter.)

8 • Scoop the batter with a ¼-cup (2-ounce) ice cream scoop or by the heaping tablespoon and drop onto the prepared baking sheets about 3 inches apart. (Note: Bake right away, before the chocolate begins to cool and harden.)

9 • Bake 10 to 12 minutes, turning the baking sheets once during the cooking time. The cookies will still be very gooey inside and soft, but do not overcook or the cooled cookies will be dry. Cool about 10 minutes on the baking sheets before gently removing the whoppers to a baking rack to cool completely.

variations: Pecans can be substituted for walnuts, or use a combination of pecans and walnuts.

"Nutty Buddy" Shortbread

We dip our shortbread into melted chocolate, then into chopped nuts, so it resembles the old-fashioned ice cream treat Nutty Buddy.

3 cups all-purpose flour

$\frac{1}{2}$ cup granulated sugar

$\frac{1}{2}$ cup firmly packed light brown sugar

$1\frac{1}{2}$ cups chopped pecans

$\frac{1}{2}$ pound (2 sticks) unsalted butter, softened

$\frac{1}{4}$ cup brewed espresso or very strong coffee

6 ounces semisweet chocolate

1 • Preheat the oven to 350 degrees.

2 • Lightly grease 2 baking sheets and set aside.

3 • Combine the flour, granulated sugar, brown sugar, and 1 cup of the pecans in a bowl and stir to mix.

4 • Add the butter to the flour mixture and mix just until the dough sticks together.

5 • Add the espresso and stir to mix until the dough starts to form a ball.

6 • Form the dough into 2 flat rectangles with lightly floured hands. Working with 1 piece at a time, roll out on a lightly floured surface into a $\frac{1}{2}$-inch-thick rectangle that is about 3 inches by 12 inches.

7 • Trim the edges with a knife to make an even edge. Slice the dough into 1 by 3-inch rectangles. Place on the prepared baking sheets about 2 inches apart.

8 • Bake 15 to 20 minutes, until light brown around the edges; do not overcook. Cool 5 to 10 minutes on the baking sheets before removing the shortbread to a baking rack to cool completely.

9 • Meanwhile, melt the chocolate in a double boiler over low heat, stirring occasionally, until the chocolate is completely melted. Remove from the heat and set aside.

10 • Dip one end of the cooled cookies about one-quarter of the way into the melted chocolate. Sprinkle the chocolate end with the remaining pecans. Place on a baking rack and let stand in a cool place until the chocolate hardens (the pecans will stick to the chocolate as it cools).

Classic Oatmeal Cookies

You can make the dough up to 1 week in advance and store it in the refrigerator until ready to bake. The cookies can be made slightly crispy or chewy, according to your taste.

MAKES ABOUT 2 DOZEN 2½- TO 3-INCH COOKIES

½ pound (2 sticks) unsalted
　butter, softened

1¼ cups firmly packed light
　brown sugar

¾ cup granulated sugar

2 large eggs

1 teaspoon pure vanilla extract

2 cups all-purpose flour

4 cups rolled oats

1 teaspoon baking soda

1 teaspoon ground cinnamon

½ teaspoon ground nutmeg

½ teaspoon salt

2 cups raisins

1 • Preheat the oven to 350 degrees.

2 • Lightly grease 2 baking sheets and set aside.

3 • Cream together the butter, brown sugar, and granulated sugar in a large bowl with an electric mixer until light and fluffy.

4 • Add the eggs to the butter mixture one at a time, beating well after each addition. Add the vanilla and beat until well blended.

5 • Combine the flour, oats, baking soda, cinnamon, nutmeg, and salt in a separate bowl. Stir to mix.

6 • Add the flour mixture to the egg mixture and stir just until the dry ingredients are moist and blended. Do not overmix. Add the raisins and stir just until combined.

7 • Scoop the dough with a ¼-cup (2-ounce) ice cream scoop or by the heaping tablespoon and drop onto the prepared baking sheets about 3 inches apart. Press the cookies flat with the back of a spatula to a thickness of about ¼ to ½ inch.

8 • Bake 12 to 14 minutes for soft, chewy cookies; 15 to 18 minutes for crunchy cookies. Cool 5 to 10 minutes on the baking sheet before removing the cookies to a baking rack to cool completely.

variations: Substitute dried cherries or dried cranberries for the raisins; add 1 cup chocolate chips or coarsely chopped walnuts for a chunkier cookie.

Blondies

Try these rich, chewy bars topped with vanilla, caramel, or coffee ice cream and drizzled with chocolate sauce.

4 cups all-purpose flour

1$\frac{1}{2}$ teaspoons baking powder

$\frac{1}{2}$ teaspoon salt

$\frac{3}{4}$ pound (3 sticks) unsalted butter, softened

4 cups firmly packed light brown sugar

4 large eggs

1 tablespoon pure vanilla extract

2 cups (12 ounces) semisweet chocolate chips

2 cups coarsely chopped pecans

1 • Preheat the oven to 325 degrees.

2 • Lightly grease the bottom and sides of a 17 by 12 by 1-inch pan (a half-sheet pan) and set aside.

3 • Sift together the flour, baking powder, and salt in a bowl, stir to mix, and set aside.

4 • Combine the butter and brown sugar in a separate bowl and cream together with an electric mixer until light and creamy.

5 • Add the eggs, one at a time, blending thoroughly after each addition until well blended. Add the vanilla and continue to beat until light and fluffy.

6 • Stir the flour mixture into the butter and sugar mixture and combine just until the dry ingredients are moist and blended. Do not overmix.

7 • Fold in the chocolate chips and pecans to blend. Pour the batter into the prepared pan.

8 • Bake 45 to 50 minutes, until a toothpick inserted in the center comes out clean. Remove from the oven and cool 30 to 40 minutes before cutting. Trim the edges and cut into 2$\frac{1}{2}$ by 3-inch bars. (For a smaller blondie, cut the bar in half down the center or on the diagonal.)

variations: Use butterscotch or peanut butter chips in place of chocolate chips or add 1 cup flaked sweetened coconut.

Foster's Brownies

These moist, fudgy brownies are easy to make and they keep well, too. For a special dessert, warm the brownies slightly and top with ice cream and your favorite hot fudge sauce or chocolate espresso sauce.

MAKES 2 DOZEN 2½ BY 3-INCH BROWNIES

2 cups all-purpose flour

1⅓ cups unsweetened cocoa
    powder

1 teaspoon salt

8 large eggs

4 cups sugar

1 pound (4 sticks) unsalted butter,
    melted

1 tablespoon plus 2 teaspoons
    pure vanilla extract

2 cups coarsely chopped walnuts

2 cups (12 ounces) semisweet
    chocolate chips

1 • Preheat the oven to 325 degrees.

2 • Lightly grease and flour a 17 by 12 by 1-inch baking pan and set aside.

3 • Sift together the flour, cocoa powder, and salt in a bowl and stir to mix. Set aside.

4 • Cream together the eggs, sugar, butter, and vanilla in a separate bowl with an electric mixer until well blended.

5 • Add the flour mixture to the butter mixture and mix just until all the dry ingredients are moist and blended. Do not overmix.

6 • Fold in the walnuts and chocolate chips and stir to blend. Spread the batter evenly in the prepared pan.

7 • Bake 35 to 40 minutes, until the brownies are firm to the touch. They will be slightly soft in the center when tested with a toothpick. Remove from the oven and cool 30 to 40 minutes before cutting.

8 • Trim the edges and cut into 2½ by 3-inch bars. (For a smaller brownie, cut the bar in half down the center or on the diagonal.)

variations: Instead of chocolate chips, you can add white chocolate chips or peanut butter chips. Pecans can be substituted for the walnuts.

MARKET DESSERTS | 253

Bench Scrapers

At the Market, we use a bench scraper—also called a bench cutter—to cut brownies and other bars as well as bread and scone dough. The metal edge is sharp enough to cut brownies and other bars, but dull enough that it won't scratch your baking pans as much as a knife would. Bench scrapers are available at cookware stores nationwide.

Lemon Bars with Blueberries

Everyone loves these! Cut them into tiny squares and serve with espresso for an elegant touch at the end of a special dinner.

MAKES 2 DOZEN 2½ BY 3-INCH LEMON BARS

Crust

4 cups all-purpose flour

1 cup confectioners' sugar

1 pound plus 4 tablespoons
(4½ sticks) unsalted butter,
cut into ½-inch cubes and
chilled

1 • Preheat the oven to 350 degrees.

2 • Lightly grease a 17 by 12 by 1-inch baking pan and set aside.

3 • Mix the flour and sugar in the bowl of a food processor fitted with the metal blade and pulse 2 or 3 times to blend. Add the cubed butter and pulse until the mixture resembles coarse meal and begins to stick together. Remove from the food processor and form into a ball.

4 • Flatten the dough with lightly floured hands and press evenly into the bottom and ¼ inch up the sides of the prepared pan. The dough will be about ¼ inch thick.

5 • Bake 12 to 15 minutes, until light brown but not quite done. Remove from the oven and set aside to cool.

- -

Filling

3 cups granulated sugar

¼ cup all-purpose flour

½ teaspoon baking powder

7 large eggs, lightly beaten

Grated zest and juice of 4 lemons

1 cup fresh blueberries, cleaned

¼ cup confectioners' sugar

1 • Mix together the granulated sugar, flour, and baking powder in a bowl and set aside.

2 • Mix the eggs, lemon zest, and lemon juice in a separate bowl and whisk until smooth and well blended. Sift the flour-sugar mixture into the egg mixture and stir until well blended.

3 • Pour the filling on top of the crust and sprinkle evenly with the blueberries; they will sink slightly. Bake 30 to 35 minutes at 350 degrees or until set. Remove from the oven and allow to cool for several hours before cutting.

4 • Trim the edges and cut into 2½ by 3-inch bars. Dust

with confectioners' sugar just before serving. (For smaller bars, cut the bar in half down the center or on the diagonal.)

variation: Substitute raspberries for the blueberries.

Chewy Apple-Pecan Bars

These bars are delicious topped with vanilla or butter-pecan ice cream.

Crust

2$\frac{1}{2}$ cups all-purpose flour

$\frac{1}{2}$ cup rolled oats

1 cup confectioners' sugar

$\frac{1}{2}$ teaspoon salt

12 tablespoons (1$\frac{1}{2}$ sticks)
   unsalted butter, softened

12 ounces cream cheese, softened

1 • Preheat the oven to 350 degrees.

2 • Lightly grease a 17 by 12 by 1-inch baking pan and set aside.

3 • Mix the flour, oats, confectioners' sugar, and salt in a bowl and set aside.

4 • Cream together the butter and cream cheese in a separate bowl with an electric mixer until smooth and creamy. Add the flour mixture to the butter mixture and mix by hand just until it forms a soft ball.

5 • Flatten the dough with lightly floured hands and press evenly into the bottom and $\frac{1}{4}$ inch up the sides of the prepared pan. The dough will be about $\frac{1}{4}$ inch thick. Prick the crust with a fork 8 to 10 times.

6 • Bake 12 to 15 minutes, until light brown but not quite done. Remove from the oven and set aside to cool.

Filling

6 large eggs

1 cup sugar

4 tablespoons ($\frac{1}{2}$ stick) unsalted
   butter, melted

2 cups dark corn syrup

2 cups Easy Applesauce (page
   211)

$\frac{1}{4}$ cup dark rum

1 tablespoon pure vanilla extract

1$\frac{1}{2}$ cups coarsely chopped pecans

1 cup Granny Smith or other tart
   apples, peeled, cored, and
   diced

1 • Preheat the oven to 350 degrees.

2 • Whisk the eggs and sugar in a bowl until well blended. Add the butter, corn syrup, applesauce, rum, and vanilla and stir to mix. Fold in the pecans and apples.

3 • Pour on top of the crust and bake 45 to 50 minutes, until the filling is firm around the edges; the center will be slightly loose. Remove from the oven and cool several hours before cutting. Trim the edges and cut into 2$\frac{1}{2}$ by 3-inch bars. (For a smaller bar, cut the bar in half down the center or on the diagonal.)

Super-Moist Carrot Cake
with Cream Cheese Frosting

This classic carrot cake is one of our favorites. It's a great cake to make year-round or for a special occasion.

4 cups peeled and grated carrots

1½ cups coarsely chopped walnuts

1 cup dark raisins

2 cups all-purpose flour

1 tablespoon ground cinnamon

1 teaspoon ground cloves

2 teaspoons baking powder

1 teaspoon baking soda

1 teaspoon salt

4 large eggs

1 cup canola or safflower oil

1 cup granulated sugar

1 cup firmly packed light brown sugar

1 tablespoon pure vanilla extract

1 recipe Cream Cheese Frosting (recipe follows)

1 • Preheat the oven to 350 degrees.

2 • Grease and lightly flour two 9-inch cake pans and set aside.

3 • Mix the carrots, walnuts, and raisins in a bowl and set aside.

4 • Sift together the flour, cinnamon, cloves, baking powder, baking soda, and salt in a separate bowl and stir to mix. Set aside.

5 • Combine the eggs, oil, granulated sugar, brown sugar, and vanilla together in a separate bowl and whisk until well blended.

6 • Slowly fold the flour mixture into the egg mixture and stir to blend just until all the dry ingredients are moist and blended. Do not overmix. Fold in the carrot mixture and stir just until combined.

7 • Divide the batter evenly between the 2 prepared pans and bake 45 to 50 minutes, until the cakes are firm to the touch and a toothpick inserted in the center of each cake comes out clean.

8 • Remove from the oven and cool the cakes 10 to 15 minutes in the pans. Remove from the pans and continue to cool on a baking rack.

9 • Once the cakes have cooled completely, use a long, serrated knife to slice off the top rounded portion of each cake to make a flat, even surface. Discard the trimmings.

10 • Place one of the layers cut side down on a cake plate. Top with about one-third of the frosting and spread evenly to cover the top of the cake layer. Place the next layer, cut side down, on top of the frosting and spread the top of the cake with about one-half of the remaining frosting. Use the remaining frosting to cover the sides of the cake.

11 • Slice into portions and serve immediately or refrigerate until ready to serve. This cake keeps well for several days.

variation: Cover the sides with finely chopped walnuts.

Cream Cheese Frosting

$\frac{1}{2}$ pound (2 sticks) unsalted butter, softened

Two 8-ounce packages cream cheese, softened

5 cups confectioners' sugar

2 tablespoons grated orange zest or lemon zest

1 teaspoon pure vanilla extract

1 • Place the butter and cream cheese in a bowl and cream together with an electric mixer until light and smooth.

2 • Add the confectioners' sugar, 1 cup at a time, beating well after each addition until smooth.

3 • Add the orange zest and vanilla and continue to mix on high speed about 1 minute to make the frosting light and fluffy.

variations:

Blackberry Cream Cheese Frosting: Fold in 1 cup fresh blackberries, which will swirl a bit of color into the frosting.

Coconut Cream Cheese Frosting: Add 2 cups sweetened flaked coconut and stir until well blended.

Chocolate Espresso Layer Cake with Mocha Latte Frosting

This super-moist cake is one of our customers' favorites. It's easy to make, and keeps well, too. If you don't have an espresso maker, use strong coffee instead.

3 cups all-purpose flour

2 teaspoons baking powder

1 teaspoon baking soda

$1/2$ teaspoon salt

7 ounces unsweetened chocolate, chopped

4 large eggs

$3/4$ cup canola or safflower oil

4 cups sugar

$3/4$ cup sour cream

1 cup brewed strong coffee or espresso, cooled

1 recipe Mocha Latte Frosting (recipe follows) or Chocolate Satin Frosting (page 264)

1 • Preheat the oven to 350 degrees.

2 • Grease and lightly flour two 9-inch cake pans and set aside.

3 • Sift together the flour, baking powder, baking soda, and salt in a bowl and stir to mix. Set aside.

4 • Place the chocolate in a double boiler over simmering water. Stir occasionally until the chocolate has melted. Remove from the heat and cool slightly. (Note: Do not cool too much or the chocolate will harden.)

5 • Meanwhile, combine the eggs, oil, and sugar in a large bowl and whisk until well blended. Stir in the melted chocolate and set aside.

6 • Mix the sour cream and coffee in a separate bowl and whisk until well blended.

7 • Add the flour mixture to the egg mixture, alternating with the sour cream mixture. Blend just until combined. Do not overmix.

8 • Divide the batter evenly between the prepared pans and bake 40 to 45 minutes, until the cakes are firm to the touch and a toothpick inserted in the center comes out clean.

9 • Remove from the oven and cool the cakes 10 to 15 minutes in the pans, then remove from the pans and continue to cool on a baking rack. Frost the cakes.

chocolate espresso

Mocha Latte Frosting

This is also delicious on Devil's Food Cake (page 263) and Buttermilk Cake (page 266).

5 ounces semisweet chocolate, chopped

1 egg white

$\frac{1}{4}$ cup heavy cream

1 tablespoon pure vanilla extract

2 tablespoons instant coffee or espresso powder

$\frac{1}{2}$ pound (2 sticks) unsalted butter, softened

$4\frac{1}{2}$ cups confectioners' sugar

1 • Melt the chocolate in a double boiler over medium heat, stirring occasionally. Remove from the heat and set aside to cool slightly. (Note: If the chocolate cools too much, it will be difficult to work with. If this happens, just return the mixture to the heat for a few minutes, or put the chocolate in a microwave-proof container and heat the chocolate 20 to 30 seconds.)

2 • Whisk the egg white, cream, vanilla, and coffee in a small bowl until the coffee has dissolved; set aside.

3 • Meanwhile, beat the butter in a large bowl with an electric mixer until soft and creamy. Add the confectioners' sugar, about $\frac{1}{2}$ cup at a time, until thoroughly blended.

4 • Slowly add the melted chocolate to the butter mixture, alternating with the cream mixture, until the frosting is smooth. Add 1 to 3 tablespoons additional cream if the frosting seems too stiff. Leave at room temperature until ready to use. (Note: Don't refrigerate this frosting; it will become too stiff to spread.)

Devil's Food Cake with Chocolate Satin Frosting

Our version of this classic cake is rich, moist, and easy to make.

MAKES ONE 9-INCH LAYER CAKE; SERVES 10 TO 12

5 ounces unsweetened chocolate,
   chopped

3 cups all-purpose flour

2 teaspoons baking soda

1/2 teaspoon salt

12 tablespoons (1 1/2 sticks)
   unsalted butter, softened

1 3/4 cups firmly packed light
   brown sugar

3 large eggs

1 tablespoon pure vanilla extract

1 1/2 cups sour cream

1 1/2 cups boiling water

1 recipe Chocolate Satin Frosting
   (recipe follows)

1 • Preheat the oven to 350 degrees.

2 • Grease and lightly flour two 9-inch cake pans and set aside.

3 • Place the chocolate in a double boiler and melt over medium-low heat, stirring occasionally, until the chocolate melts. (Note: Do not let the chocolate cool too much or it will harden. If this happens, place the pan back on the heat for a few minutes, or put the chocolate in a microwave-proof container and heat 20 to 30 seconds.)

4 • Sift together the flour, baking soda, and salt in a bowl and set aside.

5 • Cream together the butter and brown sugar in a separate bowl with an electric mixer until light and fluffy.

6 • Add the eggs, one at a time, to the butter mixture, beating well after each addition. Beat until well blended. Add the vanilla and melted chocolate and stir by hand to mix. (Do not use the electric mixer to complete the batter because an overmixed batter will lead to a heavier, tougher cake.)

7 • Add the flour mixture, alternating with the sour cream, to the egg-butter mixture and stir just until the dry ingredients are moist and blended. Do not overmix.

8 • Stir in the boiling water and mix until well blended (the batter will be fairly liquid and runny).

9 • Divide the batter evenly between the prepared pans. Bake 45 to 50 minutes, until the cakes are firm to the touch and a toothpick inserted in the center of each cake comes out clean.

10 • Remove from the oven and cool the cakes for 10 to 15 minutes in the pans. Remove from the pans and continue to cool on a baking rack.

11 • Once the cakes have cooled completely, use a ser-

rated knife to slice off the top rounded portion of each cake to make a flat, even surface. Discard the trimmings.

12 • Place one of the layers cut side down on a cake plate. Top with about one-third of the frosting and spread evenly over the top of the cake. Place the other layer on top, cut side down. Top with the remaining frosting and spread over the top and sides of cake.

Chocolate Satin Frosting

This creamy frosting is also good on Chocolate Espresso Layer Cake (page 260) or Buttermilk Cake (page 266).

MAKES ABOUT 5 CUPS FROSTING

1½ cups heavy cream
⅔ cup sugar
5 large egg yolks
1 teaspoon pure vanilla extract
20 ounces (1¼ pounds) good-quality semisweet chocolate (such as Valrhona or Callebaut), very finely chopped (Note: The chocolate should be in very small pieces, almost shaved or shredded)
½ pound (2 sticks) unsalted butter, cut into ¼-inch cubes
⅓ cup light corn syrup
⅓ cup sour cream

1 • Combine the cream and sugar in a medium saucepan over medium-low heat and bring to a low boil, stirring constantly, until all the sugar has dissolved. Set aside.

2 • Combine the egg yolks and vanilla in a small bowl and whisk until well blended. Whisk ½ cup of the warm cream mixture into the yolks. Add the yolk mixture to the saucepan and cook, whisking constantly, over very low heat for 3 to 4 minutes, until the mixture coats the back of a spoon. (Note: It is important that the heat be very low and that you whisk constantly, otherwise the yolks may cook.)

3 • Add the chocolate and butter and whisk several times. Remove from the heat and whisk until the chocolate and butter have melted completely and the mixture is smooth.

4 • Add the corn syrup and sour cream and whisk until well blended. Transfer the frosting from the saucepan to a shallow bowl and refrigerate 30 to 40 minutes until cooled, stirring occasionally, until the mixture becomes thick and creamy. (Note: If you refrigerate it too long, the frosting will become too hard to work with.) Frost cake while the frosting is smooth and creamy.

Blackberry Jam Cake with Blackberry Cream Cheese Frosting

I found this old-fashioned recipe for a 4-layer cake in my grandmother's recipe collection. It's delicious!

MAKES ONE 9-INCH 4-LAYER CAKE; SERVES 12 TO 16

4 cups all-purpose flour

2 teaspoons baking soda

2 teaspoons ground cloves

2 teaspoons ground cinnamon

2 teaspoons ground allspice

1 teaspoon salt

$\frac{1}{2}$ pound (2 sticks) unsalted
  butter, softened

$1\frac{1}{2}$ cups sugar

4 large eggs

$\frac{3}{4}$ cup buttermilk

2 cups blackberry jam

1 cup chopped pecans

One 8-ounce jar Blackberry Spoon
  Fruit (made by American Spoon
  Foods) or your favorite
  blackberry jam

1 recipe Blackberry Cream Cheese
  Frosting (page 259)

1 pint fresh blackberries

1 • Preheat the oven to 350 degrees.

2 • Grease and lightly flour two 9-inch cake pans and set aside.

3 • Sift together the flour, baking soda, cloves, cinnamon, allspice, and salt in a bowl and stir to mix. Set aside.

4 • Cream the butter and sugar together in a bowl with an electric mixer until light and fluffy.

5 • Add the eggs, one at a time, and blend well. Stir in the buttermilk and mix well. Add the jam and stir to mix thoroughly.

6 • Mix the flour mixture with the egg mixture and stir to moisten the dry ingredients. Fold in the pecans.

7 • Divide the batter evenly between the prepared pans and bake 45 to 50 minutes, until the cakes are firm to the touch and a toothpick inserted in the center of each cake comes out clean.

8 • Remove from the oven and cool the cakes 10 to 15 minutes in the pans. Remove from the pans and continue to cool on a baking rack.

9 • Once the cakes have cooled completely, use a serrated knife to slice off the top rounded portion of each cake to make a flat, even surface. Discard the trimmings. Cut each layer in half horizontally through the center to make 4 layers.

10 • Place 1 layer on a plate cut side down and spread evenly with $\frac{1}{3}$ of the Blackberry Spoon Fruit. Top with about 1 cup frosting and spread evenly. Sprinkle with one-fourth of the blackberries. Repeat the process with the next 2 layers. Top with the final layer, cut side down, and spread the top and sides with the remaining frosting. Garnish the top of the cake with fresh blackberries if desired.

Buttermilk Cake with Fresh Strawberries and Cream

Our pastry chef, Amy Buckner, makes this cake in square pans, which gives it a unique look. Although it's delicious with strawberries, it's also great with a mix of seasonal berries.

MAKES ONE 9-INCH 4-LAYER CAKE; SERVES 12 TO 16

4½ cups all-purpose flour

1 tablespoon baking powder

1 teaspoon baking soda

½ teaspoon salt

¾ pound (3 sticks) unsalted butter

2½ cups granulated sugar

6 large eggs

2 teaspoons pure vanilla extract

2 cups buttermilk

3 cups heavy cream

3 pints fresh strawberries, hulled, and cut into ½-inch lengthwise slices

1 pint fresh strawberries, hulled

Confectioners' sugar, to garnish, optional

1 • Preheat the oven to 325 degrees.

2 • Grease and lightly flour two 9-inch by 2-inch deep round or square cake pans and set aside.

3 • Sift together the flour, baking powder, baking soda, and salt in a bowl and stir to mix. Set aside.

4 • Cream together the butter and 2¼ cups of the sugar in a separate bowl with an electric mixer.

5 • Add the eggs, one at a time, to the butter mixture and beat several minutes until light and fluffy. Add the vanilla and stir by hand to mix.

6 • Add the buttermilk to the flour mixture, alternating with the egg mixture, and stir until well combined.

7 • Divide the batter evenly between the prepared pans and bake 45 to 50 minutes, until the cakes are firm to the touch and a toothpick inserted in the center of each cake comes out clean.

8 • Remove from the oven and cool the cakes 10 to 15 minutes in the pans. Remove from the pans and continue to cool on a baking rack.

9 • Once the cakes have cooled completely, use a serrated knife to slice off the rounded top part of each layer to make a flat, even surface. Cut each layer in half horizontally through the center to make 4 layers. Discard the trimmings.

10 • Meanwhile, whip the cream in a bowl with the remaining one-quarter cup sugar until soft peaks form.

11 • Place one of the layers, cut side down, on a cake plate. Top with about one-third of the whipped cream and one-third of the sliced berries. Repeat the process with the next 2 layers and the remaining cream and sliced berries. Place the fourth layer on

top, cut side down. Top with the whole hulled berries and sprinkle with confectioners' sugar just before serving. (Note: If you are going to refrigerate the cake, add the confectioners' sugar just before serving. The cake can be refrigerated up to 1 day ahead.)

variations: Instead of only strawberries, use 2 pints strawberries and 1 pint blueberries, blackberries, or raspberries. You can also use Lemon Curd (page 270) between the cake layers, alternating Lemon Curd with whipped cream.

Coconut Cake with Lemon Curd Filling and Seven-Minute Frosting

Our coconut cake is a little different from the classic recipe in that we flavor the cake with coconut cream, and spread tangy Lemon Curd (page 270) between the layers. We then top the cake with Seven-Minute Frosting (page 270), an old-fashioned meringue-like topping that takes about that long to make, and is best served the same day it is made. The cake is also great with Coconut Cream Cheese Frosting (page 259), which will keep for several days.

MAKES ONE 9-INCH LAYER CAKE; SERVES 10 TO 12

2½ cups all-purpose flour

2 teaspoons baking powder

½ teaspoon baking soda

½ teaspoon salt

12 tablespoons (1½ sticks) unsalted butter, softened

1¾ cups sugar

6 large eggs, separated

1 teaspoon pure vanilla extract

1½ cups buttermilk

¼ cup canned coconut cream (such as Coco Lopez)

1 cup Lemon Curd (page 270)

1 cup sweetened flaked coconut

1 recipe Seven-Minute Frosting (page 270)

1 • Preheat the oven to 325 degrees.

2 • Grease and lightly flour two 9-inch cake pans and set aside.

3 • Sift together the flour, baking powder, baking soda, and salt in a large bowl and stir to mix. Set aside.

4 • Cream together the butter and sugar in a separate bowl with an electric mixer.

5 • Add the egg yolks, one at a time, beating well after each addition until mixture is light and fluffy. Add the vanilla and stir by hand to mix well.

6 • Add the flour mixture to the butter mixture, alternating with the buttermilk and coconut cream. Stir just until all the dry ingredients are moist and blended. Do not overmix.

7 • With an electric mixer whip the egg whites in a separate bowl 2 to 3 minutes, until soft peaks form. Gently fold the egg whites into the cake batter.

8 • Divide the batter evenly between the prepared pans and bake 40 to 45 minutes, until the cakes are firm to the touch and a toothpick inserted in the center of each cake comes out clean.

9 • Remove from the oven and cool the cakes 10 to 15 minutes in the pans. Remove from the pans and continue to cool on a baking rack.

10 • Once the cakes have cooled completely, use a long, serrated knife to slice off the top rounded portion of each cake to make a flat, even surface. Discard the trimmings.

11 • Place 1 layer cut side down on a cake plate. Spread

with all the Lemon Curd, and sprinkle with ½ cup coconut. Place the other cake layer cut side down on the coconut. Spread top and sides of the cake with Seven-Minute Frosting and sprinkle with remaining coconut.

Lemon Curd

3 large eggs
3 large egg yolks
1 cup sugar
1 cup fresh lemon juice (4 to 6 lemons)
2 tablespoons unsalted butter

1 • Place the eggs and egg yolks in a heavy, medium nonaluminum saucepan and whisk in the sugar until well blended.

2 • Slowly whisk in the lemon juice and place over low heat, whisking constantly, 10 to 15 minutes, until the mixture thickens. (Note: Be careful not to let the mixture get too hot or the eggs will curdle.)

3 • Remove from the heat and whisk in the butter. Cool to room temperature. Refrigerate in an airtight container until ready to use or up to 2 weeks.

Seven-Minute Frosting

2 large egg whites
1½ cups sugar
¼ cup cold water
1 tablespoon light corn syrup
1 teaspoon pure vanilla extract

1 • Combine the egg whites, sugar, water, and corn syrup in a double boiler set over simmering water over low heat.

2 • Beat with a handheld electric mixer 3 to 4 minutes on low speed. Increase speed to high and mix 3 to 4 minutes longer. The icing will become shiny and satiny and form soft peaks.

3 • Remove from the heat, add the vanilla, and continue to beat on high speed 1 to 2 minutes longer, until the mixture becomes thick. (Note: This frosting becomes slightly crusty as it stands and therefore should be made and spread on the cake no more than 2 to 3 hours before serving.) Although the frosting doesn't refrigerate well, it is worth the effort because it complements this cake so beautifully. If you prefer a make-ahead frosting, try Coconut Cream Cheese Frosting (page 259).

German Chocolate Cake with Coconut-Pecan Caramel Frosting

This traditional layer cake—with its delightfully gooey frosting—is a great addition to casual buffets, potlucks, tailgates, and picnics.

MAKES ONE 9-INCH 4-LAYER CAKE;
SERVES 12 TO 16

3³/₄ cups all-purpose flour

2 cups unsweetened cocoa powder

2 teaspoons baking powder

1 teaspoon baking soda

¹/₂ teaspoon salt

3¹/₂ cups sugar

4 large eggs

1 cup hot water

1 cup milk

1 cup canola or safflower oil

2 teaspoons pure vanilla extract

1 recipe Coconut-Pecan Caramel
   Frosting (recipe follows)

1 • Preheat the oven to 350 degrees.

2 • Grease and lightly flour two 9-inch cake pans and set aside.

3 • Sift together the flour, cocoa, baking powder, baking soda, and salt in a bowl and stir to mix. Set aside.

4 • Combine the sugar, eggs, water, milk, oil, and vanilla in a separate bowl and whisk until well blended.

5 • Slowly add the flour mixture to the egg mixture, about one-quarter at a time, scraping the sides of the bowl and blending well after each addition.

6 • Divide the batter evenly between the prepared pans and bake 50 to 55 minutes, until the cakes are firm to the touch and a toothpick inserted in the center of each cake comes out clean.

7 • Remove from the oven and cool the cakes 10 to 15 minutes in the pans. Remove from the pans and continue to cool on a baking rack.

8 • Once the cakes have cooled completely, use a long, serrated knife to slice off the top rounded portion of each cake to make a flat, even surface. Cut each layer in half horizontally through the center to make 4 layers. Discard the trimmings.

9 • Place the first layer on a cake plate, cut side down, and top with one-quarter of the frosting. Repeat with the remaining 3 layers. At Foster's, we don't frost the sides of the cake; we love the way the frosting oozes down the sides, creating a homey, casual look.

Coconut-Pecan Caramel Frosting

3 cups sugar

3 cups heavy cream

1 teaspoon pure vanilla extract

3 cups (8 ounces) sweetened
flaked coconut, lightly toasted

4 cups coarsely chopped pecans,
lightly toasted

1 • Place the sugar in a very large, dry skillet over medium heat. (Note: Be sure to use a large skillet. Otherwise, the hot, syrupy mixture may boil over when you add the cream in step 3.)

2 • Without stirring, let the mixture melt and cook for 8 to 10 minutes, until it turns amber in color. (Note: If the mixture begins to turn dark around the edges, do not stir, but shake or rotate the pan so the mixture cooks evenly. Stirring will cause the mixture to be lumpy.)

3 • Slowly and carefully stir in the cream and vanilla and stir for 2 to 3 minutes, until smooth and all the lumps dissolve.

4 • Mix the coconut and pecans together in a large bowl. Add the cream mixture and stir to mix. Cool to room temperature before frosting the cake. (Note: Do not refrigerate the frosting; it will become too hard to work with.)

Four-Layer Blueberry Gingerbread Cake with Mocha Cream

Kathy Edwards, a pastry chef at Nana's Restaurant in Durham, North Carolina, worked with us one summer and created this luscious cake. We continue to make it every summer and it's always a hit, especially during blueberry season.

MAKES ONE 9-INCH 4-LAYER CAKE;
SERVES 12 TO 16

4 cups plus 2 tablespoons all-purpose flour

2 teaspoons baking powder

1 teaspoon baking soda

2 teaspoons ground cinnamon

2 teaspoons ground ginger

1 teaspoon ground nutmeg

$\frac{1}{2}$ teaspoon salt

2 large eggs

$\frac{1}{3}$ cup sugar

1 cup canola or safflower oil

1 cup molasses

2 cups buttermilk

3 cups fresh or frozen blueberries

1 recipe Mocha Cream (recipe follows)

Confectioners' sugar, to garnish, optional

1 • Preheat the oven to 350 degrees.

2 • Grease and lightly flour two 9-inch cake pans and set aside.

3 • Sift together 4 cups of the flour, baking powder, baking soda, cinnamon, ginger, nutmeg, and salt in a bowl and stir to mix. Set aside.

4 • Mix together the eggs and sugar in a separate bowl and beat with an electric mixer until light and fluffy.

5 • Slowly add the oil and molasses to the egg mixture while beating constantly until well combined.

6 • Add the flour mixture to the egg mixture, alternating with the buttermilk, stirring after each addition just until all the dry ingredients are moist and blended. Do not overmix.

7 • Toss 2 cups of the blueberries with the remaining flour in a separate bowl and fold into the batter.

8 • Divide the batter evenly between the prepared pans and bake 35 to 40 minutes, until the cakes are firm to the touch and a toothpick inserted in the center of each cake comes out clean.

9 • Remove from the oven and cool the cakes 10 to 15 minutes in the pans. Remove from the pans and continue to cool on a baking rack.

10 • Once the cakes have cooled completely, use a long, serrated knife to slice off the top rounded portion of each cake to make a flat, even surface. Discard the trimmings. Slice each cake horizontally through the center to make 4 thin layers.

11 • Place 1 layer, cut side down, on a cake plate and top with about one-third of the Mocha Cream. Sprinkle with about one-third of the remaining blueberries.

Repeat the process with the second and third layers. Place the fourth layer cut side down on the Mocha Cream and berries. Just before serving, dust generously with confectioners' sugar through a fine sieve if desired. (Note: If you are going to refrigerate the cake, add the confectioners' sugar just before serving. The cake can be assembled and refrigerated up to 1 day ahead.)

Mocha Cream

MAKES ABOUT 4 CUPS MOCHA CREAM

2 cups heavy cream
1/2 cup firmly packed light brown sugar
1 tablespoon unsweetened cocoa powder
2 teaspoons instant espresso powder

1 • Whip the cream in a bowl at high speed with an electric mixer until soft peaks form.

2 • Add the brown sugar, cocoa, and instant espresso and whip lightly until the sugar and espresso dissolve. Refrigerate in an airtight container until ready to use or up to 1 day.

Chocolate Pound Cake

This not-too-sweet variation on the classic pound cake is wonderful served with a dollop of lightly sweetened whipped cream and fresh berries. The cake keeps well, and can be frozen, too.

MAKES ONE 10-INCH BUNDT CAKE; SERVES 10 TO 12

3 cups all-purpose flour

$1/2$ cup unsweetened cocoa powder

2 teaspoons baking powder

$1/2$ teaspoon salt

$3/4$ pound (3 sticks) unsalted butter, softened

3 cups sugar

5 large eggs

1 cup milk

2 tablespoons pure vanilla extract or coffee-flavored liqueur

Melted chocolate, to garnish, optional

Cocoa powder, to garnish, optional

Confectioners' sugar, to garnish, optional

1 • Preheat the oven to 350 degrees.

2 • Grease and lightly flour a 10-inch Bundt pan and set aside.

3 • Sift together the flour, cocoa, baking powder, and salt in a bowl and stir to mix. Set aside.

4 • Cream the butter and sugar together in a separate bowl with an electric mixer until light and fluffy.

5 • Add the eggs one at a time, beating well after each addition until the batter is smooth.

6 • Mix together the milk and vanilla in a small bowl. Add to the butter mixture, alternating with the flour mixture, scraping down the sides of the bowl several times. Mix just until smooth and all the ingredients are moist and well blended. Do not overmix. The batter will be slightly stiff.

7 • Pour and spread the batter into the prepared pan and bake 1 to $1\frac{1}{4}$ hours or until a toothpick inserted in the center of the cake comes out clean.

8 • Remove from the oven and cool 20 to 30 minutes in the pan. Turn the cake out of the pan and continue to cool on a baking rack before slicing. Drizzle with melted chocolate or dust with cocoa powder or confectioners' sugar, if desired.

Lemon-Almond Pound Cake

This dense, moist cake is brushed with a tart, lemony glaze that soaks into the cake. It's addictive! Try it with fresh strawberries or raspberries and some whipped cream or ice cream.

4½ cups all-purpose flour

1 tablespoon baking powder

½ teaspoon baking soda

½ teaspoon salt

¾ pound (3 sticks) unsalted butter, softened

3 cups sugar

6 large eggs

Grated zest and juice of 3 lemons

1¼ cups milk

3 cups sliced almonds

Lemon Glaze (recipe follows)

1 • Preheat the oven to 350 degrees.

2 • Grease and lightly flour two 9 by 5 by 3-inch loaf pans and set aside.

3 • Sift together the flour, baking powder, baking soda, and salt in a bowl and stir to mix. Set aside.

4 • Cream together the butter and sugar in a separate bowl with an electric mixer until light and fluffy.

5 • Add the eggs, one at a time, beating well after each addition.

6 • Combine the lemon zest, lemon juice, and milk in a small bowl and stir until well combined.

7 • Add the flour mixture to the egg mixture alternating with the milk mixture and stir until well combined. Fold in the almonds and stir to mix.

8 • Pour the batter into the prepared pans and bake 50 to 60 minutes, until the loaves have risen and a toothpick inserted in the center of each loaf comes out clean.

9 • Remove from the oven and cool 10 to 15 minutes in the pans. Meanwhile, make the glaze.

10 • Turn the loaves out of the pans, and while the loaves are still warm, brush with the glaze. Serve immediately or continue to cool on a baking rack.

- -

Lemon Glaze

Juice of 3 lemons

½ cup sugar

Place the lemon juice and sugar in a small saucepan over medium heat and bring to a low boil. Cook, stirring occasionally, 7 to 10 minutes or until the sugar has dissolved and mixture has thickened slightly. Drizzle immediately on top of the cake.

Cream Cheese Pound Cake

This rich, dense cake keeps well and freezes beautifully. Try it with fresh peaches, sorbet, ice cream, or fruit compote.

3 cups all-purpose flour

1 teaspoon baking powder

$\frac{1}{2}$ teaspoon baking soda

$\frac{1}{2}$ teaspoon salt

One 8-ounce package cream cheese, softened

$\frac{3}{4}$ pound (3 sticks) unsalted butter, softened

3 cups sugar

6 large eggs

2 teaspoons pure vanilla extract

1 • Preheat the oven to 350 degrees.

2 • Grease and lightly flour a 10-inch bundt pan and set aside.

3 • Sift together the flour, baking powder, baking soda, and salt in a bowl and stir to mix. Set aside.

4 • Cream together the cream cheese, butter, and sugar in a separate bowl with an electric mixer until light and fluffy.

5 • Slowly add the eggs, one at a time, beating well after each addition. Add the vanilla and mix until well blended.

6 • Add the flour mixture to the butter mixture and beat just until the dry ingredients are moist and blended. Do not overmix.

7 • Pour the batter into the prepared pan and spread evenly. (Note: The batter will be very thick.) Bake 1 to 1¼ hours until the cake is golden brown and a toothpick inserted in the center comes out clean.

8 • Remove from the oven and cool 20 to 30 minutes in the pan. Turn the cake out of the pan and continue to cool on a baking rack.

variations: You can also add spices—up to 2 teaspoons total—such as cinnamon, cardamom, nutmeg, or allspice, to the batter. Try lemon or almond extract instead of vanilla; fold in chopped dried fruit or nuts, if desired. One cup sour cream can be substituted for the cream cheese for a slightly different taste and texture.

Turtle Cheesecake

Cheesecake is a staple at the Market, but it's different nearly every day because we vary the toppings, crusts, and flavorings. Cookie crusts are particularly good with cheesecakes. If you prefer your cheesecake plain, just serve it without the topping.

MAKES ONE 9-INCH CHEESECAKE; SERVES 10 TO 12

Crust

1½ cups graham cracker crumbs

½ cup finely chopped pecans (pulse in a food processor several times)

6 tablespoons (¾ stick) unsalted butter, melted

1 • Grease a 9-inch springform pan. Wrap the outside of the pan, including the bottom, with a large square of aluminum foil. Set aside.

2 • Combine the graham cracker crumbs, pecans, and butter in a bowl and mix until the crumbs and pecans are moistened. Press the mixture into the bottom and about 1 inch up the inside of the prepared pan. Place in the refrigerator to chill until ready to use.

Filling

1½ pounds cream cheese, softened

¾ cup sugar

2 tablespoons all-purpose flour

3 large eggs

1 large egg yolk

½ cup heavy cream

2 teaspoons pure vanilla extract

1 recipe Turtle Cheesecake Topping (recipe follows)

1 • Preheat the oven to 325 degrees.

2 • Cut the cream cheese into small pieces and place in a bowl. Blend with an electric mixer until soft and creamy.

3 • Add the sugar and flour slowly until they are completely incorporated and the mixture is smooth. Scrape the sides of the bowl several times during this process. Add the eggs and the egg yolk one at a time, beating thoroughly after each addition.

4 • Combine the cream with the vanilla in a small bowl and slowly add to the cream cheese mixture. Mix until thoroughly blended.

5 • Pour the filling into the prepared pan. Place the cheesecake in a large roasting pan or baking dish. Add enough water to come 1 inch up the sides of the pan to make a water bath.

6 • Place the roasting pan with the cheesecake in the water bath in the oven and bake 1 to 1¼ hours, until the cheesecake sets and is firm about three-fourths of the way into the center; the center will be slightly loose.

7 • Remove the cheesecake from the oven; remove the

cheesecake from the water bath. Place the cheesecake on a baking rack to cool completely. Leave in
the springform pan and place in the refrigerator to
chill several hours or overnight. Add the topping. Refrigerate the cheesecake until ready to serve.

Turtle Cheesecake Topping

1 cup sugar

1 cup heavy cream

$\frac{1}{2}$ teaspoon pure vanilla extract

$\frac{1}{2}$ cup coarsely chopped pecans,
  toasted (page 141)

2 ounces semisweet chocolate,
  melted

1 • Place the sugar in a very large, dry skillet over medium heat. (Note: Be sure to use a large skillet; otherwise, the hot, syrupy mixture may boil over when
you add the cream.)

2 • Without stirring, let the mixture melt and cook 8 to
10 minutes, until it turns amber in color. (Note: If
the mixture begins to turn dark around the edges, do
not stir, but shake or rotate the pan so the mixture
cooks evenly. Stirring will cause the mixture to be
lumpy.)

3 • Slowly and carefully stir in the cream and stir to
mix. Simmer 5 to 6 minutes longer, stirring constantly, until the lumps dissolve. Stir in the vanilla
and pecans; remove from the heat. Pour the caramel
mixture from the skillet into a bowl and cool completely to room temperature. (Note: Do not refrigerate the topping until after you've put it on the
cheesecake; it will be too hard to spread.)

4 • Spread a thin layer of the caramel on top of the
chilled cheesecake. Dip a fork into the melted chocolate and drizzle it over the caramel topping.

variation: Kahlúa Cheesecake

Prepare the cheesecake as the recipe directs
through step 5. Prepare the Kahlúa topping as follows: Place 2 ounces chopped bittersweet chocolate,
2 tablespoons brewed coffee, $\frac{1}{4}$ cup Kahlúa, and
2 teaspoons instant espresso powder into a small
stainless steel bowl over a pan of simmering water
or a double boiler. Stir the mixture constantly until
the chocolate melts and the mixture is smooth. Remove the bowl from heat and stir in 2 teaspoons

pure vanilla extract. Cool to room temperature. Pour the chocolate and Kahlúa mixture on top of the cheesecake mixture, after it is in the prepared pan, then drag it through the mixture from the center of the cake to the outside edges with a knife to get a swirled effect. Proceed as the recipe directs at step 6.

variation: Pumpkin Cheesecake

Prepare the cheesecake as the recipe directs through step 4. Combine ½ cup canned pumpkin, ½ teaspoon ground cinnamon, and ½ teaspoon ground allspice in a small bowl and mix until thoroughly blended. Pour the pumpkin mixture into the filling and stir until well blended. Proceed as recipe directs at step 5.

Basic Piecrust

We use this recipe at the Market for most of our single-crust pies, including Lemon Chess Pie with Sour Cherries (page 283), Coconut Custard Pie (page 284), Chocolate Meringue Pie (page 287), Bourbon-Pecan Pie (page 288), and Silky Pumpkin Pie (page 289). It's easy, and can be made several days in advance. The recipe can be doubled, so it's sensible to make enough for several pies at a time. The extra dough can be rolled, placed in a pie pan, wrapped with plastic wrap, and frozen until ready to use. The next time you want to bake a pie, half the work is already done. We add vegetable shortening because it makes the crust exceptionally flaky, but if you prefer the taste of butter, by all means use all butter.

MAKES TWO 9-INCH PIECRUSTS

3 cups all-purpose flour

½ cup vegetable shortening

8 tablespoons (1 stick) cold, unsalted butter, cut into ¼-inch cubes

1 large egg

⅓ cup plus 2 to 3 tablespoons ice-cold water

1 teaspoon salt

1 teaspoon distilled white vinegar

1 • Place the flour in a large bowl.

2 • Cut the shortening and butter into the flour with a pastry blender or 2 knives until the mixture resembles coarse meal. (Or pulse in the bowl of a food processor fitted with the metal blade 10 to 12 times. Transfer to a large bowl to continue making the dough.)

3 • In a separate bowl, beat the egg, ⅓ cup of the water, salt, and vinegar. Add to the flour mixture, stirring just until the dough comes together in a round ball; do not overmix. Add additional water—1 tablespoon at a time—if the dough seems too dry.

4 • With lightly floured hands, place the dough on a lightly floured work surface and divide into 2 pieces. Form each piece into a flat round about 1½ inches thick. Wrap each with plastic wrap and refrigerate at least 60 minutes, or up to 3 days.

5 • Working with 1 piece of dough at a time, roll the chilled dough on a lightly floured work surface to form a 12-inch circle. Roll up the dough onto the rolling pin, and then lay it into the pie pan. Press the dough lightly into the bottom and sides of the pie pan.

6 • Trim the edges of the dough, leaving about a 1½-inch overhang, and make a crimped or flattened edge. Cover with plastic wrap and refrigerate at least 50

minutes, or up to 3 days, until ready to use, or proceed as follows for a prebaked pie shell.

7 • To prepare a prebaked pie shell, preheat the oven to 425 degrees.

8 • Line the pie shell with aluminum foil or parchment paper. Fill the lined pie shell with uncooked dried beans or pie weights. Bake 15 to 20 minutes.

9 • Remove the beans and foil and return the pie shell to the oven and bake about 5 minutes, until golden brown.

Lemon Chess Pie with Sour Cherries

This variation on a classic southern pie is so rich and tangy, a small slice is often enough—even for those with an insatiable sweet tooth. The addition of sour cherries makes this pie unique.

MAKES ONE 9-INCH PIE; SERVES 8 TO 10

1½ cups sugar

1 tablespoon yellow cornmeal

1 tablespoon all-purpose flour

3 large eggs, lightly beaten

Grated zest and juice of 2 lemons

4 tablespoons (½ stick) unsalted
    butter, melted and cooled

½ cup heavy cream

1 teaspoon pure vanilla extract

½ cup fresh sour cherries, pitted,
    or 1 cup dried cherries (soak in
    hot water for 1 hour, then drain)

1 unbaked piecrust (Basic
    Piecrust, page 281)

1 • Preheat the oven to 350 degrees.

2 • Mix together the sugar, cornmeal, and flour in a bowl and stir until well blended.

3 • Add the eggs to the sugar mixture and whisk until the ingredients are smooth and well blended.

4 • Add the lemon zest, lemon juice, butter, cream, and vanilla and mix until well blended.

5 • Place the cherries in the bottom of the chilled, unbaked piecrust.

6 • Pour the filling on top of the cherries. Bake 50 to 55 minutes or until the top is golden brown and a toothpick inserted into the center of the pie comes out clean.

7 • Cool the pie completely on a baking rack before slicing.

variations: This pie is great with other dried or fresh berries added. Scatter about ½ cup fresh (or drained, reconstituted) berries evenly over the bottom of the pie shell before adding the filling. For a Holiday Eggnog Pie, eliminate the lemon zest and lemon juice. Replace the heavy cream with 1 cup good-quality eggnog and add 1 egg, 3 tablespoons dark rum, and 1 teaspoon ground nutmeg in step 4. Proceed as directed. For a Chocolate Chess Pie with Fresh Raspberries, eliminate the lemon zest and lemon juice. Mix ½ cup unsweetened cocoa powder into the sugar-flour mixture. Add an additional ½ cup heavy cream and 2 teaspoons pure vanilla extract to the filling in step 4. Place ½ cup fresh raspberries in the bottom of the piecrust and pour the filling over the raspberries. Proceed as directed.

Coconut Custard Pie

We love the simplicity of this old-fashioned pie.

¹/₂ cup milk

1¹/₄ cups sweetened flaked
   coconut

4 tablespoons (¹/₂ stick) unsalted
   butter, melted and cooled

³/₄ cup sugar

3 large eggs

1 teaspoon pure vanilla extract

Grated zest and juice of 1 lemon

1 unbaked piecrust (Basic
   Piecrust, page 281)

1 • Preheat the oven to 350 degrees.

2 • Combine the milk and coconut in a bowl. Stir to mix
   and set aside.

3 • Stir together the butter and sugar in a separate bowl
   until well blended.

4 • Add the eggs, one at a time, to the butter mixture
   and stir until well blended.

5 • Stir the coconut mixture, vanilla, lemon zest, and
   lemon juice into the egg mixture and mix well.

6 • Pour into the prepared piecrust and bake 40 to 45
   minutes, until the pie is lightly golden on the top and
   firm to the touch.

7 • Cool the pie completely on a baking rack before slicing.

French Silk Pie

As luxurious as its name suggests, this refrigerator pie has just a hint of port to add depth and complexity. French silk pie can be made up to 4 days in advance and topped with lightly sweetened whipped cream just before serving.

MAKES ONE 9-INCH PIE; SERVES 8 TO 10

Crust

1½ cups chocolate wafer cookie (or other chocolate cookie) crumbs or graham cracker crumbs

½ cup finely ground walnuts (pulse in food processor several times)

6 tablespoons (¾ stick) unsalted butter, melted

¼ cup sugar

1 • Preheat the oven to 325 degrees.

2 • Combine the chocolate wafer crumbs, walnuts, butter, and sugar in a bowl and stir until the crumbs are moistened.

3 • Spread the mixture evenly on the bottom and sides of a 9-inch pie pan, then press the mixture with your fingers or the back of a spoon on the bottom and sides of the pan to form the crust.

4 • Bake 10 to 12 minutes, until the crust is firm. Set aside on a baking rack to cool completely.

Filling

6 ounces unsweetened chocolate

4 tablespoons (½ stick) unsalted butter

1 cup sugar

4 large eggs

¼ cup port

1 teaspoon pure vanilla extract

¼ teaspoon salt

1 cup heavy cream, whipped and lightly sweetened with ¼ cup sugar

Chocolate curls, to garnish, optional

1 • Place the chocolate, butter, and sugar in a double boiler. Warm the mixture over medium-low heat until the chocolate and butter melt, stirring occasionally. Remove from the heat and let the mixture cool to room temperature.

2 • Combine the eggs, port, vanilla, and salt in a bowl and stir until well blended.

3 • Slowly add the egg mixture to the chocolate mixture in the double boiler. Continue to cook, whisking constantly, 5 to 6 minutes, until well blended and the mixture thickens.

4 • Pour the filling into the baked piecrust and chill at least 4 hours or overnight before serving.

5 • When ready to serve, top with whipped cream and garnish with chocolate curls.

Key Lime Pie with Walnut–Graham Cracker Crust

Like our blueberry muffins, we've made Key lime pie every day for over ten years. And, like the muffins, this pie is one of our customers' favorites. The walnut-flavored crust and the grated lime zest in the filling give this pie additional flavor.

MAKES ONE 9-INCH PIE; SERVES 8 TO 10

Crust

1½ cups graham cracker crumbs

½ cup ground walnuts (pulse in the food processor a few times)

3 tablespoons sugar

6 tablespoons (¾ stick) unsalted butter, melted

1 • Preheat the oven to 325 degrees.

2 • Combine the graham cracker crumbs, walnuts, and sugar in a bowl and stir to mix.

3 • Add the butter and stir until all the ingredients are moistened.

4 • Spread the mixture evenly on the bottom and sides of a 9-inch pie pan, then press the mixture with your fingers or the back of a spoon on the bottom and sides of the pan to form the crust.

5 • Bake 8 to 10 minutes, just until golden brown and firm. Remove from the oven and set aside to cool.

Filling

3 large eggs

One 14-ounce can sweetened condensed milk

Grated zest and juice of 10 to 12 Key limes or 6 regular limes

1 teaspoon pure vanilla extract

1 cup heavy cream, whipped and lightly sweetened with ¼ cup sugar

1 • Preheat the oven to 325 degrees.

2 • Combine the eggs, condensed milk, lime zest, lime juice, and vanilla in a bowl and whisk until well blended.

3 • Pour the batter into the baked, cooled pie shell and bake 20 to 25 minutes, until firm.

4 • Remove from the oven and allow to cool completely. Place in the refrigerator and chill for several hours or overnight.

5 • When ready to serve, top with whipped cream.

Chocolate Meringue Pie

My mother has been making this pie for as long as I can remember. It's homey, easy to make, comforting, and truly delicious.

MAKES ONE 9-INCH PIE; SERVES 8 TO 10

1¼ cups plus 3 tablespoons sugar

2 tablespoons all-purpose flour

½ cup unsweetened cocoa
    powder

2 cups milk

2 tablespoons cornstarch

4 large eggs, separated

1 teaspoon pure vanilla extract

4 tablespoons (½ stick) unsalted
    butter, cut into ½-inch pieces

1 prebaked piecrust (Basic
    Piecrust, page 281)

1 tablespoon sugar, to garnish,
    optional

1 • Preheat the oven to 350 degrees.

2 • Combine 1¼ cups of the sugar, flour, and cocoa in a bowl and stir to mix. Set aside.

3 • Whisk together the milk, cornstarch, and egg yolks in a separate bowl until well mixed.

4 • Slowly add the milk-egg mixture to the flour mixture and whisk to blend thoroughly.

5 • Add the filling mixture to a saucepan and cook and stir over low heat 8 to 10 minutes, until the mixture becomes thick and smooth. Remove from the heat and stir in the vanilla and butter. This can be made several days in advance and refrigerated, with plastic wrap placed on the surface of the filling to prevent a film from forming.

6 • Whip the egg whites in a bowl with an electric mixer for 2 to 3 minutes, or until soft peaks form. Add the remaining sugar and beat just to mix.

7 • Pour the filling into the prepared piecrust. Top with the beaten egg whites, spreading evenly to cover the chocolate mixture. Sprinkle with additional sugar if desired.

8 • Bake 5 to 7 minutes, until the meringue topping is golden brown. Remove the pie from the oven and cool for 2 hours before slicing.

Bourbon-Pecan Pie

We've added bourbon to classic southern pecan pie for extra flavor; if you prefer, you can use dark rum instead. (It's equally good without alcohol, too.) This is one of our top-selling desserts, particularly at Thanksgiving, when we make about five hundred pies!

4 large eggs

1 cup sugar

2 tablespoons unsalted butter, melted

1 cup dark corn syrup

2 tablespoons bourbon

1 teaspoon pure vanilla extract

2 cups coarsely chopped pecans

1 unbaked piecrust (Basic Piecrust, page 281)

1 • Preheat the oven to 350 degrees.

2 • Mix together the eggs, sugar, butter, corn syrup, bourbon, and vanilla in a bowl and stir to thoroughly combine all the ingredients.

3 • Fold in the pecans and pour the pie filling into the prepared pie shell. Bake 50 minutes to 1 hour, until the pie is firm around the edges and slightly loose in the center.

4 • Cool the pie completely on a baking rack before slicing.

variations: Add 1 cup semisweet chocolate chips for an even richer pie. Or add 1 cup peeled, diced Granny Smith or other tart apples and only 1 cup pecans for a Bourbon-Apple-Pecan Pie.

Silky Pumpkin Pie

Inspired by the creamy, flan-type desserts that I tasted on a trip to Argentina, this pie is much smoother than classic American pumpkin pie. (Sweetened condensed milk is the secret.) The pie will keep several days in the refrigerator, but make sure to serve it warm or at room temperature.

MAKES ONE 9-INCH PIE; SERVES 8 TO 10

3 large eggs

$^1/_3$ cup sugar

One 14-ounce can sweetened
   condensed milk

$1^1/_2$ cups (one 15-ounce can)
   cooked pureed pumpkin

3 tablespoons unsalted butter,
   melted and cooled

1 tablespoon all-purpose flour

$^1/_2$ teaspoon ground ginger

$^1/_2$ teaspoon ground cinnamon

$^1/_4$ teaspoon ground nutmeg

$^1/_4$ teaspoon ground cloves

$^1/_8$ teaspoon salt

1 unbaked piecrust (Basic
   Piecrust, page 281)

Lightly sweetened whipped cream
   or ice cream, to garnish,
   optional

1 • Preheat the oven to 325 degrees.

2 • Combine the eggs, sugar, sweetened condensed milk, and pumpkin in a large bowl and whisk until well blended. Add the butter and stir until thoroughly blended.

3 • Mix the flour, ginger, cinnamon, nutmeg, cloves, and salt in a separate bowl. Stir into the pumpkin mixture.

4 • Pour into the prepared piecrust and bake 45 to 50 minutes, until the pie is light golden on top, firm to the touch, and set in the center when you shake it gently.

5 • Cool completely on a baking rack before slicing. Serve with whipped cream or vanilla ice cream if desired.

Fresh Peach Pie with Cream Cheese Crust

My mother makes the best peach pie I've ever had. The rich cream cheese crust complements the simple flavor of really ripe peaches and the lightly sweetened whipped cream topping. Although the crust is baked, the filling is not, so this pie is great in summer, when you want to keep the kitchen cool. In fact, we advise that you make this only in summer, when peaches are at their peak.

MAKES ONE 9-INCH PIE; SERVES 8 TO 10

Cream Cheese Crust

1¼ cups all-purpose flour

1½ teaspoons baking powder

½ teaspoon salt

6 ounces cream cheese, softened

6 tablespoons (¾ stick) unsalted
   butter, softened

1½ teaspoons pure vanilla extract

½ cup sugar

1 • Sift the flour, baking powder, and salt in a bowl and stir to mix. Set aside.

2 • Beat together the cream cheese and butter with an electric mixer until well blended. Add the vanilla and stir to blend. Add the sugar and blend until well mixed.

3 • Add the flour mixture to the cream cheese mixture and mix thoroughly just until all the ingredients are well blended. Do not overmix.

4 • With lightly floured hands, form the dough into a flat round. Wrap and refrigerate 30 to 40 minutes, until firm enough to handle. The dough will be slightly sticky.

5 • Remove from the refrigerator and roll out on a lightly floured work surface into a 10- to 11-inch round that is ¼ to ½ inch thick. Roll up the dough onto the rolling pin, then lay it into a deep, 9-inch pie pan. Press the dough lightly into the bottom and sides of the pie pan.

6 • Trim the edges and use a fork to press the edges of the pastry down on the lip of the pie pan. Cover with plastic wrap and refrigerate 30 to 40 minutes or overnight before baking.

7 • Preheat the oven to 350 degrees.

8 • Bake 25 to 30 minutes, until the crust is light brown and puffy. Set aside to cool completely.

Peach Filling

5 cups peeled, pitted, sliced
    peaches (about 2$\frac{1}{2}$ to
    3 pounds, or 6 to 8 peaches)
$\frac{3}{4}$ cup sugar
1 cup heavy cream

1 • Mix the peaches with $\frac{1}{2}$ cup of the sugar and spread out evenly over the prepared piecrust.

2 • Whip the cream in a bowl with an electric mixer until soft peaks form. Add the remaining sugar and beat until stiff. Top the peaches with the cream mixture and refrigerate up to 8 hours or until ready to serve.

variation: Substitute 5 cups (about 3 pints) hulled, sliced strawberries for the peaches.

Fresh Strawberry Shortcake

Everyone loves strawberry shortcake—it's a sign that spring has truly come. That said, we suggest that you make this only when strawberries are in season. The shortcakes are like sweet biscuits, and really easy to make.

Topping

2 pints fresh strawberries, hulled
    and sliced
¾ cup sugar
1 cup heavy cream

1 • Mix half the strawberries with ½ cup of the sugar in a bowl and mash gently with a potato masher to release the juices. Toss with the remaining sliced strawberries and set aside 10 to 15 minutes or until the sugar has dissolved. You can refrigerate up to 6 hours, until ready to use.

2 • Whip the cream in a separate bowl with an electric mixer until soft peaks form. Add the remaining sugar and continue to whip about 1 minute more, until stiff peaks form. Refrigerate up to 6 hours, until ready to use.

Shortcakes

2 cups all-purpose flour
¼ cup sugar
1 teaspoon baking powder
1 teaspoon baking soda
½ teaspoon salt
8 tablespoons (1 stick) cold,
    unsalted butter, cut into
    ¼-inch cubes
¾ cup heavy cream

1 • Preheat the oven to 375 degrees.

2 • Grease a baking sheet and set aside.

3 • Combine the flour, sugar, baking powder, baking soda, and salt in a bowl and stir to mix.

4 • Add the butter and cut into the flour with a pastry blender or your fingertips until the mixture resembles coarse meal.

5 • Add the cream and stir to mix until the dough starts to come together. Do not overwork the dough or the shortcakes will be tough.

6 • Turn the dough out onto a lightly floured work surface and press together in a flat, round shape.

7 • Roll the dough to a thickness of ½ to ¾ inch. Cut six 3-inch rounds with a biscuit cutter or cookie cutter. Place on the prepared baking sheet and bake 12 to 15 minutes, until golden brown. Place on a baking rack to cool. These can be made several hours in advance.

8 • After the shortcakes have cooled, slice each one through the center (like a sandwich) to make 12 halves. For each shortcake, place the bottom half of 1 shortcake cut side up on a plate. Place a large spoonful of the strawberry mixture on top, add a spoonful of whipped cream, and add the top half of the shortcake. Top this with another spoonful of fresh berries, some whipped cream, and a few more berries. Serve immediately.

Strawberry-Rhubarb Crisp

This crisp is slightly tangy. You may want to add more sugar if you prefer a sweeter dessert. And, as with most crisps, vanilla ice cream or lightly sweetened whipped cream is a wonderful complement to this dish.

Topping

1 cup all-purpose flour

$\frac{1}{2}$ cup firmly packed light brown sugar

$\frac{1}{2}$ cup rolled oats

$\frac{1}{2}$ cup sliced almonds

2 teaspoons ground cinnamon

$\frac{1}{2}$ teaspoon ground cloves

$\frac{1}{4}$ teaspoon salt

12 tablespoons ($1\frac{1}{2}$ sticks) cold unsalted butter, cut into $\frac{1}{2}$-inch cubes

1 • Combine the flour, brown sugar, oats, almonds, cinnamon, cloves, and salt in a large bowl and stir to mix.

2 • Add the butter and cut it into the mixture with a pastry blender or 2 knives until the mixture resembles coarse meal.

- -

Filling

2 cups hulled, halved strawberries

4 cups chopped rhubarb

1 cup sugar (or up to $1\frac{1}{4}$ cups sugar for a sweeter crisp)

3 tablespoons all-purpose flour

1 tablespoon cornstarch

1 • Preheat the oven to 375 degrees.

2 • Grease an 11 by 7 by 3-inch baking dish and set aside.

3 • Combine the strawberries, rhubarb, sugar, flour, and cornstarch in a bowl and stir to mix. Pour into the prepared baking dish.

4 • Sprinkle the topping over the strawberry mixture and bake 40 to 45 minutes, until the fruit is bubbling around the edges and the top is crisp and golden brown. Cool slightly before serving. Serve warm.

variation: For an Apple Crisp, substitute 6 cups peeled, chopped, and cored apples for the strawberry and rhubarb. Increase the sugar to $1\frac{1}{4}$ cups and add the grated zest and juice of 1 lemon.

Say's Bread Pudding with Bourbon Icing

This is actually a variation on my mother's bread pudding. My mother, Say, adds much more butter and bourbon than we do at the Market, but our version is just as delicious.

12 tablespoons (1½ sticks) unsalted butter, melted

¾ cup firmly packed light brown sugar

½ of a baguette or 9 cups cubed bread (day-old or leave to dry for several hours after it has been cubed or torn into large pieces)

4 cups milk

5 large eggs

¾ cup granulated sugar

3 tablespoons pure vanilla extract

1 cup raisins

¼ cup bourbon

1 recipe Bourbon Icing (recipe follows)

1 • Preheat the oven to 350 degrees.

2 • Brush a 13 by 9 by 3-inch glass baking dish with 4 tablespoons of the melted butter. Sprinkle the brown sugar evenly over the bottom of the dish and set aside.

3 • Cut or tear the bread into 1-inch pieces and place in a bowl. Pour the milk over the bread and let stand 4 to 5 minutes, until the bread is soft.

4 • Combine the eggs, granulated sugar, remaining butter, and vanilla in a separate bowl and whisk together until well blended.

5 • Pour the egg mixture over the bread-and-milk mixture; add the raisins and stir to mix.

6 • Pour the mixture into the prepared baking dish, cover, and bake 50 to 60 minutes. Uncover, return to the oven, and continue to bake an additional 15 to 20 minutes, until the pudding is puffy and golden brown.

7 • Remove from the oven, pour the bourbon over the top of the pudding, and set aside to cool 10 to 15 minutes before serving. Top with the icing while the pudding is still warm.

Bourbon Icing

8 tablespoons (1 stick) unsalted butter

2 cups confectioners' sugar

1 cup heavy cream

¼ cup bourbon

1 • Place the butter in a saucepan and melt over medium heat. Remove from the heat.

2 • Whisk in the sugar, about ½ cup at time, and stir to mix until all the sugar is blended.

3 • Stir in the cream and bourbon and whisk to blend thoroughly, until the icing is thick and creamy. Pour directly onto the top of the pudding while it is still warm. Serve immediately.

bread pudding

Fresh Peach Cobbler

So easy and so good! This homey dessert can be assembled in no time, then popped into the oven when you sit down to dinner. Serve it warm, topped with vanilla ice cream or softly whipped cream.

Filling

8 cups peeled, pitted, sliced
    peaches (about 10 peaches)
1 cup sugar
3 tablespoons all-purpose flour
Grated zest and juice of 1 lemon

Toss together the peaches, sugar, flour, lemon zest, and lemon juice in a bowl until all the fruit is lightly coated and well mixed. Set aside or refrigerate up to 4 hours until ready to use.

Crust

12 tablespoons (1½ sticks)
    unsalted butter, melted
2½ cups all-purpose flour
¼ cup plus 3 tablespoons sugar
2 teaspoons baking powder
1 teaspoon baking soda
½ teaspoon salt
¾ cup buttermilk

1 • Preheat the oven to 375 degrees.

2 • Grease an 11 by 9 by 3-inch baking dish with 2 tablespoons of the butter. Pour in the peach mixture and set aside.

3 • Mix together the flour, ¼ cup of the sugar, baking powder, baking soda, and salt in a bowl and stir to blend thoroughly.

4 • Combine the buttermilk and ½ cup (8 tablespoons) butter in a separate bowl and stir to mix.

5 • Slowly add the buttermilk mixture to the flour mixture and stir to form a soft dough. With lightly floured hands turn the dough out on a lightly floured work surface and roll into a 12- to 14-inch round, about ¼ inch thick.

6 • To make a lattice topping, use a ruler and pastry cutter or pizza cutter to cut straight, even strips of pastry that are about 1 inch wide. Lay the dough strips parallel to one another on top of the peach filling, leaving about 1 inch between strips. (Note: The space between the dough strips allows for steam to escape as the cobbler cooks.) Fold alternate strips back and lay a strip across the unfolded strips.

Unfold the folded strips over it. Fold back the strips that are not under the crosswise piece, and lay a second crosswise strip parallel to the first, about 1 inch away. Unfold the folded strips over it. Repeat the process until the filling is evenly covered. Crimp the edges and trim off the excess pastry around the edges.

7 • Brush the tops of the lattice strips with the remaining butter and sprinkle with the remaining sugar. Bake 40 to 45 minutes, until the top is golden brown and the filling is bubbling around the edges.

variations: You can use almost any fresh fruit —except very soft fruits like bananas, mangoes, or papaya—or a combination of fruits for this cobbler. We particularly like diced Granny Smith or other tart apples, diced firm pears (such as Anjou), berries, plums, and cherries.

Bibliography

Alexander, Stephanie, and Maggie Beer. *Stephanie Alexander and Maggie Beer's Tuscan Cookbook.* New York: Viking, 1998.

Alston, Elizabeth. *Muffins.* New York: Crown, 1985.

Anderson, Kenneth N., and Lois E. Anderson. *The International Menu Speller.* New York: John Wiley and Sons, 1993.

Berolzheimer, Ruth. *Culinary Arts Institute Encyclopedia Cookbook.* New York: Penguin Putnam, 1976.

Brown, Ellen. *Southwest Tastes.* United States: H.P. Books, 1987.

Chiarello, Michael. *The Tra Vigne Cookbook: Seasons in the California Wine Country.* San Francisco: Chronicle Books, 1999.

Conran, Caroline. *English Country Cooking at Its Best.* New York: Villard, 1985.

Corriber, Shirley O. *Cookwise.* New York: William Morrow Company, 1997.

Davidson, Alan. *The Oxford Companion to Food.* New York: Oxford University Press, 1999.

Donovan, Mary Deirdre, ed. *The New Professional Chef.* 6th ed. New York: Van Nostrand Reinhold, 1996.

Glenn, Camile. *The Heritage of Southern Cooking.* New York: Workman Publishing, 1986.

Grigson, Jane. *Jane Grigson's Fruit Book.* New York: Atheneum, 1982.

Heatter, Maida. *Book of Great Chocolate Desserts.* New York: Alfred A. Knopf, 1983.

Herbst, Sharon Tyler. *Food Lover's Companion.* 2nd ed. Hauppauge, New York: Barrons, 1995.

——. *The Food Lover's Tiptionary.* New York: Hearst Books, 1994.

Innes, Jocasta. *The Country Kitchen.* London: Frances Lincoln Publishers, 1979.

Junior League of Baton Rouge. *River Road Recipes.* Baton Rouge, Louisiana: Junior League of Baton Rouge, 1972.

Killeen, Johanne, and George Germon. *Cucina Simpatica.* New York: HarperCollins, 1991.

La Place, Viana. *Panini, Bruschetta, Crostini.* New York: Hearst Books, 1994.

Levine, Carrie, and Ann Nickinson. *Good Enough to Eat.* New York: Simon & Schuster, 1987.

Madison, Deborah. *The Greens Cookbook.* New York: Bantam Books, 1987.

——. *The Savory Way.* New York: Bantam Books, 1990.

Mariani, John F. *The Dictionary of American Food and Drink.* New York: Tichnor and Fields, 1983.

Martha Stewart Living, ed. *The Martha Stewart Living Cookbook.* New York: Clarkson Potter, 2000.

McGee, Harold. *On Food and Cooking.* New York: Simon & Schuster, 1984.

Miller, Mark. *Coyote Café.* Berkeley, California: Ten Speed Press, 1989.

Neal, Bill. *Bill Neal's Southern Cooking.* Chapel Hill, North Carolina: University of North Carolina Press, 1985.

Olney, Richard. *Good Cook: Soups.* Alexandria, Virginia: Time-Life Books, 1979.

Ostmann, Barbara Gibbs, and Jane L. Baker. *The Recipe Writer's Handbook.* New York: John Wiley and Sons, 1997.

Piccolo, Jack. *Timing Is Everything: The Complete Timing Guide to Cooking.* New York: Three Rivers Press, 2000.

Prudhomme, Paul. *Chef Paul Prudhomme's Louisiana Kitchen.* New York: William Morrow and Company, 1984.

Purdy, Susan G. *The Perfect Pie*. New York: Broadway Books, 2000.

——. *A Piece of Cake*. New York: Collier Books Publishing Company, 1989.

Robertson, Laurel, Carol Flinders, and Brian Ruppenthal. *The New Laurel's Kitchen*. Berkeley, California: Ten Speed Press, 1986.

Rosengarten, David, with Joel Dean and Georgio DeLuca. *The Dean and DeLuca Cookbook*. New York: Random House, 1996.

Russo, Julie, and Sheila Lukins. *The New Basics*. New York: Workman Publishing, 1989.

Scherer, Francine, and Madeline Poley. *The SoHo Charcuterie Cookbook*. New York: William Morrow and Company, 1983.

Schmidt, Arno. *Chef's Book of Formulas, Yields and Sizes*. 2nd ed. New York: Van Nostrand Reinhold, 1996.

Stearns, Maggie, and Sallie Y. Williams. *The Hayday Cookbook*. New York: Atheneum, 1986.

Stewart, Martha. *Martha Stewart's Hors d'Oeuvres Handbook*. New York: Clarkson Potter, 1999.

Time-Life Books, ed. *Foods of the World, Kitchen Guide*. Alexandria, Virginia: Time-Life Books, 1968.

Waters, Alice. *Chez Panisse Café Cookbook*. New York: HarperCollins, 1999.

Whaley, Emily. *Mrs. Whaley's Charleston Kitchen*. New York: Simon & Schuster, 1998.

Willan, Anne. *French Regional Cooking*. New York: William Morrow and Company, 1981.

Index

Granny Smith apples, tarragon
chicken salad with red grapes
and, 137–38
grapes, red, tarragon chicken salad
with Granny Smith apples and,
137–38
gratin, potato, with tomatoes,
chèvre, and thyme,
226–27
green beans, pesto, with three types
of tomatoes, 117
greens:
baby, sesame noodles with
cucumbers and, 118–19
mixed, with baby beets, chèvre,
and walnuts, 110
see also spinach
grilled, grilling, 176
asparagus with roasted shallots
and cranberry vinaigrette,
132–33
butterflied leg of lamb with fresh
mint-pepper jelly, 177–78
eggplant Parmesan with fresh
mozzarella and zesty tomato
sauce, 220–22
pimiento cheese sandwich with
grilled ham, 88
portobello mushrooms stuffed
with Parmesan mashed
potatoes, 212
standing rib roast, spicy,
175–76
tuna with balsamic-glazed
scallions and wasabi mustard,
188–89
turkey club on focaccia, 86
zucchini, orzo with sun-dried
tomato and, 126
grilled chicken:
breasts, 60
Caesar on sourdough bread, 86
fajita on Syrian bread, 86
salad with Provençal vinaigrette,
129–30
salad with tomatoes, spinach, and
dijon vinaigrette, 139
grilled ham:
grilled pimiento cheese sandwich
with, 88
mushroom-risotto hash with
fried eggs and, 36–37

grilled vegetable:
antipasto with herbed chèvre and
crostini, 122–23
ratatouille, 124
ratatouille omelet, 34
grits soufflé, 35
grouper, Provençal fish stew with
rouille, 199–200
gumbo, chicken, with chicken-apple
sausage, 65–66

h

habanero peppers, 209
half-and-half, in soups, 54
ham:
country, split pea soup with, 71
grilled, grilled pimiento cheese
sandwich with, 88
grilled, mushroom-risotto hash
with fried eggs and, 36–37
hash:
mushroom-risotto, with fried
eggs and grilled ham,
36–37
turkey-sweet potato, 48
heavy cream, in soups, 54
herb(s), herbed:
balsamic vinaigrette, 131
chèvre, 123
chèvre, grilled vegetable antipasto
with crostini and, 122–23
cream cheese, 96
cream cheese, and smoked
salmon omelet, 34
dried vs. fresh, for soups, 53
-grilled salmon with fresh
tomato-orange chutney,
190–91
potato crisps with, 103
herb biscuits, 17
cheese, 17
Foster's, chicken potpie with,
204
hoisin sauce, Asian-style roasted
vegetables with bok choy and,
157
honey:
–cider vinegar dressing, 112
mustard, 91
mustard-jalapeño glaze, rack of
lamb with balsamic reduction
and, 181–82

horseradish:
-beet mustard, 92
-beet mustard, roast beef with,
88
mustard, 91
sauce, sweet and spicy, 184
sauce, sweet and spicy, slow-
roasted pork roast with,
183–84
hot cross buns with raisins, apricots,
and cranberries, 25–26
huevos rancheros with Granny
Foster's chili sauce, 41–43
hummus, 98

i

icing:
bourbon, Say's bread pudding
with, 296
royal, 244
see also frosting
Italian:
-style chicken and mushroom
soup with orecchiette, 63
sweet peppers, 209
vinaigrette, 151
white beans, roast leg of lamb
stuffed with spinach and,
179–80

j

jalapeño(s), 209
corn muffins, 7
-honey mustard glaze, rack of
lamb with balsamic reduction
and, 181–82
jam, blackberry, cake, with
blackberry cream cheese
frosting, 265
Jamaican black bean soup, 82
jelly:
Foster's seven pepper, with fresh
mint, 178
fresh mint-pepper, grilled
butterflied leg of lamb with,
177–78

k

Kahlúa cheesecake, 279–80
key lime pie with walnut-graham
cracker crust, 286
killer pecan sticky buns, 27

butternut squash soup with
tomatoes, thyme, and corn
bread croutons, 77–79
leg of lamb stuffed with Italian
white beans and spinach,
179–80
new potato salad with dijon
vinaigrette, 134–35
root vegetable puree, 172
root vegetable puree, braised
short ribs with, 171–72
shallots, grilled asparagus with
cranberry vinaigrette and,
132–33
roast(ed) chicken:
breasts, 59
salad on toasted baguette, 86
for salads, 128
sweet potato, and arugula salad,
131
roasted pepper(s), 40
red, and corn chowder, 72–73
red, and eggplant soup, 80–81
red, sauce, 217
red, sauce, creamy corn pudding
with, 216–17
roasted tomato(es):
braised fillet of beef with
mushrooms and, 169
fresh mozzarella, and pesto
omelet, 33
mushroom, and caramelized
shallot pie, deep-dish,
228–29
oven-, 235
risotto cakes with Foster's arugula
pesto and, 234–36
vinaigrette, 239
vinaigrette, squash pudding with,
238–39
roasted vegetables:
Asian-style, with bok choy and
hoisin sauce, 157
and garlic, 81
roast pork:
slow-roasted, with sweet and
spicy horseradish sauce,
183–84
tenderloin with dried cherries
and rosemary, 185
rolls, Granny Foster's refrigerator,
23–24

root vegetable puree, roasted, 172
braised short ribs with, 171–72
rosemary:
focaccia, 107
roast pork tenderloin with dried
cherries and, 186
rouille, 200
Provençal fish stew with, 199–200
roux, in soups, 54
royal icing, 244
rum-raisin apple bread, 19

S
sage, wine-braised boneless turkey
breast with thyme and, 168
salad:
Asian cole slaw with corn and
frisée, 111–12
black beans and yellow rice,
115
Cobb, sandwich, 88
cucumber, avocado, and tomato,
145–46
grilled vegetable antipasto with
herbed chèvre and crostini,
122–23
lentil, spinach, and feta, with sour
cherry vinaigrette, 120–21
mixed greens with baby beets,
chèvre, and walnuts, 110
olive oil for, 112
pesto green beans with three types
of tomatoes, 117
potatoes for, 134
roasted new potato, with dijon
vinaigrette, 134–35
sesame noodles with baby greens
and cucumbers, 117
shrimp, with lemon-dill
vinaigrette, 143–44
succotash, with garden tomatoes,
149
turkey Waldorf, with dried
apricots and chèvre dressing,
140–41
Tuscan white bean, with spinach,
olives, and sun-dried
tomatoes, 150–51
see also chicken salad
salad dressing, old-fashioned,
125
see also dressing; vinaigrette

salmon:
cakes with crunchy corn relish,
192–93
herb-grilled, with fresh tomato-
orange chutney, 190–91
smoked, and herbed cream
cheese omelet, 34
smoked, bagel with, 88
salsa:
cucumber-lime, for sautéed soft-
shell crabs, 198
Foster's, 90–91
spicy tomatillo, for chicken
chilaquiles, 207
teriyaki orange, lemon-roasted
asparagus with, 148
sandwiches:
bacon, avocado, cucumber, and
sprouts, 88
bagel with smoked salmon, 88
Cobb salad, 88
curried chicken salad, 88
grilled chicken Caesar on
sourdough bread, 86
grilled chicken fajita on Syrian
bread, 86
grilled pimiento cheese with
grilled ham, 88
grilled turkey club on focaccia,
86
meat loaf, 88
Mediterranean vegetarian, 89
quick-cooked chicken for, 58–60
roast beef with beet-horseradish
mustard, 88
roasted chicken salad on toasted
baguette, 86
Thai chicken wrap, 89
tomato and mozzarella with pesto,
88
turkey barbecue on sweet potato
biscuit, 86
sauce:
barbecue, Foster's sweet and
tangy, 167
Granny Foster's chili, for huevos
rancheros, 43
hoisin, for Asian-style roasted
vegetables with bok choy, 157
roasted red pepper, for creamy
corn pudding, 216–17
spicy pepper (rouille), 200

SARA FOSTER is the founder and owner of Foster's Markets, two café takeout shops in Durham and Chapel Hill, North Carolina. She has worked as a chef for Martha Stewart's catering company as well as for several well-known New York chefs and caterers. Sara has been featured in *Martha Stewart Living, House Beautiful, Country Home,* and *Southern Living* and appears regularly on *Martha Stewart Living Television.* She lives on a farm outside Durham with her husband, Peter Sellers.

SARAH BELK KING is a contributing editor for *Bon Appétit* magazine and a freelance writer. Her articles have appeared in *Wine Spectator, Country Home, House Beautiful, Diversions, The New York Times Magazine,* and other national publications. She is the author of *Around the Southern Table* and *The Hungry Traveler: France.*

a b o u t   t h e   t y p e

The text of this book was set in Filosofia. It was designed
in 1996 by Zuzana Licko, who created it for digital typesetting
as an interpretation of the sixteenth-century typeface Bodoni.
Filosofia, an example of Licko's unusual font designs, has
classical proportions with a strong vertical feeling, softened by
rounded droplike serifs. She has designed many typefaces and is
the cofounder of *Emigre* magazine, where many of them first
appeared. Born in Bratislava, Czechoslovakia, Licko came to
the United States in 1968. She studied graphic communications
at the University of California, Berkeley, graduating in 1984.